Women of ʿAmran

A village girl, wearing the virgin's bonnet under her veil.

Women of ʿAmran
A Middle Eastern Ethnographic Study

Susan Dorsky

University of Utah Press
Salt Lake City

Copyright © 1986 University of Utah Press
All rights reserved

Library of Congress Cataloging-in-Publication Data

Dorsky, Susan, 1946–
   Women of ʿAmran.

   Bibliography: p.
   Includes index.
   1. Women—Yemen—ʿAmrān—Social conditions.
2. Women, Muslim—Yemen—ʿAmrān.   3. ʿAmrān (Yemen)—
Social life and customs.   I. Title.
HQ1730.7.Z8A473   1986   305.4′0953′32   85-26534
ISBN 0-87480-250-4

This book is dedicated to my parents and to Tom

Fond and grateful acknowledgments also to Charles Callender
and to the women, children, and men of ʿAmran

Contents

Illustrations viii
Note on Transliteration ix
Prologue 3
Chapter 1. Introduction 9
Chapter 2. Historical Background and Social Setting 23
Chapter 3. Fieldwork: Collecting and Connecting 41
Chapter 4. A Typical Day 53
Chapter 5. Daughters and Sons 75
Chapter 6. Marriage: Arrangements, Celebrations, and Consummation 99
Mashjab at the Groom's House 111. *Mashjab* at the Bride's House 113. The Wedding Eve 115. The Wedding Day 116. The Groom's Celebrations 117. The Women of the Groom's Household 119. The Wedding Day at the Bride's Household 120. Postwedding Celebrations 128. *Yawm al Sābᶜa* (The Seventh Day) 129. *Shikma* 131.

Chapter 7. Marriage: Relations and Conflict 133
Sexual Relations 134. Early Years of Marriage 139. Separation 141. Polygyny 145. Divorce 150.

Chapter 8. Pregnancy, Birth, and Motherhood 153
Childbirth 155. The Forty Days after Childbirth 158. Return to Normal Life 164. Relations with Sons and Daughters 166.

Chapter 9. Neighbors and Friendships 171

Chapter 10. Women's Perceptions 185

Chapter 11. Conclusions 197

Notes 207

Glossary 213

Bibliography 215

Index 225

Illustrations

Frontispiece: A village girl, wearing the virgin's bonnet under her veil

Susan Dorsky and her husband, Thomas Stevenson, outside their front door in ʿAmran   2

A girl carries midmorning breakfast   33

Neighborhood children outside author's front door   55

Men in the marketplace   57

A ʿAmrani man plows a terraced field   59

A village woman carrying purchases   61

Veiled woman carrying alfalfa   61

Women carrying laundry and bread   62

A young married woman washing clothes next to her house   63

A young father with his firstborn   67

Cousins enjoying lollipops   86

Young girls wearing peaked bonnets   86

Older girls caring for younger ones   90

Girls dressed up in the Sanʿa-style *sharshaf* for the holiday   96

Girls playing on a swing   98

Tribesmen perform a traditional dance at a wedding   132

One of the oldest and most popular women in ʿAmran   180

Fully veiled woman crossing paths with a man   201

Maps

Sketch map of Yemen   24
Sketch map of ʿAmran   54

Note on Transliteration

The transliteration system used in the text and the glossary follows that of *Arabian Studies* (Middle East Center, University of Cambridge). I have not transliterated place names, but have used common spellings. In accordance with Yemeni pronunciation, I have changed the letter *qaf* to *gaf*. In ʿAmran, *gīm* is pronounced *jīm*. Words beginning with an ʿ*ayn* have an "a" following the initial sound for ease of reading. The singular forms of Arabic words have the appropriate masculine and feminine endings; the plural is formed by adding a terminal "s" to the Arabic word for the sake of simplicity.

Women of ʿAmran

Susan Dorsky and her husband, Thomas Stevenson, outside their front door in ʿAmran.

Prologue

The neighbor women and I often laughed over our different memories of my first trip to ᶜAmran, a market town in the northern tribal region of the Yemen Arab Republic. My husband and I had just entered the town after a delightful visit in a nearby village, when two small girls seized my hands. They led us firmly past groups of yelling children and staring adults on what seemed at the time to be a winding, confusing route. We ended up on a dead-end street deserted except for two veiled women and their children. I was thrilled when they beckoned for us to join them.

My purpose in coming to Yemen was to make an ethnographic study of the women, but I had begun to worry whether I would establish contact. In public the women were inaccessible, concealed behind complicated layers of veiling, and I had no access to their private domains. These women, it appeared, were interested in meeting us, and we approached them eagerly.

"Want to buy my coral necklace?" asked one of the two women. When I answered negatively, she suggested, "Perhaps my *shub-shub*?" as she removed her rubber sandals for me to consider. The other woman readjusted my scarf to conceal escaping strands of hair.

I was crushed. Not only were they apparently more interested in our money than in us, but also after all my pains to dress modestly they clearly had not approved of the results. One of my first encounters with Yemeni women, a failure. "The people in that village were really nice," I told my husband as we taxied back to Sanᶜa, the capital, "but I'd never want to live in that town!" Either those women were shockingly mercenary or they were laughing at us, and I wasn't sure which was worse.

It turned out that we did move to ᶜAmran and, by sheer accident, into that very street. After about a month in our new house, I vaguely realized that I might have been in this neighborhood before. It wasn't until the neighbors volunteered their versions of that day, however, that I realized I was living in the midst of the women who had so upset me.

A group of us were sitting around a doorway, when Huria was reminded of her first view of me. "You turned the corner with your husband, and you were wearing your red dress and black pants. You didn't understand anything anyone said to you. I asked if you wanted to buy my *shubshub*!"

"It was you?" I gasped, as the memory flooded my consciousness. "Ohhh yes, of course." Laughing heartily, we reviewed the encounter in detail. We were neighbors now.

The episode became one of many shared stories to be brought up by any one of us in a reminiscing mood. I would reiterate how mad I'd been at their rudeness, and they would marvel over how dense I'd been. I, then, would defend myself by insisting that English was entirely different from Arabic and that they'd look dense in America. Then usually one of them would make a soothing comment on how much better I'd gotten at Arabic. "Susan knows all the words now," she might say.

I'd laugh delightedly and, with becoming modesty, demur, "Oh no! Only a quarter of them, or less."

"We'll say 'half,'" was the decisive retort, and the subject would be changed.

That first encounter had taken place early in January 1978. Later that month we had the good fortune to meet three young men from ʿAmran who were high-school students in Sanʿa, Yemen's capital. They offered to help us locate and rent a house in ʿAmran. After inquiring as to available houses and owners' willingness to rent to *naṣāra* (Christians), they showed us our choices. The first few houses were relatively new and in the more desirable part of town, across a paved road from the original walled town (the *madīna*). I couldn't hide my profound reservations about each one. So, with apparent reluctance, they decided to show us one more house. It was in "the village of the Jews" (often referred to just as "the village"), an enclosed community of seventy-four houses. Adjacent to the walled part of ʿAmran, it had been the Jewish quarter until the late 1940s departure of ᶜAmran Jews for Israel. The houses had been purchased by Muslims, and most had been remodeled in conformity with Islamic architectural conventions.

Our almost immediate decision to rent this house was to have immeasurable consequences for my sixteen-month stay in ᶜAmran. I learned that most women, in contrast with men, are intensely involved with their neighbors. The frequently quoted aphorism, "Neighbors are greater [more important] than relatives," indicates the ideal of neighborhood solidarity. The message was: relatives may be physically distant, or simply unable or unwilling to help, but neighbors are always there, obligated to help you as you are to help them.

We had several reasons for choosing the old "village" house over the more modern "suburban" ones. Architecturally, it had far more character, and its history in a Jewish enclave had romantic appeal. Practically, its advantages were that it was cheap and we'd been assured it could be connected with the town waterline. Most important was its location in a crowded, narrow dead-end street. We thought we would be less "ignorable" in this cramped setting than in the new area where houses are widely scattered and many secluded within walls. As the first foreigners to live in ᶜAmran since the Turkish departure at the end of World War I, we were wary of how we would be received. The dangers of isolation seeming to us greater in the smart part of town, we felt more than justified in opting for a house with aesthetic and romantic appeal. We told the students to arrange the lease, and returned to Sanᶜa to await clearance from the North Yemeni government to do our research.

When the landlord's agent refused to deal directly with us, one of the students generously assumed a year's lease on our behalf. He and two other students arranged for essential work to be done on the house. One of them visited us regularly in Sanᶜa, where we impatiently awaited our research clearance. When it came, he supervised our actual move to ᶜAmran. Two months after our first sight of the town, we were finally moving.

Our arrival, so it seemed, brought everyone out of their houses. In no time at all, our many possessions had been carried up the stairs and into our central hall. Understanding little of what was said and overwhelmed by my neighbors' helpfulness, I quickly gave up arguing with their notions of how our mats and cushions should be arranged. They knew which room should be used for what and the implications for decorating far better than I did. They could see, I imagine, that I knew close to nothing about everything.

What had seemed like the entire neighborhood helping us move in was in fact an all-female group. Once they had launched the ordering of the household, most of them departed as rapidly as they had appeared. We were left alone with three girls, aged roughly fifteen, thirteen, and nine. Although I found the talk of all three close to incomprehensible that first day, I soon learned that communication with adult women was even harder.

Neighborhood women tried from the first day to include and befriend me. My appeal was based, I think, on a combination of genuine near helplessness, apparent good cheer, the perception of my strangeness as more funny than threatening, and a belief by some that my friendship would enhance their status. Before our arrival, I had worried whether townswomen would tolerate my company, and never imagined the degree of enthusiasm with which the neighbors were to embrace me. From our very arrival, they took over my life, although not always with results I would have chosen myself.

After an uneasy first night in our new house, we were awakened at the crack of dawn by Kharia, the eldest of the three girls who had helped us move in. She presented us with hot bread, and left only after extracting my promise that I would rush right to her house after breakfast. She said that she knew I would want to see how her mother prepared the bread, which was to be sold in the *sūq* (market).

Interested in the bread, but wary of being manipulated, I dressed quickly, gathered courage, and went off to find Kharia's house. Only minutes after I was inside it, neighbors began appearing to gawk and joke. One complained angrily that I had chosen to visit Kharia before her or the others. All eagerness to endear myself to all and alienate none, I vowed I'd come to her house right after lunch.

I arrived while Amina was changing clothes. After a brief period of light chatter, she began speaking to me earnestly. Slowly and clearly, with her eyes fixed on mine, she told me that Kharia's family were *muzayyin* and that her own were *gabā'il*. She explained that *gabā'il* are better than *muzayyin*, and would never marry them, although they could visit back and forth. Clearly Amina was trying to convey to me why I should prefer her company over Kharia's.

Before I could question her further about the social differences she apparently considered so important, Amina urged me to accompany her on a visit. She answered my nervous questions (How many women? How far away? How long will we stay?) reassuringly. I protested that I was still in dirty work clothes. I looked fine, she said breezily, as she stuck a basil flower behind my ear and doused me with perfume. She arranged her veils, took me by the hand, and off we went.

She had told me nothing but lies. The house was far and the reception room packed with at least fifty brilliantly dressed and richly jeweled women. It was a major social event, which Amina had no intention of quitting until the evening prayer call signaled departure time for all. My shoes were taken from me at the door, and I was squeezed between two strange women. As angry as I was with perfidious Amina, and as difficult as it was to communicate with her, it was a terrible jolt to be separated from her and from my shoes as well.

All eyes were riveted on me. Although the older woman to one side of me strove to be polite, she was obviously disconcerted by my presence. I was totally overwhelmed, embarrassed by my dirty clothes and disheveled appearance, mortified by my inability to converse or even behave at all appropriately, and furious with Amina, whom I could not locate among all the unfamiliar Yemeni faces.

Once back home I decided I was not yet ready for a steady diet of such stressful afternoons. That evening, when, as was to happen for weeks to come, women and children crowded around my door, I told them how uncomfortable I'd felt amid all the strangers and that for a while I intended to spend most of my time with them in the neighborhood.

They showered sympathy upon me and berated Amina sharply for taking me to the party. Tempers flared and shoving began, as women and girls maneuvered to stake their claims on me. I watched with horrified fascination, until an older woman told me that things were going too far and I had better go inside my house for the night.

Feeling even more sought after than I had ever desired in my popularity-craving early teens, I ended my exhausting first day as a resident of ʿAmran. The promise of the support and friendship of neighbors more than made up for the mortification of the afternoon. I told myself that if I stayed close to home until my competence and confidence improved, I would be all right. The neighbors would take care of me.

It turned out to be a good plan. At first I especially relied on the girls. School children had had to learn to understand and make themselves understood to Egyptian teachers, and so had a head start over their mothers in dealing with me. A few young girls had a particular genius for reducing the complicated speeches of adults to a level I could grasp and converting my babbles into meaningful utterances. Because most of the girls were also less judgmental and more empathetic than most of the women, I basked in their company.

Soon, however, I began shifting allegiance to the grown women. The girls expressed little resentment. They looked forward to the time when they too would dress up and go out like their mothers, and did not fault me for preferring women's festivities to staying home with them and their omnipresent younger charges. And we could visit at odd times on the street, just before or after lunch or in the magical twilight time between the breakup of women's gatherings and entering our homes for the night.

Gaining little by little in mastery and comprehension, I moved inside the women's social world. Packed rooms of fifty women dressed and jeweled and "perfumed-to-kill" became my milieu; the villainous neighbor who had taken me to my traumatic first party turned into a close friend and invaluable informant. Without her cooperation and generosity and that of countless other women, my research would have been a dismal failure. This book is written with deep gratitude toward the women of ʿAmran and with the hope that this version of their lives would ring at least partially true to them were they to know its contents. I have no doubt that they would be deeply angered by my disclosure of so many secrets, but these must be revealed if we are ever to overcome the false stereotypic image of the Arab Muslim woman.

1

Introduction

This book is about the women of ʿAmran, a small town in the Yemen Arab Republic (hereafter also referred to as Yemen, North Yemen, or the YAR). It describes the day-to-day realities of female lives and reports women's thoughts and feelings about themselves, significant others, and their changing life situations. To convey a sense of women as persons—thinking, feeling, planning, active individuals—I include abundant case material. The object is to lend a three-dimensionality absent in the caricature of traditional Arab Muslim women that is part of our cultural baggage.

Both negative and positive aspects of women's lives are discussed. Arab Muslim societies undeniably discriminate against women, and Yemen lags behind almost all other Muslim nations with respect to legal reforms affecting women (Gerner 1984:91; White 1978:60–64). ʿAmrani women lack economic and political power. They have minimal control over important decisions affecting them and their children. Even those whose husbands are rarely at home because of employment in Saudi Arabia or army service are relatively powerless. Important decisions must await the husband's return or are made by his male relatives. Few women can risk alienating kinsmen and husbands upon whose support they depend. However, ʿAmrani women derive surprising advantages from a separate female social domain. It is not simply a matter of enjoying each others' company but of deriving psychological strength and a sense of emotional well-being from connectedness with other women.

The subject of Arab Muslim women is a confusing one. As Fernea and Bezirgan (1977:xviii) point out, most writings on the subject represent one of two contradictory positions: The critics tend to focus on the gross oppression of women under Islam, portraying the Middle Eastern woman as "in a state of bondage from which she has no recourse and no escape." On the other side are the apologists who portray the strict sexual code of Islam as protective of women and as an indicator of the high esteem Islam has for women. Research since 1977 reveals considerable variation in the conditions of female lives both between and within Middle Eastern nations. The subject is now known to be much more complex than had been thought. In more developed and progressive countries, some urban women are well educated, employed outside the home, and in control of their own fertility and other aspects of their lives. In these same countries as well as less developed and more conservative ones, poor women and rural women have fewer options. Even in the least-developed countries, women's life situations and values vary along class, rural and urban, religious, and other dimensions. Readers interested in the current state of research on women throughout the Middle East are referred to Fernea's *Women and the Family in the Middle East*, UNESCO's *Social Science Research and Women in the Arab World*, and Hussain's *Muslim Women*. Earlier collections particularly recommended are Beck and Keddie's *Women in the Muslim World*, Fernea and Bezirgan's *Middle Eastern Muslim Women Speak*, Smith's *Women in Contemporary Muslim Societies*, and al-Hibri's *Women and Islam*.

The surge of research on Middle Eastern women is partly attributable to the revitalization of feminism in the West. Scholars in the social sciences and humanities began in the 1970s to incorporate a feminist perspective in their research methods and theories. Within anthropology, concerted efforts developed to collect new data on women in all parts of the world and to create new methods and theories to advance the cross-cultural understanding of women. By the late 1970s the anthropology of women had entered what Rapp (1979:497) aptly refers to as "an adolescent growth spurt." Most of its advocates agree on the following positions: (1) Women are important social actors; studies that ignore them are resultantly deficient. (2) Sexual stratification is universal, or nearly so, but could change. (3) Most previous female researchers were no more effective in studying women than were male researchers because of a "double male bias," that of the discipline itself and of the societies most anthropologists studied:

> All anthropologists wear the blinders of their own civilization in approaching other cultures; our eyes are as conditioned as those of the people we study. Our own academic training reflects, supports, and extends the assumptions of male superiority to which our culture ascribes. (Reiter 1975:13)

There was a conviction, then, among many anthropologists studying women that only a feminist perspective enabled a researcher to transcend her or his training.

Among the most influential of the 1970s theoretical writers on the anthropology of women were Sherry Ortner, Nancy Chodorow, and Michelle Rosaldo, who, in related arguments, traced sexual stratification to social and cultural ramifications of differences between female and male bodies. Even their critics agree that the three theories generated highly productive research and debate. The theories are summarized here because of their special relevance to the case of Arab Muslim women in general and ʿAmrani women in particular.

Ortner (1974) argues that the universal devaluation of women is related to the fact that women are universally symbolic of nature, which is in all cultures' ideologies perceived as inferior to culture. It is through culture, with which males are symbolically associated, that nature is controlled and transcended. Culture's superiority over nature rests in this power to transform nature to human purpose.

The argument for a universal distinction between the categories of nature and culture is based on the occurrence of ritual in all cultures and particularly on beliefs and rituals of purity and pollution. In Ortner's view, rituals of purification, which are cultural products, are believed to have the power to subdue or negate harmful natural forces. Cultural power, then, is perceived as distinct from and at a higher order of existence than the raw powers of nature.

Ortner's main objective is to fix the relationship between what she believes to be a universal devaluation of women with this universal devaluation of nature in relation to culture. She argues that because the female body is constructed to bear and nurse young, there are constraints upon women's time and energy that do not apply to men. Whereas women are bound up with "species life," the lack of such limitations on men's lives leaves them free to engage in other activities. Women create only "perishables," but men, "through the medium of technology and symbols . . . create relatively lasting, external and transcendent objects" (Ortner 1974:75).

As a result of the constraints upon them, women are perceived as closer to nature than are men. Still, they are participants in culture as well and, in their role as socializers of their children, important cultural transmitters. Their position, then, is an intermediate one, more rooted than men in nature but not entirely confined to that level.

Chodorow's approach (1974) to sexual stratification is psychoanalytic. She is interested in the relationship between women's role as mothers and their low status. Focusing primarily on the mother-daughter relationship, she seeks to show that male and female personality differences are not innate but, rather, arise from the universal assignment of child care to females.

Chodorow argues that a woman tends to identify more with her daughter than with her son. Consequently she is more likely to treat her daughter as an extension of herself, to encourage her dependency implicitly if not explicitly. In contrast, a mother is likely to emphasize her son's differentness, his masculinity, and to behave toward him in ways that facilitate his differentiation and independence from her. Given greater encouragement than their sisters to separate from their mothers, males form firmer ego boundaries than do females.

She describes further salient differences in female and male socialization. One has to do with children's wider spheres of interaction. Because domestic chores are much more often assigned to daughters than to sons, boys are more free to participate in extradomestic peer groups. Competitive play with peers further contributes to the son's differentiation from his mother. Girls spend most of their time with kinswomen of several generations. They grow up in close personal contact with adult role models, observing and learning what will be expected of them when they become women. Less encouraged than their brothers to form separate identities and master novel domains, they remain embedded in household relations.

For girls, then, growing up is relatively smooth and unproblematic. The adult role is constantly visible and their education is in an intimate and easeful atmosphere. Growing up for boys is more difficult. The adult male role is in varying degrees outside the male child's observation and must be fantasized. This is different from the girl's constant, direct interaction with usually affectionate adult role models. The boy must master something he doesn't really know in much less emotionally supportive contexts, usually with weaker affective ties to his father than exist between the girl and her mother.

Each socialization pattern has its negative and positive consequences in adulthood. Female embeddedness in intimate personal relations gives women a sense of security that men lack, but it tends to prevent their formation of strong ego boundaries. Further, they tend to have social identities not of their own, but based on their relationships with men (as daughter, sister, or wife).

Men have had to struggle more in achieving the adult role. They have, in the process, acquired firm ego boundaries, but they also have come to deny their dependency and intimacy needs and to repress and devalue "feminine" qualities. Having learned to act in spheres requiring conduct that is formal and distanced, they evaluate these spheres as more important than the informal and intimate domains of women. A man "appropriates to himself and defines as superior particular social activities and cultural (moral, religious, and creative) spheres" (Chodorow 1974:50).

Chodorow sees the ranking of the female domain below the male domain as a male cultural model, and she at least implicitly recognizes that female models may differ. Explicitly she argues that neither cultural devaluation of females nor their low-status assignment necessarily results in low self-esteem among women. Additionally, she cites studies indicating that weak ego boundaries do not prevent high ego strength.

Rosaldo (1974) ties together Chodorow's psychoanalytic and Ortner's symbolic approaches with her own emphasis on the level of social organization. Like them, she takes female physiology as her starting point. Because much of women's time and energy go toward carrying and caring for their young, their social roles are primarily at the domestic level. This level, for reasons elucidated by Ortner and Chodorow, is ranked inferior to the public domain. Men dominate the public domain, having "no single commitment as enduring, time-consuming and emotionally compelling . . . as the relationship of a woman to her infant child . . . are free to form those broader associations that we call 'society' " (Rosaldo 1974:24).

One consequence of this opposition, related to Chodorow's notion of psychic differences between the sexes, is that womanhood is perceived as a more "natural" or ascribed status than is manhood. Manhood must be achieved in competitive extradomestic contexts that are the explicit social order and that form the substance of most anthropological studies. Cut off from such institutionalized roles and doing similar work in all societies, women are seen, within their own cultures and by most anthropologists as well, as living less structured and more spontaneous lives. The attribution to women of greater empathy, sensitivity, and intuition is related to the cultural perception of their apartness from the social order.

Another consequence of a separation and ranking of domestic and public domains has to do with allocation of authority. In constant, intimate interaction with their children and responsible for repetitious, mundane, and sometimes dirty domestic chores, women are too "familiar" to evoke respect. Men's social distance allows them to manipulate their images in ways women cannot. Only those apart from a situation can control it. Monopoly of authority positions by men, then, is linked to their freedom from domestic duties. Only in old age might a woman have sufficient freedom from those duties to acquire authority commensurate with that of men.

Although lacking access to positions of public authority in most societies, women frequently wield considerable indirect influence. Often defined as weak and insignificant, in actuality they may be of great importance to men (in marriage exchange, as providers of heirs, as maintainers of male honor and perpetuators of male alliances, as well as in other critical aspects of social life). When women's real power is seen as opposed to the formally legitimate authority of men, notions of female pollution may develop. Although cultural perceptions of women as anomalous and disruptive of the cultural order suggest a symbolic devaluation, they do not necessarily indicate a reduction in female power.

Rosaldo, Chodorow, and Ortner have been criticized on several grounds. It is now generally believed that, with the accumulation of data of the last several years, the subordination and devaluation of women appear to be far too complex, subtle, and variable to be reduced to facile "key" explanations. Still, their ideas have generated valuable research and rethinking of issues related to female status. Whereas their ideas do not explain the universal secondary status of women, they are relevant to cultures with certain characteristics: pronounced differentiation of domestic and public domains; high cultural evaluation of bearing and rearing children; and perception of females as psychologically different from males, and outside of or opposed to the cultural order. These characteristics are all found in Arab Muslim societies.

The notion of a female menace to the social order is illustrated vividly in a sermon delivered in a Jordanian village (in Antoun 1968:685–86):

> Oh ye people, verily women are discord. And the messenger of God did not point out to us anything more disturbing of the peace than women. And verily the discord among the people of Israel was on account of their women. And verily, this is the cause of dishonor and the rending of God's commandments and prohibitions, and the loss of family lines, and the ruin of houses, the thing that destroys societies. . . . It is an obligation on every true believer in God to forbid his wife and daughters and all over whom he holds guardianship from departing his house except for necessities; for the woman on leaving the house is accompanied by Satan until she returns to her dwelling.

Reports of cultural perceptions of women as more socially disruptive than men are common in studies of Islamic communities (Fuller 1961; Nordenstram 1968; Dwyer 1978; and others). In the view of Islam, female sexuality is dangerous, requiring social institutions that restrict women and protect male affairs. Mernissi (1975:xv) states: "Since she is considered by Allah to be a destructive element, she is to be spatially confined and excluded from matters other than those of the family. The woman's access to non-domestic space is put under the control of males."

Men must control the more important public concerns. The following statement from a thirteenth-century source spells out the male domain quite explicitly. According to al-Bayḍāwi, writing in 1846 (Levy 1957:99), Allah prefers men over women

> in the matter of mental ability and good counsel, and in their power for the performance of duties and for the carrying out of [divine] com-

mands. Hence to men have been confined prophecy, religious leadership, saintship, pilgrimage rights, the giving of evidence in the law courts, the duties of the holy war; worship in the mosque on the day of assembly, etc. They also have the privilege of electing chiefs, have a larger share of inheritance, and discretion in the matter of divorce.

While males create and maintain transcendent cultural institutions, they must take precautions to protect their domain from female contamination. Social arrangements to keep women under the control of fathers, brothers, husbands, and sons are needed because men are constantly vulnerable to female sexuality. In Mernissi's comparison (1975:13) of Freud's Western and al-Ghazāli's Islamic theories of sexuality, she points out the following contrasts:

> In the western Christian experience, it was sexuality itself which was attacked, degraded as animality and condemned as anti-civilization. . . . Islam took a substantially different path. What is attacked is not sexuality; it is the woman who is attacked as the embodiment of destruction, the symbol of disorder. She is *fitna*, the polarization of the uncontrollable, a living representative of the dangers of sexuality and its rampant disruptive potential.

There is a clear resemblance between the Islamic model, as presented by Mernissi, and Ortner's nature/culture opposition. Woman symbolizes the destructive power of nature and so must be restricted in her actions and influence. She is "a dangerous distraction . . . [who] should not, in any way, be an object of emotional investment or the focus of attention" (Mernissi 1975:14). Men have some protection through a social order that confines women to the domestic domain and removes men as much as possible from that devalued sphere.

Despite the apparent close fit between the Islamic model and Ortner's and Rosaldo's explanations of female subjugation, there remain problems with applying their explanations. First, it is not established whether the association of women with nature is causal of female subjugation or is epiphenomenal. Secondly, Ortner's contention that women accept cultural evaluations of female inferiority is arguable. Many recent writers have maintained that "dominant cultural models" (E. Ardener's term [1972]) represent male positions and perspectives not necessarily shared by women (Sweet 1974; Friedl 1967; Nelson 1974; Dwyer 1978; Reiter 1975; Safa-Isfahani 1980; and others).

Following up on ideas of E. Ardener (1972), S. Ardener (1975:xii) has suggested that the "dominant model may impede the free expression of alternative models of their world which subdominant groups may possess." In some cases the subdominant group generates "counterpart models," and in others they must "structure their world through the model (or models) of the dominant group" (S. Ardener 1975:xii). The Ardeners link the neglect of women by both female and male anthropologists to women's disadvantage in "expressing themselves through the idiom of the dominant group" (S. Ardener 1975:xii). Women's "muted structures are 'there' but cannot be 'realized' in the language of the dominant structure" (E. Ardener 1975:22). An important task for contemporary anthropologists with interest in women is to discover their "muted structures," and investigate the "little defined and seemingly vague, possibly repressed, alternative ideas which women have about the world, including those about themselves" (S. Ardener 1975:xxi).

Evidence of alternative female models comes from the Middle East (Nelson 1974; Sweet 1974; Dwyer 1978; Ahmed 1982b; and others) and other culture areas (Friedl 1967; Paulme 1963; Rogers 1978; and others). Instances have been reported of contradictions between male and female evaluations of each sex's worth and importance. Kaberry's comments (1952:150, 152) from Nsaw women and men, respectively, about women are an excellent example:

> Important things are women. Men are little. The things of women are important. What are the things of men? Men are indeed worthless. Women are indeed God. Men are nothing. Have you not seen?

> Yes a woman is like God, and like God she cannot speak. She must sit silently. It is good that she should only accept.

A return to the issue of public versus domestic orientations is in order here. Rosaldo saw the confinement of women to the domestic level as underlying their devaluation, particularly in societies characterized by sharp public/private differentiation. Clearly implicit in the argument is a recognition of cultural models that rank the public sphere above the domestic one. Yet, evidence suggests female evaluations may differ. Reiter (1975:258), for example, writes that French village women's reaction to male dominance of the public domain is to invert it:

They perceive the public areas as the sites of great playacting. They see men as overgrown children strutting around and holding onto places and roles that are really quite silly; these have less value than their own homes and roles as family cores. They even consider men's space to be inferior to their own. . . . The arenas and roles forbidden them are discounted as unimportant. They do not see the public sphere as more powerful or more imposing than the private one.

Friedl (1967) and Rogers (1978:148–49) argue that many peasant societies are in fact domestic-centered. In such societies male dominance may be more fiction than reality. They claim that female domestic authority may be more "real" than male public power, particularly when village men have little or no control over wider political and economic forces shaping village life. A "myth of male dominance" may develop to conceal the actual distribution of power. According to Quinn (1977:218):

While neither sex believes that the myth accurately reflects the actual situation, both sexes maintain the illusion of male dominance so that each can continue to exercise the forms of power allocated to them. Women retain control of their households and covertly manage their husbands' activities.

Rogers (1978:144) suggests extreme caution in accepting cultural models of male superiority, as these may only represent public male evaluations. "While important to consider, such valuations are rather lopsided grounds on which to base theories about women, if women in the same societies do not accept them, and have their own counter valuations." Women are particularly likely to have their own countervaluations in sexually segregated societies. Consequently, the frequent assumption that sexual segregation can be equated with discrimination against women is unfounded:

The barring of one sex group from the domain of the other does not necessarily have negative implications for the excluded group. Furthermore it may not be legitimate to consider one group as more excluded than the other, if neither has access to the other's domains. . . . Sexual segregation *per se* is neither discriminatory, nor a sign of discrimination. Only in the presence of other factors may the two be associated. (Rogers 1978:145)

Few scholars, however, would claim that Arab Islamic societies are sexually egalitarian. Dwyer (1978:22) grants that societies in which the sexes are separate but equal are "theoretically possible," but describes the situation in Taroudannt, Morocco, as one in which "women have less power, are accorded less authority, and are burdened with legal and extra-legal restrictions which sharply curtail even the most vital of life options."

On a more general level, Barakat (1985:32) lists a number of characteristics of Arab societies reflecting the subordination of women. These include: (1) the seclusion and segregation of the majority of women; (2) widespread veiling of women; (3) nonavailability to most women of roles other than kinship and marital ones; (4) discriminatory personal status codes, particularly with respect to marriage, divorce, and inheritance; (5) limited opportunities for women from certain classes to own property; and (6) an ideology that "considers women to be a source of evil, anarchy . . . , and trickery or deception."

In Yemen, as in Morocco (Dwyer 1978:23-26) and other Arab Islamic societies, male rights and privileges exceed those of females in inheritance, employment, purchase, physical mobility, sexual conduct, marriage choice, divorce, custody of children, office holding, voting, and legal affairs. Makhlouf points out that tribal codes and values operate in conjunction with Islamic ones in Yemen to

> celebrate the activities and virtues of men in groups and to restrict achievement in the political sphere to the males. Moreover, in the religious courts of Yemen, as in tribal law, the blood money (*diya*) paid for a woman is evaluated at half the amount paid for a man, and the testimony of a man is worth that of two women. (Makhlouf 1979:20)

Makhlouf (1979:25) goes on, however, to state that Yemeni women do not appear to possess a negative self-image, and describes them as "not nearly so tense or inhibited as women in some other cultures." Even Minces, whose *The House of Obedience* is a grim portrayal of the "incarceration" of women under Islam, acknowledges that within their homes, women do "not feel subordinate, oppressed, inferior or powerless compared to the men" (1980:44). Ahmed describes Dubai women as "singularly impervious to the assertions of the dominant ideology regarding their 'natural' inferiority and 'natural' subservience" (1982b:530). Recall that Chodorow (1974:62) maintains that neither low status nor cultural devaluation of females precludes high self-esteem in women.

In a survey of research on women in Arab countries between 1960 and 1980, Kader (1984:149) notes:

> The majority of women in the Bedouin and peasant societies and in the urban lower and lower middle classes of the Arab region seem basically satisfied with the existing social order. . . . In spite of the strictness of the moral sex code, they are well-adjusted and find implicit and covert ways for self-fulfillment and the realization of their ends.

The survey shows dissatisfaction with the social order to be almost exclusively an urban upper-class phenomenon. While Kader acknowledges that less-educated women's apparent acceptance of male dominance is related to a lack of awareness of alternatives, she links women's general satisfaction to the fact that "their lives are sometimes easier, and their role performance is often more competent than that of men" (1984:147).

Similarly, S. Ardener (1978:33–34) suggests that women in many sexually inegalitarian societies may be at least partly pleased with the restrictions placed upon them. She advocates attention to both positive and negative aspects of any institution, the perpetuation of which we are seeking to understand.

It may well be the case that the perpetuation of unequal relations between the sexes in Yemen and elsewhere will be better understood once we have examined how women's lives appear to them, focusing, as S. Ardener suggests, as much on those aspects they discern as positive as on those that they or we discern as negative. One aspect in many Arab Muslim societies that women value highly is their extensive and intensive contacts with other women. These are unquestionably important to the women themselves, and are frequently critical to male interests as well (Aswad 1967, 1978; Sweet 1974; Makhlouf 1979; Ahmed 1982b; Larson 1984; and others).

By regular visiting, North Yemeni women interact almost daily with large numbers of other women. They have "a separate sphere over which men have little control and which may constitute a source of support and even power" (Makhlouf 1979:25). Their visiting practices give women access to extensive information, and sometimes put them in a position to influence male decision making. It would not be unreasonable to maintain, in Makhlouf's view, that men are at least as excluded from the female sphere as women are from the male one. Furthermore, at certain types of women's gatherings, female folktales and real-life anecdotes criticizing male conduct and celebrating female deviance are recounted. More dramatically, informal skits are enacted in which males and their activities are ridiculed to the hilarity of all present (my own observations in ꜤAmran; Fayein 1957:191; Makhlouf 1979:46). This suggests women's countervaluations, not only of the relative importance of the sexes, but of the dominant cultural model as a whole (Makhlouf 1979:44–47). Ahmed (1982b:167) goes so far as to claim that "there is an indigenous tradition of 'feminism' . . . in the Arabian Peninsula" and that the exceptional involvement of women in the revolution of South Yemen (People's Democratic Republic of Yemen) grew out of this empowering tradition.

In North Yemen, where revolution has been partial and minimally concerned with the liberation of women, women have their own social order but remain for the most part subordinate to the men in their lives. Not surprisingly, ꜤAmrani women's ideologies are a combination of distinctive female elements and others shared with men and are derived from Islamic and tribal sources. Because these are interwoven in complex and subtle ways, women remain unconscious for the most part of inconsistencies and contradictions. A brief example may clarify this point. Women believe themselves to be men's equals with respect to moral worth and intelligence, insisting that variability on these two dimensions is related to individual rather than gender differences. Yet most also see their situation as more pitiable than that of men and are likely to attribute this unfortunate state of affairs to men's greater educational and employment opportunities. Uneducated and essentially unemployable, women, they say, have no choice but to accept the authority of the men who support them. Mothers often say they want daughters to be educated and to postpone marriage until confident and mature—to be less dependent and vulnerable than their mothers. Only a few women, however, consistently promote these avowed objectives. Most discourage or interfere with their daughters' regular school attendance and mold them toward sacrificing their own wants to those of adults and younger siblings. This inconsistency is partly related to mothers' reliance on daughters' help with baby-sitting and housework to get out of the house themselves but also to their feeling threatened by the prospect of their daughters becoming too different from themselves. What women convey to their daughters is a considerable ambivalence about fundamental change in women's lives. They know they want their daughters to be strong in the ways they are strong, and they want them to grow up to enjoy the daily round of female visiting that constitutes the good life. They are less sure whether they want their daughters to work among men. Employment would spare them some of the vulnerability to male abuse and neglect of which they complain, but it would also take them far away, both geographically and emotionally. Women also worry about what ʿAmranis would think of a daughter who is educated and employed. Others might envy her autonomy and earnings, but gossip about loss of honor incurred by working publicly among men. On this subject and many others, women think in several different, even contradictory ways about their present and future circumstances.

The sometimes obvious, sometimes subtle interplay of perspectives will be apparent throughout this description of ʿAmrani women's lives, offered in the hope of making a dent in what Fernea and Bezirgan (1977:xviii) call "the continuing confusion in Western views of Middle Eastern women" and of enhancing understanding of Yemeni society and culture as a whole.

2

Historical Background and Social Setting

ᶜAmran is located in the northern region of the Yemen Arab Republic, the home of Yemen's two powerful tribal confederations, and the area of the country most resistant to social reform. Yemen's northern and southern regions differ religiously, economically, socially, and politically. Historically, the north has been influenced by neighboring Saudi Arabia, the south by its neighbor, South Yemen, now the People's Democratic Republic of Yemen, formerly a British colony and the first Arab nation to adopt Marxism-Leninism as its official ideology.

Neither of the two Yemens produces oil at present, although a 1984 oil find in the YAR could be productive as soon as 1990 (Halliday 1985:8). To date both Yemens provide their oil-rich neighbors with unskilled labor. North Yemen exports a major proportion of its workers to Saudi Arabia. The cash remittances these workers send home to their families, in combination with other aspects of the Yemeni-Saudi relationship, have a dramatic impact on Yemen's economy, allowing purchase of imported foods and consumer goods, but undermining agricultural and other production and contributing to inflation and dependence on Saudi and other foreign assistance.

This chapter sketches Yemeni social history, concentrating on north-south differences and changes both in ᶜAmrani women's and men's lives and their evaluations of these in relation to what Stookey refers to as Yemen's "partial revolution" (1984:89). For more comprehensive treatment of ᶜAmrani and Yemeni social history see Stevenson's *Social Change in a Yemini Highlands Town*, Stookey's

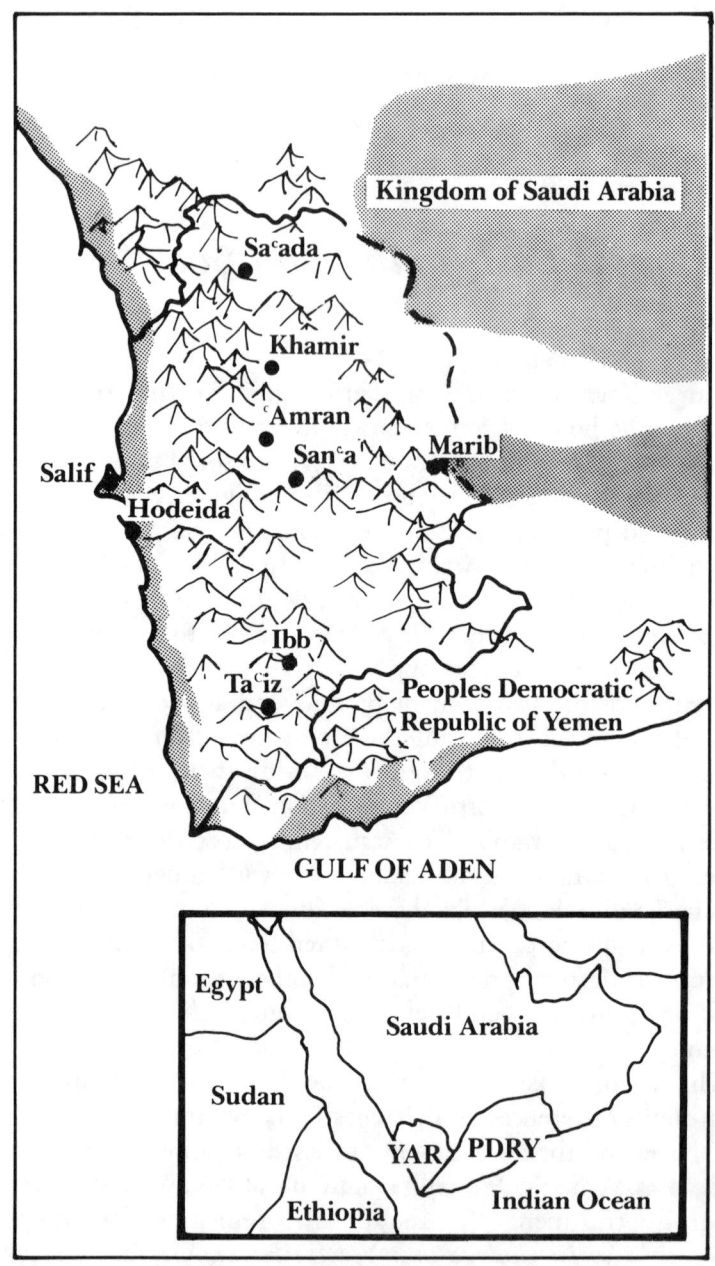

Sketch map of Yemen

Yemen: The Politics of the Yemen Arab Republic and *The Arabian Peninsula*, Wenner's *Modern Yemen*, Swanson's *Emigration and Economic Development*, Peterson's *Yemen: The Search for a Modern State*, and Bidwell's *The Two Yemens*.

Most writers on the Yemen Arab Republic emphasize its long isolation from foreign influence and consequent underdevelopment (Halliday 1974; Stookey 1978; Makhlouf 1979; Bidwell 1983; and others). Wenner (1967:17), for example, writes:

> Until well in the twentieth century, Yemen remained one of the most inaccessible countries of the world. Although under the nominal control of the Ottoman Empire during the last decades of the nineteenth century, Yemen's inhabitants remained largely ignorant of the Industrial Revolution, modern technology, and the political, social, and economic theories and practices of the Western world. While most other Middle Eastern nations were stirring under the impact of the West and its technology and ideologies, Yemenis lived as they had for centuries, cognizant only of their own immediate surroundings, indifferent to all but their closest neighbors.

To Stookey (1984:81) the most salient characteristic of Yemeni society is the split between the Shafiʿi school of Sunni Islam and the Zaydi sect of the Shiʿa. The north is Zaydi, the south and coastal region are Shafiʿi.

There are two ancient tribal confederations in the north—the Hashid and the Bakil. In Peterson's view (1982:21-22), the northern tribe was historically a "self-contained mini-state" whose members' allegiance remained with the tribe rather than the state. Although not all residents of tribal territories were tribal members, "the tribesman . . . is the 'norm' of Yemeni society." Living within each tribal area were people outside the tribe, but interlinked with it and clearly ranked above or below the normative stratum.

Above the tribespeople were the *sāda* (s. *sayyid*), whose high status rests in their descent from ʿAli and Fatima, the cousin and daughter of the Prophet Muhammad. *Sāda* originally came to Yemen to mediate conflicts between northern tribes, and stayed on, combining their "religio-social status with a domination of the political arena through the institution of the Zaydi imamate" (Peterson 1982:23). The close but problematic relationship between northern Zaydi tribes and the Zaydi Imamate is discussed below. Ranked below the *sāda* and the tribespeople were "socially deficient classes" with occupational specialties serving the tribe and marrying only among themselves. These included merchants, barbers, butchers, town criers, musicians, weavers, and bleeders. As will be seen, this rigid stratification system endures (in part) in the north well after the ousting of the imamate and formation of the Yemen Arab Republic, a phenomenon explored in depth in Stevenson (1985).[1]

For over one thousand years, until the 1962 coup, a Zaydi imam functioned as religious leader of Zaydi northerners and as political leader of all of what is now the Yemen Arab Republic. He had to be of *sayyid* descent, and he relied on other *sāda* who were administrators, tax collectors, and judges. The imam's authority was limited largely to the collection of taxes; for coercive power he had to rely on northern tribesmen. Because they were Zaydi, they were under the imam's religious rule, unlike the southern Shafiᶜi. Still, religious authority never allowed the imams to control the tribes in a strict sense:

> Although the imamate was dependent upon the brute strength of the tribes, it was unable either to make them the instrument of a strong central government, or to prevent them from pursuing aims irrelevant, or hostile, to those of the Zaidi regime. (Stookey 1978:151)

Consequently the imams utilized tactics such as taking sons of tribal leaders as hostages to ensure tribal loyalty. Occasionally imams called upon one tribe to discipline or punish another for disloyalty to the imamate.

In the south, where large-scale intertribal organization had not developed, settlements were highly vulnerable to raiding by northern tribesmen. Some raids were carried out in the confederations' capacity as "wings of the imamate"; others were simply for the tribes' benefit. Southerners viewed northerners as barbaric. An informant of Messick's from Ibb expresses traditional southern notions of the differences between southern and northern characteristics: "The men of al-yaman al-asfal [the south] are known for their eloquence, wealth, and knowledge, and are great poets. Those from the north are known only for killing" (Messick 1978:52). Another of Messick's informants, an Ibb resident of northern origin, provides a typical statement of the opposite, northern point of view: "Men of the north are known for their severity and heroism, whereas those of al-yaman al-asfal are subject peoples; . . . there are no men of distinction . . . down here as there are in the north" (1978:52).

Some authors link chronic conflict between north and south to religious differences: the southerners' adherence to the Shafiʿi school of Islam as opposed to the northerners' adherence, in company with the imams, to the Zaydi sect (Stanford Research Institute 1971: 41–42; and others). Halliday (1974:82–84) and Messick (1978:46) argue that social and economic divisions between the regions are of greater importance, Messick (1978:60) claiming that "the differences of legal schools is only a metaphor for a broader gauged political antagonism." Still, it is significant that the imams' rule was legitimized by their religious authority in the north but not in the south (Wenner 1967:18).

Southern dissatisfaction with imamic rule and tribal raiding was undoubtedly of long standing, but is thought to have intensified in the early 1940s (Messick 1978:65–73; Boals 1971:220). For years Shafiʿi southerners had been objects of discrimination, since Zaydi officials exercised authority over them. They were taxed more heavily than northerners and excluded from important positions in the army and government. This "ascriptive inferiority was understandably a source of resentment for the Shafiʿis" (Stookey 1978:173). Closed off from other options, many of them became merchants and traders. It was these Shafiʿi who were particularly angry when Imam Yahya (1904–1948) sought to concentrate control of foreign trade within his own family (Boals 1971:220). Boals (1971:220–21) summarizes some of the factors leading to the creation of Shafiʿi-dominated movements for political change in the 1940s:

> The Imam's policy of putting members of his own family into all the positions of political and economic power in the society and monopolizing trade and commercial relations with the outside world . . . alienated . . . the merchants and traders, most of whom were Shafiʿis and had no love for Zaydi rule in any case. The Shafiʿi element of the population . . . were further alienated by the fact that the Imam used administrators in the Shafiʿi districts who were almost all Zaydis. Zaydi dominance in society was also increased by the fact that the regular army was composed primarily of northern Zaydi tribesmen who were only too happy to oppress the Shafiʿis in the name of the Imam.

Also important in the growth of political resistance was the diffusion of foreign ideas into Yemen, which occurred despite the self-protective isolationist policies of twentieth-century imams. New concepts of freedom, constitutional government, and the assignment of status according to achieved rather than ascribed factors spread widely throughout Yemen from the 1940s onward. Although southerners' proximity to British-controlled Aden and their history as traders and merchants gave them greater access and receptiveness to these powerful new secular ideas, they were not alone in embracing them:

> Despite the apparent control of the imamate, significant changes took place within the Yemeni polity. Traditional values had been abandoned or downgraded, and a long list of new ones adopted, satisfaction of which was considered the duty of those in authority. . . . More and more Yemenis, belonging to traditional as well as to newly formed social components, came to believe that their own efforts could force the political system to provide gratification of the newly acquired aspirations.
>
> These changes did not permeate the society uniformly, and . . . many of the (northern) tribesmen remained attached to the imamate itself as the legitimate form of authority beyond the tribe. (Stookey 1978:211)

The Free Yemenis' Movement was formed in Aden in 1945 to work for the desired political reforms. Coup attempts in 1948 and 1955 failed in part because of the "xenophobic and ultraconservative" northern tribes' military support of the imam (Boals 1971:228). The ultimate success of the 1962 coup can be attributed, among other factors, to Imam Ahmad's (1948–1962) alienation of some of these tribes, including the tribe of ᶜAmran.

In 1959 Imam Ahmad was attempting to resolve a conflict between the Hashid confederation and the national government. Following normal practice for such situations, he sent his son to the Hashid paramount *shaykh* with an offer of safe-conduct to Sanᶜa to discuss the problem. The paramount *shaykh* accepted, and travelled to Sanᶜa to see the imam:

> A heated argument took place during which the imam impetuously ordered both guests (the paramount sheikh and his son) seized and sent to Hajja, where they were to be decapitated. This breach of faith, and of tribal custom, alienated many Yemeni tribes. Major military campaigns were necessary to put down the ensuing rebellions in the north and the east. Imam Ahmed was discredited beyond redemption among the Hashid tribes. (Stookey 1978:206)

Three years later, when the imam and the *sāda* were overthrown and a republic declared, some Hashid tribes, still angry at Imam

Ahmad's treachery, allied with the rebels. Most tribes, however, remained loyal, allowing the royalists (as they came to be called) to organize a strong resistance. Tribal military support for the imam forced the republicans to seek outside aid. An eight-year civil war ensued, with the republicans supported by Egyptian arms, funds, and troops and the royalists by arms and funds from Saudi Arabia. The Yemeni civil war became "a struggle between two of the several value systems then competing for supremacy in the Arab world at large" (Stookey 1978:229–30).

The organizers of the coup had achieved their shared goal of ousting the imam and the *sāda* from power, only to find themselves troubled by internal conflicts. The Zaydi organizers were unwilling to give up their longstanding position of political preeminence, whereas the Shafiʿi felt that their large contribution to the revolution had earned them the right to at least equal political power (Stookey 1978:233).

The political strength of the Zaydi leaders was further enhanced as more and more of their tribes switched their support to the republican side, even though most of the reversals were based more on self-serving than ideological considerations. Tribal abandonment of the royalists was one of several developments leading to the 1970 termination of warfare and the formation of a compromise government. Approximately 200,000 Yemenis, or about 4 percent of the population had been killed (Halliday 1974:106).

Two years after the cessation of warfare the Yemeni government was still Zaydi dominated and oppressive to areas of the south. A Shafiʿi described the political situation in 1972 as follows:

> The Army is afraid to clash with the tribes, and the tribes with the Army—both are afraid of the "educated youth," namely the politically indoctrinated of the towns, who in turn lack the force to confront either. (Quoted in Serjeant 1973:9)

After al-Hamdi (1974–1977) seized control of the government there occurred a definite erosion of tribal power, effected in part by the entry of the Hashid paramount *shaykh*, al-Ahmar, into an important role in national government. Concerned that the north was far behind the south in material progress, al-Ahmar tried to convince lesser tribal leaders that by working with the government, the quality of life in their towns and villages could be improved. When he realized that the side effects of this cooperation were diminished tribal autonomy and *shaykh*ly status and objected to growing leftist influence in the North Yemen government, he withdrew from that government. From his headquarters in Khamir, just north of ʿAmran, he entered into negotiations with Saudi Arabia for support against al-Hamdi's regime. This support could be expected because al-Hamdi's politics were too far to the left for Saudi comfort. Reportedly the Saudis have continued to provide aid to certain tribal leaders who actively oppose any political changes within North Yemen that menace Saudi interests (Swanson 1979:34; Halliday 1985:8).

Periodic conflict continues in the north. Neither the national government's construction of schools, wells, and clinics (with foreign-aid funds) nor its payments of subsidies to tribal leaders has subdued the more belligerent tribes. Occasional roadblocks, seizure of private property, and other hostile tribal actions ensure the endurance of the image of the "barbaric north." The reduction in tribal power has made northern "barbarism" far less threatening than in the past, but, in the opinion of the new Yemeni powerholders, tribalism is still an obstacle to national progress. Stookey (1978:280) expresses the commonly held developmental perspective:

> A fundamental aim of the government is gradually to take power from the traditional leaders and to place it in the hands of new elites possessing the technical skills needed for modernization and enhancement of the people's material and cultural well being. The leadership pattern in northern Yemen, laid down two millennia ago, retains considerable vitality, but is becoming less and less suited to the contemporary era; the open question is whether change in its nature will be evolutionary and orderly, or abrupt and violent.

In the modern view, then, the term *gabīlī* (tribal) has entirely negative connotations. Its meaning in the major cities and the relatively progressive south, is similar to that of our "hick" or "hillbilly," suggesting ignorance and backwardness. This contrasts sharply with the enduring northern pride in the traditional *gabīlī* virtues of strength, courage, and independence. Even though many tribespeople are poor in a society that increasingly values material success and despite the indications that other elements of the tribal image reflect reality less than ever, the image remains entrenched in most northerners' consciousness that

> the tribesman epitomizes traditional Arab virtues: he is courageous and generous, aggressive and virile, proud and self-reliant. He feels himself an equal to any member of his own tribe and superior to those of most other tribes. He is ready to defend his honor at the slightest provocation. . . . The only worthy enemy of a *gabili* is another *gabili*. . . . He may ridicule those who are "weak" (*daᶜif*) or "deficient" (*naqīs*), but by laying hand on them he would lose his honor. . . . The traditional *gabili* is one who is independent and who gives protection; others are dependent and receive protection. (Gerholm 1977:115–16)

Traditionally tribespeople looked down upon merchants and craftsmen. Although they were dependent upon the *sūq* (marketplace), tribesmen emphasized the warrior component of their status and tried to conceal their roles as cultivators. They did this by means of middlemen:

> The peasant himself does not take his produce to the market which economically would be the most rational procedure. Instead he is visited in his village by someone from the market who buys his crops, transports it to the market and sells it either to another merchant or directly to the customers. . . . This reduces the gain made by the farmer, but it protects him from the contagion of the *suq*. On the market day, then, the *gabili* is able to enter the *suq* as an outsider and not as an insider, a patron and not a client. (Gerholm 1977:117)

In ᶜAmran both the traditional positive and the modern negative images of the term *gabīlī* operate, often simultaneously. Tribal membership is still important and valuable, and males are expected to present themselves with prideful toughness appropriate to a potential warrior. The great majority of adult males still carry arms daily. With ᶜAmran's growth and proximity to Sanᶜa, however, the inhabitants have acquired new self-images as modern, sophisticated townspeople. They emphasize their separation from the dirt and toil of village tribespeople. The *sūq* has lost some of its stigma, so that many tribesmen now work as merchants. Although they still will not marry into *sūq* families, the notion of the *gabīlī* as above and apart from the market sphere is much diminished. With reference to themselves, ᶜAmranis define *gabīlī* in terms of superior descent. When they and other ᶜAmranis refer to the villager as a *gabīlī*, they are not alluding to his ancestry, but to his naïveté or crudeness. Still, the ᶜAmranis' perception of themselves as sophisticates in comparison to villagers is countered by their relations with Sanᶜanis who, they rightly fear, lump them in the same lowly category as the villagers.

In the preceding historical sketch, particular attention was given to the past and present roles and images of the northern tribes. The scholars whose works I consulted in tracing Yemeni history differed, sometimes in their facts, more often in their interpretations of the same facts. When I narrow the focus to the town of ᶜAmran and base the reconstruction of its history on the accounts of primarily female informants, I find a similar situation. Just as the scholars see history through the lenses of their theoretical orientations, so are informants' recollections and present perceptions colored by factors such as age, sex, class, and education. Class differences still matter very much to women, their socializing across class lines notwithstanding. For example, an impoverished elderly *sharīfa* (female *sayyid*) who regrets the diminished status of her group can be counted on to describe the past and see the present in terms very different from those of the newly wealthy *muzayyina* (female in one of the lower strata). The following discussion of past and present ᶜAmran, then, will focus not just on actual changes over time, but also on status-related differences in women's evaluations of these changes.

In *zamān* (the "past," used for any time period prior to the 1962 coup), ᶜAmran was a small market town, most of its homes contained within the ancient walled city and the adjacent walled Jewish *guriyya* (literally "village"). The tribe of ᶜAmran, which includes some but not all surrounding villages, was and still is affiliated with the Hashid tribal confederation. Other neighboring villages belonged, and still belong, to the Bakil tribal confederation and were, in the past, in frequent bitter conflict with ᶜAmranis. The Bakil villages supported the royalists in the civil war and suffered considerable damage from Egyptian bombers. ᶜAmran's support of the republicans from the outset of the war paid off in very few casualties and minimal destruction of property. (Of the thirty-six town residents said to have died in the war, several were women,

Historical Background and Social Setting / 33

A girl carries midmorning breakfast to male relatives working outside of town. The wall of old ʿAmran is in the background.

and a number of the men reportedly lost their lives while scavenging in bombed Bakil villages.) Since the end of the war, with the dramatic growth of the town and its market, large numbers of Bakil villagers have come to live and work in ᶜAmran. Although tolerated, they are still viewed with suspicion and kept at a marked social distance by many ᶜAmranis.

ᶜAmran is located in a fertile valley rich in cultivable land. In the past, most ᶜAmran families farmed, with labor contributed by women and men. Although very large tracts of land were owned by a few wealthy tribesmen, there were other tribesmen, *sūq* families, *sāda*, and Jews who were landowners. Those who owned little or no land could work as sharecroppers (*shurakā'*, s. *sharīk*). Then, as now, there are two sharecropping arrangements, the *sharīk* receiving three quarters of the yield when he provides all the labor or two thirds when the landlord contributes additional labor. The staple crops were millet, wheat, barley, and sorghum. These grains are still grown today, but their production has declined greatly due to the availability of relatively inexpensive imported wheat and to an increasing preference for more profitable town occupations. Formerly, almost everything consumed in ᶜAmran was locally produced, but this is very far from being the case today.

All informants speak of how long and hard women and men had to work in the past, but some older women see the easiness of modern life as a mixed blessing. They claim that without arduous labor, people have become weak and prone to illness. Often I was told, "look at the *gabā'il* [meaning, in this context, villagers]. They never get sick because they work hard and are strong. That is how we used to be too." Many of these same informants are often critical of townswomen's new visiting patterns. In the old days, they say, there was barely time for an occasional late afternoon get-together, whereas now women are gadding about all day long.

The grinding of grain is at the heart of women's recollections of the past. Regardless of husbands' and fathers' status, all women spent long hours every day hand-grinding grain for the family's food, often returning to the task in the evening after the children were asleep. Now, most grain processing is done at the mills, although a few operations still require hand-grinding. Most younger women, the postmill generation, cannot grind, and are dependent upon their mothers or other older women to do this extremely difficult and tiring work. Only a few homes still have working grindstones, and these are available for use by all women.

In discussions of the "old days," the topic of grinding inevitably is raised. One of the older women is certain to act out the grinding motion and chant one of the old accompanying story-songs, with staccato rhythms dictated by the precise regularity of the toil. Her delight in the performance is always met, if not surpassed, by that of the younger women, for whom the songs represent a past never known.

Although female work was essentially the same in all families, definite social and economic distinctions existed. There were descent-based prestige groups as well as economic divisions. These hierarchies only partially overlapped, as many *sayyid* and *gabīlī* families were considerably poorer than some merchant families. The economic differences, however, were extremely slight in comparison to those of today. Informants agree that prior to the post-civil-war increase in consumer goods, the standard of living was uniformly low. The primary contrast in life-style between economically "big" and "weak" households was that the former ate meat twice a week, the latter only once.

Informants are keenly aware that now in ʿAmran, there are significant differences in standards of living, and they appear to have what they consider to be an accurate knowledge of others' economic status. Poor tribespeople say that others now look down on them for their poverty, whereas in the past all tribal members were respected for reasons of descent. Formerly wealthy and influential *sāda* also bemoan their losses in the revolution.[2] Economic expansion, labor migration, entry of tribesmen and *sāda* into formerly stigmatized mercantile activity, devaluation of agricultural work, and the national government's inroads on tribal power and prestige have all contributed to altering ʿAmran's status hierarchy. These issues are addressed in Stevenson (1985).

Women of the *sayyid* and *gabīlī* groups, not unexpectedly, describe the past more favorably than do women of *sūq* families. Some *sayyid* women speak bitterly of the republican government's seizure of family property; others talk wistfully of the greater deference paid them in the past.

Now, as in the past, a *sayyid* woman is addressed and referred to as *sharifa* X (the honorable X). Formerly, the norms governing her conduct were far stricter than those applied to women of lower descent. Circumspection was particularly required of the *sharifa* whose kinsmen, husband, or in-laws occupied important public positions. A *sharifa* told me the following story of a *sharifa* of the past. It conveys the special limits, the price of the prestige enjoyed by *sayyid* women:

> Prior to the civil war, a *sharifa* married a *sayyid*, as all *sayyid* women were required to do. She cared deeply for him, and he for her. But she liked to gad about all the time, instead of staying home as a *sharifa* should, and she fraternized too freely with non-*sayyid* women. As her father-in-law was a government official, the family had a reputation to uphold. So her husband, despite his affection for her, had no choice but to divorce her. The *sharifa* became sick at heart, and remained ill for the rest of her life.

Whereas some *sayyid* women strive to adhere to the paragon-of-virtue role, those who behave more freely need not fear severe reprisal. They may, however, receive mild reproach. For example, if a *sharifa* makes a joke at another woman's expense, its target is likely to retort: "And she's a *sharifa!*" The sting of this kind of half-joking, half-censorious retaliation reminds the audience of what is expected from a *sharifa* and how far her antagonist has deviated from that norm.

Tribeswomen, like *sayyid* women, remember the past as a time of high status for their group. Although their families may have been poor, they had pride and prestige by virtue of their ancestry. Now those few tribal families who have maintained old wealth and the many tribesmen who have become successful merchants suffer relatively little at the loss of ascribed *gabīlī* prestige. Rather, it is from the poor tribal families who have failed to capitalize on new economic opportunities that criticisms of the new order are most likely to be heard.

In an extreme example, one old tribeswoman told me that everything new is bad. In the past, all the food was tasty and nourishing, unlike the abysmal imports. She was the only informant to mark the separation between the past and present by reference to a specific event, all others speaking broadly and vaguely of "the past" (*zamān*) or "the present" (*dhalḥīn*, "now"). "When Imam Yahya died," she said, "everyone cried. Even the sky cried."

It is far more common for informants to value some aspects of the new order, even if passionately critical of others. Tribeswomen may regret their loss of prestige and resent gains made by nontribal families and at the same time welcome consumer goods, new economic opportunities, the clinic, and the schools. The following account of changes in the status of ʿAmran's leading *muzayyina* (female entertainer) comes from such a tribeswoman. Of considerable descriptive interest, it is also a rich divulgence of injured *gabīlī* pride:

> In the old days the *muzayyina*'s role in weddings was very different from today. Now, you have to beg her to sing, pay her whatever outrageous fee she demands, and you can't expect her to do any other of the wedding-related work. In the past, as soon as she heard that a wedding might be in the offing, she would come to *you*, and ask *you* humbly to use her services.
>
> She had lots of hard work to do, personally inviting all the guests, making the broad beans to be served at the prewedding parties, preparing the bride and her friends, singing so the guests could dance, and escorting the bride to the groom's house on the wedding night. Each dancer had to give her only a penny or two, and the parents of the bride paid her in whatever grain was in season. Whatever they gave her, she had to accept. She made so little doing weddings that she had to go out to the villages where she cut children's hair for meager payments.
>
> Now it's all different. The *muzayyina* has a very high fixed price (approximately 1,000 riyals or $220), which she demands even of the poorest families. Each dancer must pay her five riyals, in advance, for the right to dance a single time. The groom is obliged to give her a sizable payment, as well, for delivering him his bride. She makes all this money, and no longer invites the guests or prepares the broad beans, and is more likely than not to show up late to prepare the bride for her groom.
>
> What is really disgraceful about this is that the *muzayyina* does not lower her fees for poor families. It is impossible in ʿAmran to marry your children without the services of a *muzayyina*, so what can we do? To demand so much money from the poor is *ḥarām* [a sin]! In the past, were a *muzayyina* to get uppity with tribespeople, the *shaykh* would simply put her in jail. Now, everything has changed, and the positions are reversed.

This *muzayyina* occupies a central place in ᶜAmrani women's society. She delights in her new wealth and power, but is sensitive to slights and snubs linked to the inferiority still ascribed to her status. Just as the tribesmen of the past strove to emphasize the warrior aspect of their status and mask the peasant component, so this *muzayyina* wants to be envied (if not respected) for her wealth and to have her ancestry forgotten. Once in my presence, when referred to as "the *muzayyina*," she snapped that she was not to be referred to as a *muzayyina* but by her personal name. Still, she is at least as aware as any other woman in ᶜAmran that only a woman of her ancestry can perform at weddings. Her wealth accrued as a result of her manipulation of her ascribed status, not in spite of it. She owes her success to the revolution, but to maintain it must hope that the new order does not progress to the point of making her services dispensable, which they have become in other parts of the country.

Perhaps it is not surprising that this *muzayyina* and other women of *sūq* families almost never spoke to me or in my presence of their prerevolution status. Their discussions of the past focus, rather, on hard work and deprivation, which they contrast with what they see as the vastly improved life-style of today. Differences in past and present meat consumption are mentioned more frequently and feelingly than any others. One old woman, typically, spoke of her little son Salah having plagued her with constant plaintive questioning as to "How many days until Sunday, Mother?," Sunday being market day and the only day of the week that their household and most others eat meat. Salah, who is a grandfather now himself, is today in a position, along with most town residents, to consume meat daily.

Tribeswomen and female *sāda* also talk of how much harder life was in the past, but many of them have the reasons just discussed for regretting the passing of the old ways. Although older *sūq* women did express nostalgia for some aspects of the past, the majority of them appeared to have less mixed evaluations of the relative desirability of the old and new orders.

Certainly, most women welcome some elements of the new order. Technological advances reducing work and increasing comfort and pleasure are widely valued, although some of them (piped water, electricity, butane gas stoves, television) are beyond the financial reach of many. The first few wringer washing machines appeared in ᶜAmran during my stay there, so I could observe directly the keen interest and enthusiasm they evoked. In a very short time, large numbers of women had watched the machines being used and were speaking of urging their husbands to buy one.

There is considerable approval of the wide variety of imported food and other items for sale in the *sūq*. Fresh and canned fruits are particularly enjoyed, whereas other imports are purchased for reasons of economy rather than quality. Local eggs, for example, are considered much tastier and healthier than imported eggs, but are so expensive that they are bought only to prepare special-occasion dishes and to give strength to the ill and convalescent. For ordinary purposes, most households use inferior imports, which, called "factory eggs," by some, are thought to be synthetic, unlike local eggs that come from chickens. Similarly, imported frozen chickens cost far less than any local meat or poultry and are eaten by most families with great frequency. Without them, it would be difficult if not impossible for most families to afford meat daily. However, the local chickens are considered to be vastly superior and, as with the local eggs, are prescribed in cases of sickness and convalescence.

Most women see the town's clinic as a positive development. They rely heavily on the clinic when their children are ill, although this in no way prevents them from carrying out traditional magical practices as well. Their simultaneous reliance on both Western and local treatments does not appear contradictory to them, but is little appreciated by the clinic's staff. Women set clear limits as to what clinic ideas they implement, ignoring those that they consider wrong from their own notions of healing. The clinic's staff often sees this as a problem; yet, from another perspective, this can be viewed as an indication of the vitality of traditional beliefs.

The women and men of ᶜAmran live in a time of rapid cultural change. With ᶜAmran only one hour's drive from Sanᶜa and a growing market town, intermediate in size and amenities between the capital and its surrounding villages, ᶜAmranis (even those not of tribal descent) constantly juggle the modern devaluation of "*gabīlī*-ness" with traditional tribal pride. The two images coexist, but, as in Manakha (a town west of Sanᶜa on the road to Hodeida), the proud, independent *gabīlī* image is "a model which Yemenis . . . find difficult to discard—even though they find it even harder to emulate" (Gerholm 1977:115).

Gerholm's reference is to men. Women's difficulties in reconciling "tradition" and "modernity" are related to, yet different from men's. They never were warriors, but they have lost some of the privileges or the penalties of the traditional hierarchy as articulated in the female domain. On the one hand, women continue to follow and value tradition in many aspects of their lives and to define many traditions as God-given. On the other hand, they are sometimes aware that the new national elite sees aspects of their way of life as obsolete and undesirable. Many younger women are attracted by what they see on television and in San'a as the glamour, ease, and romance in other women's lives. Yet, they and their mothers are usually sharply critical of the few San'ani women who have given up the veil or deviated in other ways from what are seen as the inspired teachings of Muhammad. This study, then, will describe how 'Amrani women, in this culturally conflicted atmosphere, live and perceive their lives.

3

Fieldwork: Collecting and Connecting

Most women were cooking lunch, most men still at work or mosque. The sun was directly overhead and the streets deserted. Only ancient Ummi Atigha lingered outside in the hope a passerby might stop to chat. This much I guessed as I approached her, squatting in a patch of shade, and pondered my chances of quick escape. She pulled on my skirt and motioned for me to squat beside her. Whatever she had to say had to be whispered. I obeyed.

"You know my grandson's wife miscarried yesterday? Well, this morning a _____ came out!"

The word was unfamiliar, and between Ummi Atigha's toothless diction and hissy whisper, I hadn't caught it. "Wasn't it the baby that came out?"

"That was yesterday," she answered impatiently. "This morning an ʿaūgari came out!"

"What's that?" I asked.

"It's a little animal, like a rat, that gets inside the womb and eats the baby. Sometimes it kills the mother too. It's not like an ordinary rat; it has eyes all over its body—eyes, eyes, everywhere."

Six months' research had passed when I learned from Ummi Atigha about the ʿaūgari belief. I could easily have missed hearing about it at all since the subject never came up in general company. The discovery was partly, but not entirely, due to luck. Equally important was Ummi Atigha's perception of me as an appropriate recipient of her gossip.

An obvious contributor to this perception was my deliberate avoidance of men. I spoke with them only occasionally and then usually in the company of their wives or kinswomen or of my husband. This dissociation eased women's initial acceptance and hastened their comfort in my presence. Also relevant was Ummi Atigha's and others' awareness that, like them, I cared enormously (too much?) about my friendships and feuds. Because I became personally involved, I made emotional sense to them despite the always obvious differences between us. A third factor was my preference for informal, minimally obtrusive research—for learning in naturally occurring situations—and as a result I had become a familiar, no longer particularly interesting participant in neighborhood social life.

My daily activities were patterned on those of most ᶜAmrani women. Ordinarily morning visits were confined to the immediate neighborhood. Some weeks Ummi Atigha and I had found ourselves in the same house more days than not. We had got to know each other well.

I had three favorite morning locations, each with its own research value. One was in the house of a popular male healer, whose services included protection against evil eye and treatment for mental and emotional disturbances. The majority of his clients were women from nearby villages, who sat with his widowed mother Ummi Amina while they waited to see him. The two other women of the household, the healer's present wife and his adult daughter from a previous one, joined them when free from other tasks. Other visitors included relatives, friends, and women bringing cloth for the widow or her granddaughter to make into dresses for them.

I was interested in the healer's clients. Many volunteered accounts of their maladies, tracing their origin to stresses or violations they had suffered. I sometimes wondered if the healer's alleged effectiveness had as much to do with his mother's calm sympathy as with his own expertise and theatricality. In any case, his clients' stories and others' comments gave me unique access to women's ideas about causes and manifestations of female suffering.

There was much more to be learned at the healer's house, from its individual members and by observing the changes in their internal and external relations. Despite Ummi Amina's exceptional integrity and dignity, the household was, like most others, troubled by periodic conflict. A temperamental and controlling man, the healer was the source of most tensions that developed, but there were also problems among the three women. Strains between Ummi

Amina and her daughter-in-law Fauzia appeared to stem much less from competition over the healer than from Fauzia's occasional resentment at Ummi Amina's partiality to her grandaughter Bilghis. Ummi Amina had raised Bilghis and loved her like a daughter. Separated from her husband in San ͨa shortly before our arrival, Bilghis was staying in her father's house waiting for her husband to reclaim or divorce her. Fauzia felt that her mother-in-law coddled Bilghis and let her get away with doing less than her share of the household work. Like other young wives, Fauzia returned to her parents' house when life at her husband's became unbearable. Only after lengthy maneuvering did her husband succeed in reclaiming her.

Bilghis was considered by herself and others to be a perfect friend for me. She was literate and had lived in San ͨa during her brief marriage—a young sophisticate in short. Dramatic and emotional like her father, Bilghis spoke ceaselessly about matters of the heart: her love for her husband and tortured hopes for reconciliation; her fear of her mother-in-law; then of her pain at the divorce. Later it was the excitement of several prospective matches, then wedding preparations, and of the actual marriage itself that she spoke. It was an eventful year and a half for Bilghis, and I was grateful for her confidences; but my real affection was for her grandmother.

It wasn't exactly that Ummi Amina reminded me of my own mother, yet when I tried to imagine my mother in ͨAmran (and speaking Arabic), it was only with Ummi Amina that I could picture her establishing rapport. As discussed in chapter 8, most ͨAmrani women care intensely about their friendships but have difficulty sustaining them. Jealousies, quarrels, and resentments are common. Ummi Amina, however, seemed above them. Neither cold nor sanctimonious, Ummi Amina was self-contained and serene. She participated minimally in female society, not out of pride or a desire to convey an image of moral superiority but because she preferred productive work at home alone or in the company of her immediate circle. Rarely idle, Ummi Amina sewed dresses for customers and taught young women to use the sewing machine. She was as patient with me as with her students and taught me a great deal about the past and about differences between town and village life. We made several visits to her natal village, also the home of her daughter-in-law, Fauzia. Besides being the source of much useful information of a general sort, Ummi Amina provided me a haven from the strains of fieldwork among women far less dispassionate than she.

In sharp contrast with the atmosphere at Ummi Amina's was the racy, often raucous one at Karima's house, another of my favorite morning locations. Karima's past was less than circumspect, as were those of most of her visitors. Now all were more or less respectable married women who behaved with at least token propriety in public, but they let their hair down in private. They joked about sex, clowned, and gossiped. Little kindness was reserved for those outside their intimate group, membership in which fluctuated dramatically due to feuds and jealousies. I lived on the same short street as the group's three core members and had my share of conflict with each one. When peace prevailed, I enjoyed their lively, irreverent ways enormously, and learned about areas of life little discussed elsewhere in my hearing. Their conflicts were enlightening as well, albeit painful when my role was more participant than observer.

Ummi Atigha (who told me about the eye-covered womb creature) was Karima's mother-in-law, but lived a few streets away with Karima's older co-wife. Sometimes she came for a second breakfast to Karima's, carrying her own kettle of unsweetened *gishr* (coffee-husk brew). I was always happy to see her, mainly for her wit and stories, but also because I shared her preference for unsweetened *gishr* and always was given a cup or two. This was more likely in my other favorite morning setting, Tagiya's, than at Karima's.

Tagiya's house was ideal for those of us, like Ummi Atigha and me, who favored leisurely morning visits, because Tagiya did little work and loved company. Tubercular and weak, Tagiya relied heavily on her daughters' help. Her soldier husband was rarely in ᶜAmran and she had no sons, so the house was a totally female domain. I spent a great deal of time alone with Tagiya in addition to my frequent appearances at the regular hour for morning get-togethers. She was in many ways an ideal informant, extremely bright, patient, gregarious, knowledgeable, and rich in free time. Tagiya liked the role of teacher and was unusually comfortable with on-the-spot note-taking. She helped me enormously with genealogies, mapping, and many other tedious endeavors besides sharing with me her life history and a wealth of information about scores of ᶜAmran families.

Tagiya delighted in visitors, was eager for news of anyone and everything, and especially enjoyed having an appreciative audience for her wit and counsel. Her regular visitors were women outside the mainstream of society, poor or lowborn or only recently moved from their villages (greenhorns). Tagiya herself was poor but highborn and, although not a native ᶜAmrania, well established after over a decade's residence. The single star of the group, she seemed to prefer friends who were grateful for their association with her.

It was Tagiya who arranged for me to visit local female healers, although she considered them amusing fakes. We went together, sometimes accompanied by one or two of her friends—once howling with laughter all the way home after a conspicuously poor performance. Whatever excursions we made together Tagiya enjoyed to the hilt. She stopped to chat with any acquaintance who crossed our path, and more often than not suggested second and third places where we ought to call. Knowing that her illness would soon again confine her to her house, she was hungry for contact and stimulation; and I was her perfect companion.

There was also great interest for me in following the preparations for and marriage of Tagiya's older daughter Nuria. This match was unique in that Nuria was the first ᶜAmrani girl of *sayyid* descent (from the line of the Prophet through his cousin ᶜAli) to marry a tribesman. It was Tagiya rather than her husband who accepted the proposal despite the acute disapproval of many *sayyid* families, and I tried very hard to understand her reasons. She had known and liked the young man and his village family for a very long time, and may have felt that, as a poor woman without sons, her future prospects were best protected by selecting a son-in-law who would be bound in gratitude to her. Additionally, Nuria was frail, and Tagiya might have feared no better offers would be made. Another factor may have been Tagiya's regretful perception that deference toward *sāda* was a thing of the past. At any rate, even before the wedding the prospective son-in-law visited Tagiya and Nuria frequently, and I observed their behavior together as well as community reaction to them.

Not all my morning visiting was at Ummi Amina's, Karima's, or Tagiya's. Less regularly I called on other neighbors and women in other parts of town, and there were occasional formal morning parties as well. Most formal visiting, however, took place in the afternoon, and for that I, like most ᶜAmrani women, sought diversity rather than familiarity.

As described in chapters 4, 6, and 8, most households receive afternoon guests after a birth, marriage, or death. They are visited by any (ideally all) women with whom they have social ties, whose houses they have previously visited. Neighbors, relatives, in-laws, former neighbors, and friends are expected to make one or several appearances, or risk damaging their relationship with the celebrants. Women with extensive networks are kept busy meeting their obligations. Most delight in having a wide choice of houses to visit and coming in contact with women outside their immediate networks. One doesn't know who will show up on a given day and this unpredictability adds great interest to afternoon social life.

As soon as my language skills and courage allowed, I began using the visiting patterns to gain access to new people. Curiosity about me remained high outside my neighborhood, and invitations poured in. Some men even asked my husband to send me to their wives' receptions, usually at the women's request.

At first I learned much more from watching and listening than from conversing at afternoon gatherings. While most talk was about women both present and absent and their families, there were also discussions of local and national politics. Banter was lively and witty, sometimes with a sharp competitive edge. In many houses we watched television, not a total research waste because comments about the "worldly" themes of the mostly imported programs gave me insight into evaluations of Yemeni versus "modern" foreign ways. Still, I preferred houses without television, where women had to be their own entertainment and where there was always a chance of hearing folk tales.

Of course I also talked with women sitting near me and arranged later visits with those who seemed good potential informants. Over half of the fifty women to whom I administered a structured interview schedule were initially met in this way.[1]

With the approach of nightfall, gatherings broke up and women headed home. I often spent the next half hour or hour sitting with neighbors on one of our front stoops. We exchanged information about where each had gone, the quality of the setting and company, interesting news acquired, and funny or dramatic episodes observed.

Occasionally a few of us reassembled outside again after our separate evening meals.

Other evenings I stopped to see a good friend before returning home. When Tagiya was too ill to go out, I passed this time with her. There was about a month, late in my research, when I spent the early evening with another ailing neighbor, Amina, one of the Karima klatch mentioned earlier. This was the Amina who, on my first day in ᶜAmran, had deceived me into accompanying her to a formal party. She angered me on a few other occasions as well, like the time she accidentally recorded over my precious tape of a rare performance by a retired local comedienne. For the most part, however, Amina was great fun, a loyal, helpful friend, and a superb informant.

Amina's long, bizarre illness and treatments (from town and village healers as well as from physicians in the capital) were of immense interest to me, as were the reactions of her family and friends. After several weeks of only very slow improvement, she was moved to her sister's house on the opposite end of town. She seemed to me to be making steady progress, but Amina considered her condition unchanged and was hurt that few friends took time to come visit her. I knew the crisis had finally passed when one late afternoon she greeted me with a strong hint of her old high spirits. "Any minute now," she said, "scads of women are going to walk up these stairs. They're coming," she explained, laughing almost uncontrollably, "because some other woman died around here today and my sister says the story got garbled and everyone thinks it was me!" Obviously that rumor was the external trigger, but I never understood what internal development allowed Amina to give up her invalid role at that time. She continued to improve and regain strength and was almost fully recovered when I left ᶜAmran. She was pregnant with her second child when I last had news of her in 1982.

My favorite place to go following afternoon visits was the house of my closest friend Arwa. This chapter closes with a description of Arwa and our relationship. There were of course other good friends and informants who have not been mentioned here; but of all those mentioned or not, Arwa stands out as the woman whose friendship meant most to me in my year and a half in ᶜAmran.

Arwa was late in a pregnancy when I began fieldwork and too

busy and tired from caring for her small children to make many social calls. When she saw me pass her rented house, a few streets from my own, and heard about me from other women, she decided she wanted to meet me. A friendship with an educated ᶜAdeni woman had been the high point of an earlier residence in Sanᶜa, where her soldier husband was still posted. I think she hoped for similar stimulation from knowing an American.

After her son was born and her month of receiving afternoon guests began, she asked her husband, who came home every weekend, to induce me to call. His willingness may have been influenced by an expectation that my visit would enhance their prestige, but he was also genuinely eager to cheer her. They had too many small children, he told my husband and me, and it took a great toll on both of them. Ahmad's story interested me, but I did not go to see Arwa. So many invitations were proferred at that time, and I was reluctant to enter a house where I knew no one. The following weekend Ahmad spoke to my husband again, and the next one as well. Then, spotting me on his street one morning, he called to me and pointed out which house was his. That afternoon I ventured in.

Our first meeting was only a partial success. I had considerable difficulty following Arwa's quick speech, and she must have been disappointed by my thickness. She, her mother, and sister, however, treated me with exceptional tact and gentleness, as did the other guests present. Most of the afternoon calls I had made were my neighbors' suggestions: the big, lively gatherings where music played constantly and dozens of women carried out simultaneous conversations, many participating in two or three at a time. These exhausted and frustrated me, and I hadn't yet learned how to deal with hostesses' complaints about my not having visited them previously and their insistence that I spend all subsequent afternoons at their house. If there was similar pressure at Arwa's, it was applied with far greater delicacy. The atmosphere was soothingly quiet and peaceful; and, since guests were usually few and music soft, I could understand much more of what was said. I continued visiting, often arriving well before other guests and staying after their departure.

After the customary large party marked the end of Arwa's six-week confinement, she cultivated our friendship with food gifts. Within a month my husband began doing her daily shopping, taking over the job from her maddeningly incompetent older son. (Men almost invariably do the daily shopping in the *sūq*, not the women.) This regular reciprocity gave our friendship a public dimension: her neighbors saw Tom collect his order and drop off the goods and ours saw her daughter deliver our bread and sometimes other dishes as well.

My attraction for Arwa was enhanced by her relative isolation. Her mother and full sister lived most of the year in Sanᶜa; her relations with ᶜAmrani half-siblings and in-laws were not close; and no more than superficial friendliness had developed between her and her neighbors, partly because of her recent move into the neighborhood. Her husband was away except on weekends; and disciplining the children, especially the older boy, was difficult. Arwa was simply too encumbered to go out most afternoons and so eagerly looked forward to my stopping in. This I did with increasing frequency, either coming or going from my formal visits. Once in a while I spent the entire afternoon with her, and periodically, especially during the sacred month of Ramadhan, visited during the evening as well.

Arwa's was only one of several life histories I recorded, but, because her recollections and reflections flowed naturally through our lengthy, intimate relationship, they are richer in meaning. Key events and periods came up over and over again in varied mood and context, so that, over time, I gained a perception of how Arwa's sense of self and of others had evolved. This perspective was balanced by watching her interactions with her children and father-in-law every day; her husband every weekend; her mother and sister during their visits to ᶜAmran and ours to Sanᶜa; and her relatives, in-laws, neighbors, and friends who visited her occasionally and some of whom we called on together.

About six months after the birth of her son, Arwa learned she was pregnant again. This was a terrible blow. She worried that her youngest son would be unable to cope with being replaced so early, and dreaded being even more tied down than she already was. Arwa wanted to attend the Arabic class for adult women; she wanted her husband to save money so they could stop renting and buy or build a house of their own. She longed for forward movement, but with repeated pregnancies, steady inflation, and other matters outside her control none seemed possible. Despite Arwa's great resilience of spirit, there were interludes of depression and irritability.

Her mother and sister, although both busy in San'a and displeased by Arwa's pregnancy, occasionally came to 'Amran to help with the children and the special preparations for the new baby. They moved in with Arwa about two weeks before the birth was expected, and stayed in 'Amran until her six-week postpartum confinement was over. My husband and I set our departure for the same time. Arwa and I were acutely aware that our friendship was to draw to a close in the same way it had begun.

Like almost all 'Amrani women, Arwa intended to give birth at home, and it was important to both of us that I be present. Because labor is kept secret in 'Amran and no close friend had given birth during my stay, I had been unable to attend a home birth. Arwa understood my desire for firsthand observation and had her own reasons for desiring my presence as well. She had felt intense panic during previous labors when left alone. Her mother had had to attend to the children or fetch hot water from the kitchen, and, although her absences were brief, Arwa had been terrified. With me there too, someone would always be with her.

When the time came, Arwa's sister closeted herself in a downstairs room with the children, leaving her mother and me free to assist in the birth. Partly because her mother had injured her hand, my role was more that of a participant than an observer. Still, between contractions, Arwa filled me in on everything that was happening and why her mother and I were doing what we were, and I marveled at what an extraordinary friend and informant she was. The labor turned out to be much longer and more difficult than her previous ones, but eventually a daughter was born. Some 'Amranis believe a baby will resemble the person in whose company the mother has spent the most time, and one of Arwa's first comments was that the tiny girl didn't have my nose after all. She did, however, give the baby my name.

During the first several days after birth, visitors are few. The new mother rests while her family converts one of the best rooms into a richly decorated reception chamber. This responsibility fell to Arwa's sister and me. The visiting began one week after the birth and continued until Susan was six weeks old. My role, of course, was entirely different from what it had been in that reception room a year earlier, giving me a clear and poignant sense of what I had learned and how I had changed between these two births.

In most ways I felt ready to leave ᶜAmran, but I was deeply pained at losing my ᶜAmrani friends, Arwa in particular. Our already considerable intimacy had deepened since the birth, perhaps partly because of my impending departure. I promised Arwa and others that we would never forget them and that we would return within a few years. So far I have kept only the first part of that promise, but my husband was in ᶜAmran just under three years later. He found Arwa still in the same rented house. Her situation had changed little except that Susan already had two younger siblings. Arwa's message to me was that I could imagine how crazy she had become with all these babies. During her pregnancy with Susan she had frequently predicted with a desperate laugh that the new baby would be her final unhinging, so I was little comforted by Tom's report that her message had been delivered with a laugh. I wanted to know how she felt, but this of course Tom could not tell me. She had been fully veiled so he had not even seen her expression.

Tom brought news of many of my friends, but the facts gave me surprisingly little satisfaction. What I craved was more personal. In writing this book, I relied heavily on the facts and hard data I collected: genealogies, household compositions, results of structured interview schedules, detailed descriptions of specific tasks and rituals, and so on. What imbued all this with meaning, however, was my sense of informants as persons. Like Jules Henry, "I have to see *that person* before me and what I cannot see as *that actuality*, what I cannot hear as the sound of *that voice*, has little interest for me" (Henry 1973:xv).

4

A Typical Day

In ʿAmran, as in most Arab Muslim traditional communities, women are largely excluded from public space. They may not pray in mosques, and are expected to avoid the *sūq* when possible. They do not enter restaurants or tea shops or take part in local elections, although many visit the town's clinic, pharmacies, and traditional healers.

Men's absence from the home is almost as marked as that of women from the *sūq*. Even those without work or other commitments leave the house early in the morning, return briefly at lunchtime, only to absent themselves again for the rest of the day. Exceptions to this pattern are rare and deviation from it may be taken as indication that a man is ill.

If a man does return home at an irregular time, he is expected to provide a loud advance warning, in case women outside his immediate circle are present. Makhlouf (1979:29–30), who observed this practice in Sanʿa, sees it as a preventative against infringement on the separate female sphere:

> I have seen it happen that a man enters his house while there is a female gathering there. In this case, he is required to say "Allah! Allah!" loudly a number of times while climbing the stairs of his house, so that the women, hearing him, are able to change their comportment and cover their faces before he sees them. This [is an] exclusion ritual. . . . A man can never see a female gathering under normal conditions since his very presence completely changes the definition of the situation.

In contrast to men and women, young children have access to both public and private space. This freedom allows them to learn

54 / *A Typical Day*

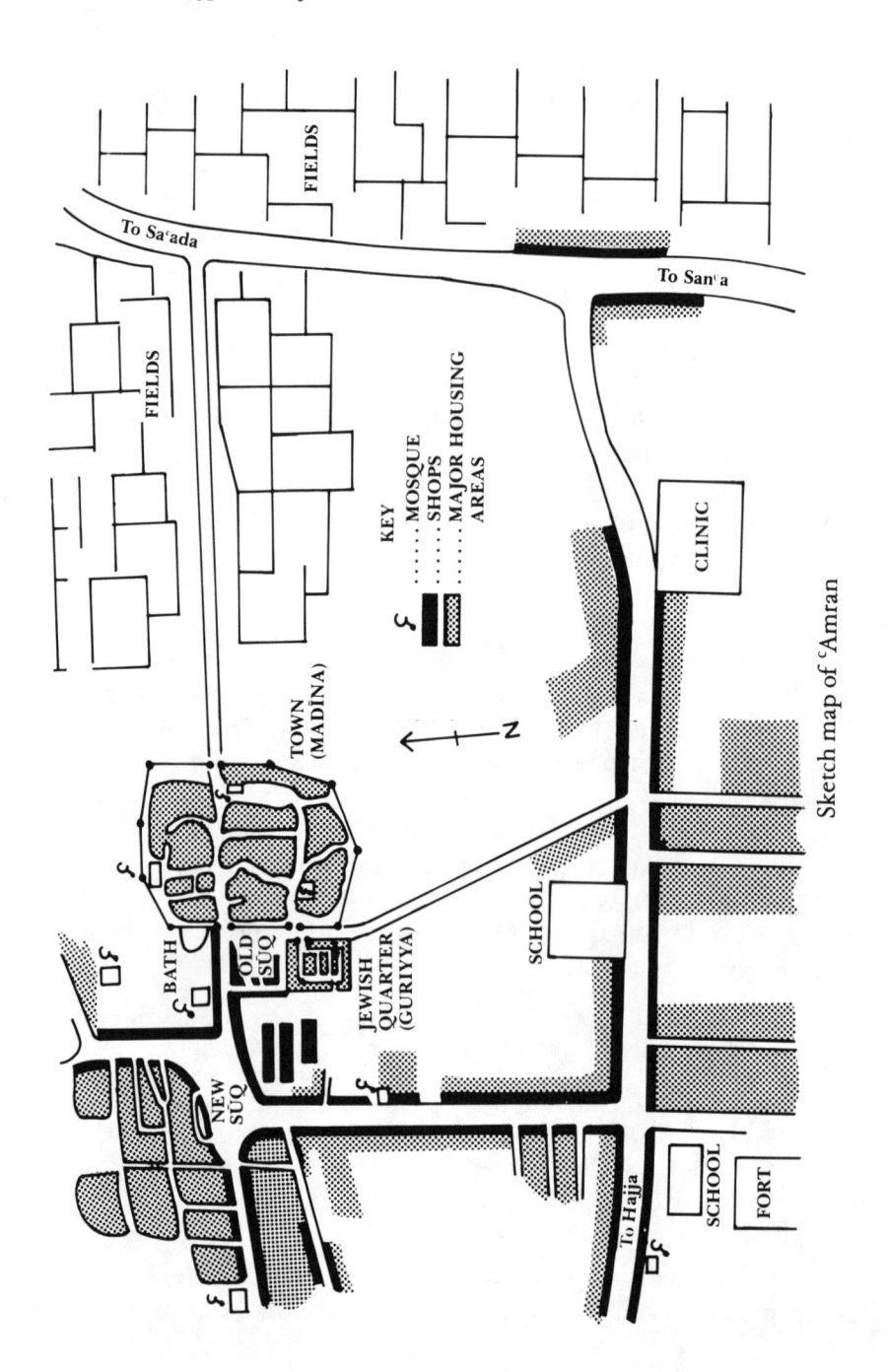

Sketch map of ʿAmran

Neighborhood children outside my front door on a particularly cluttered day. It is the responsibility of women to sweep the street in front of their houses.

about both the male and female worlds, knowledge that will be invaluable in adulthood. Many ᶜAmrani women remember the layout and atmosphere of the *sūq* from their girlhood shopping errands. Similarly, men may recall from boyhood experience the demeanor and conversation of their mothers and other women when no men were present. It is probable that each sex's model of the other derives largely from the impressions of childhood, the only period in which direct observation and interaction are allowed. As Schildkrout (1978:128) writes of the Hausa, the symbolic transition to adulthood "really comes about when the freedom to move inside and outside houses, between male and female domains, is restricted."

Although men and women do not understand (and appear to have little interest in) the subtleties of each others' social and mental worlds, they do know in a general way each others' patterns of work and leisure. This chapter is intended to provide the reader a similar broad familiarity with women's and men's typical daily activities and concerns. Subsequent chapters will add flesh to the skeletal model of the female domain presented here.

In theory the dawn prayer call starts an ᶜAmran day. Dawn is the first of five set times for ritual prayer, each with its fixed recitations from the Quran and fixed number and order of bowings (*rakᶜa*). Each prayer must be preceded by washing one's face and lower extremities. Particularly in the coldest months, people find it difficult to wake and wash by dawn. A few men do arrive at a mosque every day in time for the dawn devotion, but most men and all women perform their morning prayers at home and not always immediately following the call to prayer.

The women of some households bake fresh bread for breakfast; others serve their families bread from the previous day's lunch. Bread is eaten plain or spread with *samn* (clarified butter), and accompanied by *bin* (coffee, which is prepared only in the morning), *gishr* (coffee-husk brew), or tea. A more substantial breakfast will be eaten later in the morning, also consisting mainly of fresh bread. ᶜAmrani women make several different kinds of bread; breakfast varieties include *gurum* (also called *gafuᶜ*, made of lentil flour or a combination of lentil and sorghum flours) and *jahīn* (made of sorghum and heavy and thick like *gurum*). *Khubz* (a very thin flat bread usually made of imported wheat) and *malūj* (made of wheat, barley, or a combination of the two) are made at lunchtime,

Men in the marketplace.

sometimes in the morning as well. Despite the increasing use of imported foods, the Yemeni highlands diet remains heavily reliant on cereals, and bread is still the core of all meals in this region.

Children, having slept in their clothes, often head directly outside upon awakening. Some do not even wait for breakfast in their eagerness for the company of their friends in the *shāri^c* (street). The younger ones will pass most of the day outdoors, usually under the care of older sisters.

Like the children, men are eager to get out of the house. Most, when free of other obligations, begin their day in the *sūq* (market). In addition to making the daily household food purchases, they use the time to chat, and to begin the construction and reconstruction of their plans for the afternoon. For the majority of ʿAmrani men, who chew *gāt* (the mildly stimulant leaves of *Catha edulis*) regularly, the daily decision as to what, where, and with whom to chew is the object of much talk and keen interest.

The household purchases (an imported frozen chicken or some local meat, perhaps green onions, tomatoes, rice, or potatoes) are taken home at a man's leisure, although rarely actually carried into the house. Most men knock on the front door or simply yell the name of their eldest son, because it is considered rude for either spouse to address the other by name when outsiders might overhear them. They then wait, sometimes with visible displays of impatience, for a woman or child of the household to descend the stairs (one or several flights) to collect the groceries. (Although some of the very new houses are single-story buildings, traditional ʿAmran houses have two or more stories, the ground floor used for storing livestock, equipment, and grain; the middle floor often for storage as well; and the top floor or floors containing the kitchen(s), toilet(s), and one or several additional rooms used for sleeping, eating, and visiting. These upper rooms are almost always whitewashed and covered with mats, rugs, and mattresses.)

The considerate shopper delivers the food early enough to avoid inconveniencing his household's women, but even usually reliable ones sometimes get sidetracked. Not infrequently, women complain that lunch was a near disaster because supplies were late (the chicken, for example, was tasteless because it had to be rush-defrosted in a pot of hot water).

A ʿAmrani man plows a terraced field.

After shopping, most men spend the balance of the morning at work. Many engage in retail or wholesale trade, drive taxis, or labor in construction. There are a few legal and religious specialists, a number of pharmacists, and many government employees, including soldiers from throughout Yemen (assigned to the town fort), police, clerks, teachers, members of the local development board, and other officials. At planting and harvesting times, men of varied occupations (and some women) engage in agricultural work, but few ᶜAmrani men farm year round. As in Ibb, "townsmen have a wide range of service occupations. While material production is primarily a rural phenomenon, the town is a service economy, specializing in distribution" (Messick, 1978:135).

If at leisure, as many men appear to be, they frequently return to the *sūq*. Tea shops, restaurants, and certain retail stores are the hub of male socializing in the morning. With the arrival of the day's *gāt*, men examine and consider at length the available qualities and their going rates. After he has bargained for his *gāt*, a man still has to decide where and with whom to chew it in the afternoon. These and other highly varied matters are discussed over second breakfasts (brought from home or bought in the *sūq*) and endless cups of *gishr* and tea. Enjoying the steady stream of social encounters, men circulate through the market area, rarely returning home until after the noon prayers.

At their homes, women have been occupied during the early morning hours with housework, preliminary food preparation and child care. Although many women may share with men and children a conviction that life outside the home is far more stimulating than life within it, most are at home for the larger part of the morning. The degree of confinement varies, however, with a woman's age, the age and sex of her children, and the presence or absence of other women in the household. The least restricted women are mothers-in-law with resident daughters-in-law; mothers of mature, competent daughters; and those living compatibly with one or more sisters-in-law. Still, women with few domestic responsibilities may choose to stay home. Some are seamstresses who earn money for their own use by their work; others who believe it is unseemly for women to gad about too much stay home for propriety's sake. There are also

A Typical Day / 61

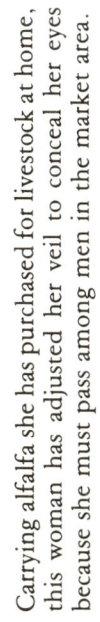

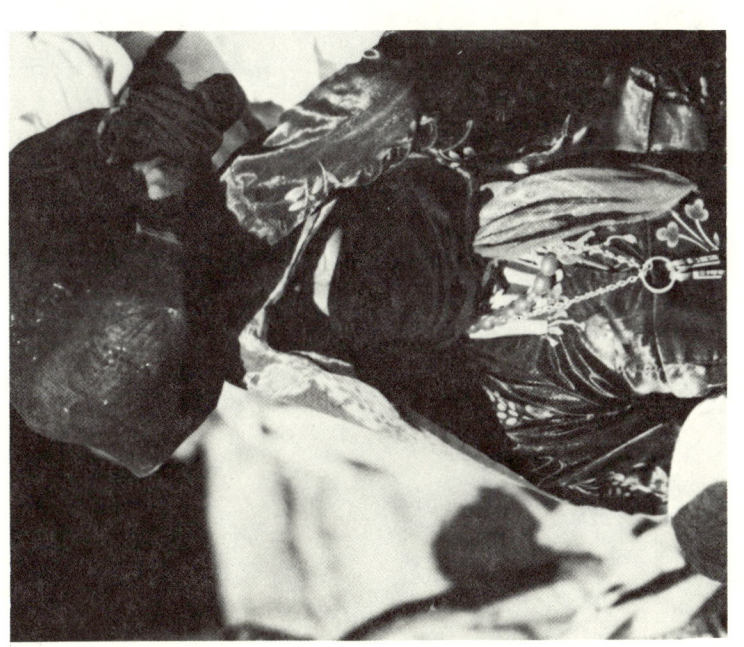

Carrying alfalfa she has purchased for livestock at home, this woman has adjusted her veil to conceal her eyes because she must pass among men in the market area.

A village woman carries a frozen chicken and other purchases.

62 / *A Typical Day*

Two women carry laundry to one of the pumps outside of town. A third woman carries bread to be sold in the marketplace.

A young married woman washes clothes next to her house.

women whose movements outside the house are severely restricted by unusually controlling husbands.

Some women's usual work loads are light. Myntti (1978:34) correctly states that the time required in daily housecleaning is very short in most North Yemeni households and that no more than three hours are spent in the kitchen on normal days. However, additional demands on female time and energy recur regularly in other households. There may be livestock that require care and milk to be converted to *laban* (skimmed sour milk) or *samn*. For women whose houses are not connected to the town's piped waterlines, there is the daily fetching of large quantities of water, either from sympathetic neighbors or from a mosque.

In all households, rooms and stairs are swept every morning. An older girl or adult woman does this. Preliminary lunch preparations (such as kneading the bread dough) also must be carried out every morning. Laundry is done at least once a week, by a woman or older girl, either at home or at one of several wells outside town. Other work is more variable. Chopping wood, processing grain, major housecleaning, and whitewashing are irregularly recurring jobs, adding significantly to the female work load. Some women, as mentioned earlier, also help their kinsmen or husbands with agricultural work.

Any of these irregular expansions of a woman's work may keep her occupied throughout the morning, in which case she will take a quick second breakfast at home. Some women breakfast at home routinely, but others savor the opportunity to get out of their houses. Most, restricted by time and by a desire to stay near the children playing outdoors, take this late-morning break with neighbors.

Women fill their thermoses or kettles with *gishr* or tea, perhaps wrap up some bread or grind a little spicy tomato relish to contribute to the pooled breakfast. Before stepping out the front door, they must pull their face veils up to cover the mouth and nose and drape themselves in the large, black cotton cloth (*fūṭa*) that is the ᶜAmran style of outer veiling. All women and older girls wear this outside the home except for the rare occasions (to go to Sanᶜa or attend a major celebration) when they wear instead the elaborate and dressy Sanᶜa style of outer garb. These hasty preparations completed, they dash to the house of their current intimate friend or to the house that has become, for any of several reasons, the current neighborhood morning gathering site.

Children are sent out to the street after eating, or fed at home prior to their mothers' departure, so women are free to enjoy each other's company and conversation with few interruptions. They linger over cup after cup of their own and their neighbor's *gishr* or tea, basking in the comfortable informality of these neighborhood get-togethers. When women are without pressing work, the breakfasts are often prolonged until someone suddenly gasps "*Gadu sharak!*" (It's almost noon!). The ambience is shattered, as women realize that returning to their kitchens cannot be put off a moment longer.

Those women who are too pressed for time to breakfast with neighbors but who are lucky enough to live on a relatively secluded street, may take their morning breaks outdoors. In the older sections of town the streets are narrow and the houses close together, if not actually connected. Not many houses have courtyards, so in most areas the entrances are right on the street and only a very short distance from those of their neighbors to either side and across the street. At all but the busiest hours of the day, any woman who appears on her own or a neighbor's stoop will probably soon be joined by others. In cool weather, women spend free moments on the sunniest of stoops. Even on hot days, despite the coolness of house interiors and the ʿAmranis' conviction that exposure to sun is debilitating and even dangerous, women's gregariousness still draws them to the street. They congregate inside a doorway if there are no shady patches on the street.

For most women the hour or two before lunch is frantic and exhausting. A four- to six-course meal must be prepared and bread baked with limited equipment and in a short time. Bread is baked in a cone-shaped oven (*tanūr*) made of mud or clay, with firewood or dung cakes used as fuel, or baked on the sides of the *tanūr* as the last stage of the lunch preparation because of the strong preference for warm bread. In some households all dishes are prepared in or on top of the *tanūr*; in others, primus stoves are also used. Two-burner stoves that operate on bottled gas are still rare but gaining in popularity. These do not replace the *tanūr* in ʿAmran, however, since breads and other local dishes can be prepared satisfactorily only in the traditional way. The drawbacks of the Yemeni highlands kitchen have been well described by Bornstein (1974:23):

> For different reasons, sometimes "to prevent anyone from looking in," sometimes "to protect from draught and dust," the windows are kept very small and the ventilation holes are completely inadequate to let the smoke out. The women spend several hours of the day in these dark places, which, when the ovens are lit, get exceedingly hot and smoky. A person who is not used to the smoke can hardly bear the atmosphere for more than a few minutes.

While women cook, most men head to one of the town's ten mosques, where they perform the noon prayers and socialize until lunchtime. Many dawdle in the company of friends, but some young fathers return home early to play with their small children. The time shortly before lunch (when most women are certain to be occupied in their kitchens) is almost the only period when men pass time on residential streets.

In most large extended households, especially those with two or more married brothers and many children, men eat separately and in advance of women and children. In households of smaller extended families or of nuclear families, lunch is consumed jointly unless male guests are present. In each case, lunch is eaten in a very simply furnished room. There are usually a few blankets spread on the floor, and a large plastic cloth is often laid down in the eating area. Household members seat themselves in no fixed order around this cloth after all dishes have been brought from the kitchen and placed on a low charcoal grill to keep warm. The courses are served one by one.

Some women say they prefer eating separately from the men because men eat so much faster than they do. When the entire household lunches together, men set the pace of the meal since, as women say, most men are eager to get out of their houses as quickly as possible. Except at weddings and other large gatherings, all-female groups tend to eat in a very leisurely manner.

Children sometimes show minimal interest in the early courses. When this happens, they are allowed to wander away from the eating area if they so choose. However, when the final course, the meat, is served, they almost always reappear. Meat is the preferred

A young father passes a few minutes with his firstborn before going in to lunch.

food for the majority of children, women, and men in ʿAmran. It and its broth are the only courses that are divided and distributed by an adult. All other courses are simply placed in the center of the eating space for each person to serve her- or himself. Children watch the distribution of the meat with keen interest, and arguments can develop as to the relative size and quality of their own and their siblings' or cousins' shares.

After the meat course, people lean back against a cushion to finish the meal with *gishr* or tea, although some men opt for tea in the clearly preferred male atmosphere of the *sūq*. Young children fall asleep or go outside to play.

The men gone (to the *sūq* or to their rooms for a rest), the women relax over several cups of tea or *gishr*. They stretch their legs, and some take brief naps. When cleaning up from lunch is delegated to older daughters, the women can relax at this time. They descend to the street to chat again with neighbors before washing for the afternoon prayer, which will mark the transition from workday to leisure time for most women.

After their tea in the *sūq*, men may head to the mosques for the afternoon prayer. Others, who retired to their rooms for naps, may pray at home. Most men chew *gāt* in the afternoons. This habit is common among ʿAmrani men and youths despite the steep price of *gāt* (approximately $5 to $20 per day) and its acknowledged unpleasant aftereffects, including loss of appetite, difficulty falling asleep, constipation, irritability, and reduced sexual potency. Most abstainers cannot afford to buy *gāt* on a regular basis, but there are a few men who abjure out of agreement with government criticisms of the economic, health, and social effects of *gāt* usage. Daily chewing, however, remains the ideal pattern, and men believe they will fall ill with flu if they miss a single day. Although a few merchants, drivers, and other workers chew alone while they work, most men spend their afternoon at leisure, gathering together for the major social occasion of the day. Some men chew in public offices, others in friends' shops, but most prefer rooms in private homes.

Men take pride in the rich furnishings and fine views from their reception rooms (*dīwān* or *mafraj*), and some host *gāt* sessions on a daily or nearly daily basis. Other households compete with these regulars on special occasions: after a member has returned from Saudi Arabia or in conjunction with a marriage or a death. With the exception of wedding celebrations, all *gāt* gatherings are open to all men; no invitations, formal or informal, are required.

Although most men chew regularly in the same places, there is considerable morning and after-lunch discussion in the *sūq* as to where each man will go. At least some of the time these are real decisions, since men do occasionally switch allegiances. A particular home will attract large numbers every day for months, only to fade gradually or abruptly in popularity, often for no obvious reasons. A house that has attracted only a handful of guests for six months or longer may suddenly become "the place to be," usually after friends and neighbors, having paid a special-occasion obligatory visit, find the setting and company to their liking and keep coming back.

Some men arrive at their chosen location shortly after lunch, but the majority arrive after performing the afternoon prayers, between three o'clock and half past three. They stay for approximately three hours, until shortly before the first evening prayer call. The afternoons pass through regular stages, although these vary somewhat with the quality of *gāt* and when men are preoccupied by important local events or conflicts:

> The real effect of the drug—which is a pleasant feeling of well-being and alertness—comes after less than an hour, but it is often anticipated by the *habitues*, so that the conversation becomes quite spirited already before the large balls have begun showing. The alert and sociable phase lasts for an hour or two. What follows is a more introvert phase, when the conversation gradually subsides and the only noise to be heard will be the heavy snoring noise of the hubble-bubble [water pipe]. . . . Each . . . is deep in his own thoughts, often quite pleasant ones: *gat* does not make one take a bleak view of the future. As the sun disappears . . . the men sit motionless in the dusk and often speechless, until someone with a barely intelligible grunt gets to his feet: "Peace be with you." No one takes much notice. The enthusiastic party that was, has fallen apart into certainly content but less talkative individuals. (Gerholm 1977:178).

Women, too, visit in the afternoons, but extremely few of them chew *gāt*. Whereas in Sanᶜa and in most villages in the ᶜAmran area it is quite acceptable for women to chew *gāt* and to smoke the water pipe (*madāᶜa*), this is not the case for ᶜAmran women. Most women and men of ᶜAmran believe it is wrong for ᶜAmrani women to chew, but tolerate the use of *gāt* by Sanᶜanias and villagers.

There are two overlapping time slots for women's afternoon visits, *gahwa ghuda* (lunch coffee) and *tūdara* (after the afternoon prayers). Most women who pay *gahwa ghuda* calls do so shortly after lunch in the work dresses they have been wearing all day. These early calls are usually to households that are in mourning or have recently experienced a birth.

Whereas men's reception rooms have their water pipes and paraphernalia specific to *gāt* use, in women's reception rooms there is always a charcoal grill and trays of small cups. Visitors usually bring either a kettle or thermos of *gishr* or tea, which they deposit upon arrival on or next to the charcoal grill. One of the women of the household sits behind the grill, filling and refilling cups all afternoon long.

Gahwa ghuda callers usually stay about one hour or sometimes until all the early visitors' *gishr* and tea have been drunk. With the first arrival of *tūdara* callers, most *gahwa ghuda* ones promptly depart. They return home to wash and pray, and to dress up for their own *tūdara* calls.

Since most women could not interrupt their cooking to pray at the time of the midday prayer call, they perform those devotions and the afternoon ones following the afternoon call, permissible because of the relative flexibility of Zaydi Islam on the combination of prayers (al-Abdin 1975:40–41). Those who are menstruating do not pray since menstruation is one of the six acts that according to Islam create the condition of "major ritual impurity" (the others are "effusion of semen, afterbirth blood, sexual connection . . . childbirth, and death" [Antoun 1968:674]). They may dress and be out visiting earlier than usual.

The degree to which women dress up for *tūdara* varies with the specific occasion. For marriage-related celebrations at which a *muzayyina* (female musician) performs, women wear their best dresses and display most of their gold and coral jewelry. These major social occasions are extremely well attended, and reception rooms get very hot and crowded. For more routine *tūdara* calls, it is sufficient for a woman to put on a fresh afternoon dress and slacks, a pretty scarf, and a clean veil. The effect is usually embellished by at least a little gold or coral jewelry, some cologne or perfume, and possibly a sweet-basil blossom worn at the ear. Some younger women regularly apply cosmetics as part of their preparations for the afternoon round of visits.

Tūdara calls are paid to households of new mothers, new brides, the bereaved, returnees from pilgrimages to Mecca, and to those who are celebrating the return of a son or husband from work in Saudi Arabia. As with men's *gāt* gatherings, no invitations are needed, although each woman has her own visiting network. Unlike men's *gāt* sessions, which are open to married and single men, women's receptions are only for married women, widows, and divorcees. Those who never married, regardless of their age, are excluded from all such gatherings, although they may join kinswomen and neighbors in more informal settings.

Whereas it is considered polite to make only one *tūdara* call a day, some women manage two or three. It is unspeakably rude to admit that one is quitting a gathering for the purpose of visiting another, and fixed formula excuses are offered. These are almost never challenged, even when recognized as patent lies. Etiquette requires dissimulation, rather than truthfulness, in this as in many other social situations.

Because *gāt* is used by so few ʿAmrani women, their gatherings are not characterized by the same mood shifts as men's sessions. They drink tea and *gishr*, eat a little popcorn, candy, and dates at larger parties, and pass the afternoon in animated conversation. Besides chatting and joking, they may listen to music, dance, watch television, and tell stories until the room becomes so dark that faces across the room are barely visible. Then women begin to leave, usually in the same groups of twos and threes as they arrived, the last stragglers often rousing themselves only when the evening prayer call is heard.

Men, after leaving their *gāt* sessions, head for the mosques and the *sūq*. They rarely appear at home promptly after praying, preferring a leisurely cup of tea, usually in the company of friends with whom they did not chew. The appetite-reducing effect of *gāt* ensures that hunger will not hasten the return home for dinner.

Knowing their husbands will linger in the *sūq* and mosques, women too can leisurely return home, unless babies or toddlers require their attention at home. In the warm months, the women of some neighborhoods settle on their stoops for a last visit with their neighbors. They exchange news of the day and comic descriptions of episodes observed while visiting, clearly enjoying the relaxed atmosphere and intimacy that characterize these twilight gatherings. Only when the men return or the needs of small children force women to rise do they, often reluctantly, enter their homes for the night.

By this hour children are usually hungry and tired, having had long days of playing, squabbling, and, if they are old enough, school. Older girls habitually help with sweeping, laundering, and food preparation and spend most of their waking hours attending to younger siblings. If allowed, they attend school in the afternoon, but otherwise remain close to home for the day. Older boys are much less likely to perform domestic or child-care work; however, some regularly help fathers or other kinsmen at their places of employment. Boys attend school (secular except in summer when it is religious) in the morning, and are far more likely than girls to play away from their own streets in their leisure time. Boys and girls both run errands in the *sūq*, but only boys linger there. They are encouraged to enter this important male social domain; girls are taught that any dawdling in the *sūq* will tarnish their reputations.

With twilight younger children are often eager to get indoors, hungry both for food and their mothers' attentions. Women, once indoors, must juggle the demands of their children with their own need to perform the two evening prayers.

After the men return the family settles down in a minimally furnished room for the rest of the evening. They watch television if they own one and eat a light meal of reheated *ḥalba* (a fenugreek-based sauce) and bread left from lunch, followed by tea or *gishr*. The children fall asleep one by one, the parents usually following suit when the television transmission halts about eleven o'clock or an hour or two earlier if they don't own a set.

Unless the house has too few rooms, each man has his own comfortably furnished bedroom. His wife may visit him there, but she usually sleeps in a shabbier room with her children. In a nuclear family household, parents may sleep in the room where they ate and watched television. In some extended households, young children sleep with their paternal grandmother, and their mother with their father.

This sketch of an ʿAmran day dealt only with routine. Marriages, births, deaths, holidays, conflicts, and seasonal and other fluctuations commonly disrupt the flow of events. Still, it provides a sense of the separation of female and male spheres, and the slightness of wife-husband contact in contrast to each one's embeddedness in relations with other women or men.

5

Daughters and Sons

> So, since I knew my husband really wanted a son, when he came in to me after I gave birth, and it was very dark, I kept slurring my pronunciation, making him think I was saying "she" instead of "he" when referring to the baby. Only after he suggested naming the child "Atigha" [a girl's name], did I laugh and reveal the truth. "Atigha?" I asked. "But it's a boy." How happy my husband was then!

Sons are preferred over daughters in ᶜAmran. In the Muslim Middle East in general, although both parents gain recognition as full adults only after the birth of a son, there are additional reasons for women's preference for male children:

> The threat of divorce [for a woman] on the basis of childlessness is eliminated and her future security is ensured by the filial obligations of her son to care for her even if she is divorced. . . . A daughter is of limited value to her mother. Although she will be there to help with housework while she is growing up, after marriage a daughter's contribution to labor or material support will be drastically reduced or eliminated. A woman's sons, on the other hand, provide labor through the daughters-in-law they bring home and material maintenance in her old age if she loses her husband. A woman who has only daughters thus lacks security in many respects. (Bybee 1978:106)

ᶜAmrani women articulate all of these points, discussing the relative advantages and disadvantages of sons and daughters quite frequently, usually humorously, but occasionally with deadly seriousness. Laughingly they point out that the news of a female birth elicits markedly less enthusiasm than the news of a male birth. Women's as well as men's obligatory formalized responses to the birth of a girl stress the importance of the mother's health; those to the birth of a boy are more congratulatory. Men, who show little active interest in infants of either sex, express less concern for daughters than for sons. Every woman who gives birth (even to a stillborn) can expect cloth for a new dress from her husband, but the quality and cost of the fabric usually is determined in part by the sex of the child.

Although women often appear more amused than troubled by the general preference for sons, they sometimes point out that it is dangerous to carry this preference too far. They are joyful for every birth, female or male, live or stillborn, because whatever the baby's sex or condition it is from God. Men who are adamant about only wanting a son may evoke divine anger or human ridicule, as illustrated in the following two accounts:

> A man divorced his wife while she was four months pregnant, stating that if she gave birth to a son, he would take him, as was his prerogative. If she gave birth to a daughter, he would forgo his rights and let her keep her. Five months later his wife gave birth to a grotesquely deformed girl, who lived only two days, but whose appearance was so dreadful that the memory of her continues to haunt all who ever saw her. The infant's deformity was attributed to her father's impiety. It is God who gives a female or male child, and not for people to stipulate.

> A man was so upset to learn that his firstborn was a girl, that, instead of making the obligatory statements to his wife about the importance of her regaining her health, he said, "Let's throw the baby down the latrine!" Of course the baby girl was not thrown down the latrine, and her father grew to love her dearly. His wife subsequently gave birth to two more daughters but no sons, and he also loves each of them. He is a good father to all three of his girls, but still must endure occasional sarcastic questioning as to whether perhaps the children might best be just thrown down the latrine.

Women agree that there are unquestionable benefits derived from daughters. Some strongly prefer their daughters over their sons and berate young women who pine for male children. They say that when sons grow up and marry, they and their wives often make more trouble than they are worth, whereas daughters remain loyal and sons-in-law can be counted on for gifts at the ʿayd (holiday). There is no longer even any certainty that sons will stay home after marriage since neolocal residence is growing in popularity with the young. Whether they stay home or move out, conflict between women and their daughters-in-law is very common.

According to Myntti (1978:22):

> Yemeni women state that the preference for sons is not so strongly felt here in Yemen. Both daughters and sons are welcomed because the joys and benefits from each sex are different and differently timed. Daughters may threaten the family honor and eventually they are married off into another house, but they are nevertheless crucial to the division of household work while they are growing up. Women admit that they could not cope without their daughters and wish no one to be so unlucky as to have none.

ᶜAmrani women are for the most part disinclined to admit the degree to which they rely on their daughters' help, and they criticize them far more often than they praise them. However, there is an intimacy between mothers and daughters that both value profoundly. As in Morocco (Maher 1974) the mother-daughter tie remains close and strong throughout life. In Taroudannt, Morocco (Dwyer 1978:88), and Isfahan, Iran (Gulick and Gulick 1978:512), as well as in Yemen, most parents want daughters in addition to sons. Among Middle Eastern peasants in general, "daughters may not be as socially desirable as are sons, but there is no doubt that . . . they are an important, and welcome, part of the household" (Bybee 1978:32).

In ᶜAmran both women and men occasionally mention that the progressive inflation of the bridewealth enhances the economic value of daughters and that girls are usually docile and reliable whereas boys are often defiant and difficult to control:

> An informant said she asked her husband if he really minded that their new baby was a girl. He replied, "Not at all, only your health matters." Dissatisfied with his formal response, she pressed him, asking if that was really true or if he were just saying it. Annoyed, he told her that their firstborn son was such a trial to both of them, that it was better that the new baby was a girl.

In the past, male births received far greater social and cultural elaboration than female births, suggesting that the preference for sons may have been greater than it is presently. One might link this to the former greater importance of male roles in warfare among the northern tribes.

Boys are still circumcised between the ages of ten days and three weeks, and some still have their heads shaved at the end of their first year. No longer, however, are these events celebrated by a *ḥalāfa* (the serving of a meal to specially invited male guests). For the vast majority of ʿAmran families, the *ḥalāfa* is now limited to marriages and deaths.

In the past, after a few male relatives watched the barber circumcise the infant, breakfast was served to large numbers of men, all of whom were obligated to give a gift to the new mother. Now, in the words of informants, most families keep the matter quiet, notifying only the mother's father and brothers of the appointed time. She receives gifts only from them and from her husband.

Presently, as in the past, the mother and other women (as well as the father in many cases) are absent from the circumcision. It is feared that they might jump or call out at the sight of the razor, dangerously startling the infant or the barber. It is preferred that the infant be held by his maternal grandfather or by a maternal uncle, but any male relative is acceptable when these are not available. (One mother with a sick husband and no male kin in ʿAmran held her son for his circumcision; and, although this was viewed as most irregular, it was not regarded as shameful or improper in any way.) Both supernatural and medical precautions are taken to insure the operation's success and the boy's speedy recovery.

First the mother washes the baby's head and body, then lavishes him with protective rue and dresses and swaddles him. He is then taken to another room, where the barber awaits him usually accompanied by a few male relatives of the family.

The barber, who is paid about 50 riyals ($11) for performing the circumcision, has ready his razor, a coagulant made from local tree bark, and a pharmaceutical powder used to prevent infections. He places a white cloth below the infant, instructs the maternal grandfather or other kinsman how to hold the baby, and requests that myrrh, which is used to counteract demons (*jinn*) and devils (*shayāṭīn*), be brought in. Household members have given the barber two eggs.

The barber begins by circling an egg over the boy's head several times, repeating prayers at the same time. He then throws the egg across the room to the doorway. (The circling of the egg over his head protects the infant and hastens his recovery; throwing it out of the room casts out *jinn* and *shayāṭīn*.) Immediately following the discarding of the egg, the barber performs the circumcision, peels off the foreskin, and squeezes out some blood. Then he breaks a bit of shell off the second egg, and briefly places the penis inside the egg. He then removes the penis from inside the egg and puts the foreskin inside it. The egg is given to the men, and later it will be buried or hidden, preferably with rue or flowering basil so that the wound will heal rapidly. The barber completes his work by covering the entire penis with the thick and sticky local bark concoction, and then sprinkles sulfamide (a pharmaceutical powder) over that. The infant is ready to be taken away to his mother or to another woman to be swaddled and consoled.

It is thought that if he does not urinate immediately after the removal of his foreskin (and if the circumcision was performed properly and all menacing spirits kept away), the baby should recover within a few days. For at least three days, his mother either holds his legs apart or keeps him very tightly swaddled so he will not hurt himself inadvertently. She must be extremely attentive to his every want during this difficult period.

Female circumcisions are extremely rare in ʿAmran. Carried out only in cases of extreme clitoral protuberance, they receive no social or cultural elaboration. They are not uncommon, however, in at least two villages just outside ʿAmran. A *muzayyina* performs the operation, and sometimes it is celebrated by a breakfast *ḥalāfa*. Women from those villages say that "it is not nice for a girl to have something like a boy" and that unless a clitoris is very small, it probably will be removed.

It is difficult to assess whether there is further differential treatment of male and female infants in ʿAmran. As Williams (1968:33-35) writes of a Lebanese village:

> Regardless of sex, the birth order of a child will very much affect the amount, kind and source of attention he or she receives. . . . The situation . . . is further modified by the size, proximity and availability of the extended kin group. . . . It is impossible to detail the infinite variability that the various mutations of sex, ordinal position, composition of residential household and size and availability of kin group can create in the environment of a newborn. . . . Any one setting or sequence described as "typical" is almost of necessity a fiction.

All infants are swaddled, but the length of time varies considerably. Those who resist energetically may be left unbound after as little time as two months, but most babies are swaddled until approximately six months old. The entire body is tightly bound for the first few months, except for brief respites during changing and bathing. Usually at four to six months, those who continue to swaddle their babies leave their arms unrestricted. Some women keep the lower body swaddled a good part of the day until the child is over a year old. The reasons given for swaddling are to ensure that the arms and legs will grow straight rather than crooked, to prevent the baby's frightening itself by its uncontrolled movements, and to keep the baby quiet to help it fall asleep.

Although women are emphatic that swaddling is essential to normal development, they recognize that infant needs are variable. An exceptionally active infant, who repeatedly fights off the binding cloths, will be given his or her way. In this, as in many other areas, women appear to have an implicit respect for the infant's right to determine the conditions of her or his own existence. An infant who clearly prefers not to be swaddled is left unbound, just as one who spits out solid foods is allowed to continue on an all-liquid diet. (This is one of many points of conflict between ᶜAmrani women and the foreign medical staff at the town clinic. The latter became exasperated when townswomen fail to follow medical advice on the grounds that their infant or toddler refused to cooperate. The ᶜAmrani view attributes to infants a kind of knowledge of what is best for them. Furthermore, townswomen fear that upsetting an unwell child will only aggravate the illness.)

Informants say that until the recent past all babies were breast-fed for at least one year and often for two or more years. According to a 1979 national survey, median duration of breast-feeding in rural Yemen was about one year, but less than six months in Sanᶜa (Goldberg et al. 1983:80). The traditional practice is thought to make for a tolerable spacing of births. Older women frequently note that among the many negative consequences of bottle-feeding is a shortening of time between pregnancies. Not only do ᶜAmrani women believe that lactation reduces the likelihood of conception but also that their own milk is superior to formulas or any other food.

Bottles and formula have been available since 1970 if not earlier and have gradually grown in popularity. In a sample of twenty-five mothers of six-month-old infants, fifteen were breast-feeding, six were bottle-feeding, and the remaining four were combining the two. Women who breast-feed do so either because they hope to postpone the next pregnancy, want to save money, consider it best for the baby, or because their mother-in-law or mother insists. Those who use the bottle offer varied reasons: to supplement their own milk (which they fear is insufficient); to have opportunities to get out of the house (whether out of necessity or for pleasure); or because they are ill, frightened or upset. There is a strong and widely held conviction that breast milk is affected by the mother's physical and emotional condition. For a sick or troubled woman to breast-feed her baby is to endanger the baby's health. Most if not all of the town's extremely influential pharmacists share this belief, frequently prescribing formula in cases of maternal or infant illness. Many women report that, having introduced the bottle as a temporary measure, they were later to find that the baby no longer wanted the breast at all. Others have had no difficulty in combining breast- and bottle-feeding as well as giving solid foods to their children.

Prior to the availability and acceptance of the bottle and formulas, wet nurses were used commonly when a mother died or was unable to breast-feed her infant. They are used only rarely now. A weak fictive filial relationship is established between infant and wet nurse, and the incest taboo is extended to include the offspring of the fictive mother.[1]

As in much of the Middle East, infants are fed on demand for most of the day, whether by breast, bottle, or both (Williams 1968:28-29; Fuller 1961:36; and others). They are, however, often left unattended for a two- or three-hour period when their mothers pay afternoon visits. After washing and completing her afternoon prayers, a mother nurses and swaddles her baby. Once it falls asleep, she leaves, closing and in some cases, locking the door of the room behind her. She hopes that the child will sleep through until her return, doing her best to ensure that it will.[2]

Aside from these few hours, most babies receive physical attention whenever they cry. Women rarely speak to their infants or offer them visual stimulation, but they do hold them a great deal and for the most part are assiduous in trying to satisfy what they see as their needs and in alleviating their discomforts. There are, however, discrepancies between ideal infant care and actual average practice. Ideally, an infant should be bathed and sunned (on the rooftop) daily and allowed to exercise briefly when being changed. Those parents who are under the influence of the foreign medical staff at the clinic also believe that solid foods should be added to their babies' diets at about six months.

In actuality, many women say they are too busy to bathe and sun their babies daily, and most let the children themselves decide what and when to eat. Some say they haven't time to sit and spoon-feed a reluctant eater, but most simply remark that the baby is unwilling to eat. The implicit assumption, once again, is that babies know best what is good for them.

Most parents are selective in their acceptance of the Western medical model. Their health-care policies for themselves and for their children are eclectic: they follow, alternatively or simultaneously, their own judgment, that of the town clinic, of Sanᶜa's doctors, one or several pharamacists, and local traditional healers. There is a definite consensus, especially among women, that infants and small children require protection from evil eye (ᶜayn). There is no doubt that there are people with wicked (*khabīth*) hearts who envy the good fortune of others and who use ᶜayn against them. Because male infants, especially large healthy ones, are thought more vulnerable than girls, mothers of sons must be particularly vigilant; yet even the mother of a scrawny daughter believes that her baby's health and well-being depend upon protection from evil eye. Both rue and varied Quranic amulets are considered effective but fallible preventatives. Consequently, infants rarely leave their houses until they are at least one year old, and are seen only by the most trusted relatives, neighbors, and friends.

The envy that underlies the use of evil eye is toward the mother. Sons are more vulnerable because mothers of sons are more fortunate and evoke greater jealousy. One informant mentioned that children are even more vulnerable to evil eye if they are robust and healthy but their father is slight and thin. She explained that this indicates the extremely good constitution of the mother and intensifies the hostility toward her. This intense and profound fear of the evil eye is an additional source of conflict between townswomen and the clinic staff. The clinic maintains a strict policy requiring all children under age two to be completely undressed and weighed at each visit. The parent who, before taking the baby out, has placed rue and amulets on its body and who has kept it completely covered since leaving home to further protect it from dangerous gazes must then completely undress him or her in the full view of other parents. This is seen as unnecessary and terribly risky by large numbers of ᶜAmrani women, many of whom say they keep their babies home even when ill, or take them to a pharmacist or traditional healer, rather than risk exposure to evil eye at the clinic.

ᶜAmran women note that babies who are swaddled for only a few months often crawl and walk earlier than those swaddled for up to a year. They also believe that protracted breast-feeding and swaddling prolong dependency and inactivity, providing a brief postponement to the obstreperous toddler stage, which usually begins between ten and eighteen months.

Once able to crawl or walk down stairs, toddlers start following their older siblings outdoors. Women are ambivalent about this development. On the one hand, there is relief that the demanding baby is finally joining the small children's street world and can be watched and cared for by an older sister (or occasionally by an older brother). On the other hand, there is worry about evil eye and about the reliability of the sibling caretaker. The older child's task is fairly easy at first, but as the toddler's locomotive skills inevitably improve, he or she can quickly vanish in any direction while the older children are distracted by their own play.

Toddlers remain very closely attached to the mother, especially if still nursing at the breast. At this age, they often accompany their mothers on afternoon calls, alternatively playing with other children and returning to their mothers' laps to nurse. If a woman does not conceive, she frequently breast-feeds a toddler until age two or older.

When a woman decides to wean, she puts soot on her nipples in the hope of frightening the child into abandoning the breast voluntarily. Unfortunately, this does not always work and, for some children, weaning is a very painful process. In the past they were given a special drink made of grapes and sugar and a gruel composed of several grains. Now, they receive bottles of milk, boiled sugar water or canned fruit, and, if old enough, special food treats.

No matter how much the child cries, he or she must not be given the breast again. It is believed that some practitioners of evil eye developed their condition by having been returned to the breast after weaning was begun. Some children adjust quickly; others fall ill or remain unhappy and difficult for a considerable time.

One girl, who was weaned at about a year and a half due to her mother's pregnancy, demanded sugar water by the quart. Her mother then weaned her from the sugar water to canned fruit juice, presumably because of the inconvenience of having to boil so much water. The girl would not go to sleep at night without a can of nectar for a period of several months. The monthly cost of the fruit juice was sixty riyals ($13), an amount the family could scarcely afford. She was finally weaned from the nectar after her brother was born.

In other areas of the toddler's life, frustration is rare. Mental and emotional maturity are thought to develop much more slowly than physical maturity. Consequently there is a strong conviction that neither discipline nor reasoning are effective tools in controlling small children. ʿAgal (responsibility, rationality) may begin to develop in a four or five year old, but even children of eight or nine cannot be counted on to show ʿāgal consistently. In women's views, female acquisition of ʿāgal tends to be earlier than for males, many men remaining deficient even through their twenties or longer.

Physical punishment is thought to be extremely dangerous to young children. Blows to the head or face are most sharply disapproved, as they may cause brain damage. An occasional swat to the hand or backside is permissible for older children, but not frequent beating. According to one informant, those treated brutally as children will become brutal adults.

Small children, then, are often coddled or manipulated through distraction and deception. As in Saufra, Egypt (Ammar 1954:133–37), Haouch el Harimi, Lebanon (Williams 1968:38), and Taroudannt, Morocco (Dwyer 1978:114), fear is sometimes used as well. In ʿAmran, it is more often a *majnūn* (crazy person) outside or around the corner than a beast or an animal that is used to intimidate the child. Sometimes mothers halt misbehavior by telling the child that "so and so is laughing at you." When an appropriate so and so is not present or the tactic is unsuccessful, the mother is much more likely to beseech than to demand proper behavior. One implores her son to please, please urinate outside, instead of scolding him for dirtying the carpet. Another uses her most lilting tones to entreat her little daughter to hand over the best tea cup, rather than ordering her to put it right down.

Most often, children under four or five years in age get their way. It is common for them to have prolonged and violent tantrums when they do not. What we called *"girsh* (penny) fits" are the most common type. Most of the time they are successful, and the child eventually receives a *girsh* to get candy or a sweet drink. Another frequent cause of tantrums is the departure of the mother. Women try to prevent these either by sneaking out of the house or by telling the child she is going to get a shot. When these tactics fail, the child often is given his or her way and taken along. As will be discussed shortly, older siblings (girls in particular) are expected to make frequent and regular sacrifices for the sake of the little ones, who are thought too immature to tolerate frustration. Little girls who rarely had a wish denied at age four are expected, only three or four years later, to devote themselves to satisfying their younger siblings' whims.

Young children need special coddling when ill or convalescent. ʿAmrani women pride themselves in the amount of time and attention they give to their babies and toddlers in general, but particularly in crisis situations. They state explicitly that children who are recovering from a serious illness such as measles must have all their requests satisfied. Weakened and vulnerable, they might die of any frustration of their desires. Convalescent toddlers often request one costly delicacy only to reject it and scream for another. This kind of erratic and demanding behavior is seen as a symptom of the child's weakened condition, never as a delighted basking in expanded power. A mother who does not devote herself exclusively to a sick or recovering child evokes sharp criticism and may be blamed if her child dies. Indeed, it is through constant attendance upon an ill child that a woman can most dramatically and unequivocally enact the role of the ideal mother. Not all women can rise to the occasion, and those who cannot may have to pay dire consequences.

Fathers express their strong concern over sick children by seeking

Cousins enjoying lollipops. Nutritionally empty sweets have become widely available in recent years and are extremely popular with children.

Young girls wearing the peaked bonnet that will not be discarded until they marry.

out remedies from numerous practitioners, but leave attending the sickbed to women. Most interact very little with infants, healthy or sick, but take an increasing interest in toddlers. Unlike their wives, however, they often expect to control the behavior of their small children and become annoyed at repeated naughtiness. Few spend more than short periods of time in direct interaction with their children. Generally less concerned than women about evil eye, fathers often encourage toddlers to play outdoors and sometimes ridicule their wives' fear in this regard.

There are some differences in the treatment of female and male toddlers, the most obvious of which are in the manner of dress. Whereas both male and female infants wear baby bonnets, male toddlers go bareheaded and females are encouraged to wear *garāgush* (s. *gargūsh*, peaked bonnets) or scarves. Girls wear pants and dresses and boys wear short *zannīn* (s. *zanna*, Saudi-style long robe) or *fuwāṭ* (s. *fūṭa*, Yemeni men's skirt). In terms of behavior, physical aggressiveness is encouraged for boys more than for girls. At women's afternoon gatherings, differences in treatment of boys and girls are sharp. When, for example, a three-year-old boy retreats to his mother's lap for comfort after having been struck by a girl his own age, his mother disparages him gently for having taken a blow from a girl. She urges him in compelling tones to go hit her back.

As part of this aggression training, mothers also tolerate punishing attacks on their own persons and expect their older daughters to do the same. A two year old, who is lying next to his mother, repeatedly kicks her stomach and breasts while drinking from a bottle. She neither stops nor reprimands him, but feebly and halfheartedly blocks his feet with her hands. A three year old continues smacking his nine-year-old sister with a sharply edged toy gun. She forces a smile as she tries to block the blows. Their mother, another woman, and several older boys and girls are present, but do not intervene or criticize the boy. Only after several minutes does an eight-year-old girl come to the older sister's aid by trying to distract the toddler's attention from the assault. Had the older sister retaliated or restrained him ungently, her mother almost certainly would have berated her.

Nevertheless, with respect to verbal aggressiveness, girls appear to receive at least as much encouragement as boys. ʿAmrani women place a very high value on the ability to engage in brisk repartee, and teach children to respond to teasing and criticism (in selected circumstances) with sharply pointed and witty counterattacks. It is considered extremely important that people retaliate through humor rather than reveal raw anger or hurt withdrawal. As in Buarij, speech possessing "vivid imagery and rich metaphor," is used as a "way of cleansing tense atmosphere" (Fuller 1961:41).

Training in teasing tolerance begins within the household and at a very early age in ᶜAmran. Adults, and more often older siblings and cousins, tease young toddlers. In Buarij as well, it is considered entertaining to tease small children, a practice Fuller (1961:39) believes is a partial substitute for punishment. There also, "children are rarely punished severely, since offenses and misdemeanors are attributed to a child's inexperience with life." In ᶜAmran the inevitable frustration, tears, and anger of the victim are treated as high comedy. Gradually the child learns that displaying feelings only makes the situation worse, and is ready to be taught to convert rage and hurt into socially approved clever retorts. Teaching is explicit and direct, as appropriate answers are fed to the child, and their delivery enthusiastically applauded. (Women also receive promptings when involved in verbal battles. Those who are especially adept at producing quick jibes regularly assist those less skilled or put temporarily at a loss by emotion. It is in no way demeaning to have one's words provided in this way.)

Children must learn to measure sometimes contradictory reactions to their budding verbal talents and to hold them in abeyance in certain company and particular settings. When a young child gives an adult a peppery retort, the mother may say, "Shame on you for speaking that way to _____." Hidden approval, however, can be detected in her eyes. Even talking back to one's own mother is implicitly applauded, although explicitly condemned. But, verbal artillery should not be fired upon the father or other male relatives unless a joking atmosphere has been established by the men themselves. As in the Lebanese village of Haouch el Harimi, children "quickly learn that of the two parents the father is the more fearsome and formidable figure" (Williams 1968:38). ᶜAmrani women say that men deal harshly with children in part because of unrealistic expectations. Fathers become particularly incensed by their sons' tears. Boys learn that to cry in front of their fathers is to invite more anger and blows, but girls' crying rarely evokes further penalty.

As children mature, they are taught increasing discretion. If an eight or nine year old talks back to her aunt, her mother will take her aside after the aunt has left the room and whisper conspiratorially to her, "Don't say things like that to her. She'll pay you back when I'm not around." She is considered ready to learn the subtleties of self-protection and manipulation that will aid her throughout life.

By age six or seven, both boys and girls have left behind the time of extreme indulgence. They have experienced frequent rebukes for misconduct and refusals of many requests, but they do not become stoic overnight. Impassioned protests against maternal conduct are common at this age, as are sibling battles. A mother of four children under nine said that if her children were left alone for long it was just like Hashid and Bakil, the two opposed tribal confederations. Children are quick to display intense, sobbing rage, and to stomp furiously out of their mother's proximity. What is most striking to the Western observer about these tantrums is how suddenly they pass. Most children reappear in a matter of moments as if nothing had happened.

Many of children's frustrations are related to the priority given to their younger siblings' wishes. The anguish of having their favored position usurped is mitigated, however, by their own fondness for the newer member or members of the family. Mothers and other relatives foster family affection in many ways. With the first acquisition of language, toddlers are asked repeatedly whether their brothers, sisters, and various other kin are *ḥālī* (nice, good) or *shūᶜa* (bad). They learn quickly that the correct response for all relatives (except those out of favor) is *ḥālī*. A little later they learn to say jokingly that sister or grandmother is *shūᶜa*, as long as the humorous intent is sufficiently clear.

When a mother is pregnant she actively promotes the older children's enthusiasm for the prospective new sibling. A game is played, for example, which pretends to identify the fetus's sex. Boys root for a brother, girls for a sister, although most children recognize the game to be more for amusement than for divination. ᶜAmrani

90 / *Daughters and Sons*

Older girls have the responsibility of caring for younger ones. Note the three types of head coverings: baby bonnet, peaked bonnet, and teenager's veiling.

women believe that even toddlers can be prepared for a new baby so as to minimize their jealousy. Children under two, however, are thought to be too young for such preparation and are expected to show fierce resentment and occasionally dangerous hostility to a new sibling.[3] No woman envies the mother who must cope with two children both under two years of age.

Women rely enormously on their older daughters for child-care assistance, although only rarely giving them credit for their aid. It is impressed upon older sons as well as upon older daughters that the young ones are still *ghāwī* (mentally undeveloped, incapable of reasoning) and that those with *ʿāgal* (the capacity to use reason and behave with responsibility) must sacrifice their wants for those of the *ghāwī*. Because girls are so much more involved than boys in child care, it is their *ʿāgal* and patience that are perpetually tested and strained. Mothers expect and require consistent self-denial from their daughters, and often deal harshly with lapses into immaturity.

A special food treat such as candy is rarely divided equally. The lion's share goes to the toddler, who may or may not respond with generosity to older sister's wheedling for a portion. If her powers of persuasion fail, the sister must accept deprivation passively. An older brother is expected to behave in the same manner, but as he often enjoys his own treats privately the occasional sacrifice is not so hard.

By school age (about seven), girls are saddled with far greater domestic and child-care duties than are boys. The timing of each sex's schooling reflects and supports this contrast. Boys attend school in the morning, just as most adult-male work is performed before lunch. Although a handful of girls attend the boys' morning classes, the vast majority study in an all-female school (except for male administrators, guards, and caretaker) in the afternoon, after having spent most of their mornings helping their mothers at home. Many girls do not attend school at all or do so irregularly, either because the parents see school as irrelevant or improper for girls or because women keep their daughters home to help with their younger siblings. Older girls can watch younger brothers and sisters on the street, listen for the cries of a sleeping baby, replenish the household water supply, and complete any chores left from the busy morning. In rare cases they can also earn money by selling candy, sweet drinks, or other treats to neighborhood children.

Nonetheless, women frequently voice the hope that their girls will receive sufficient education to lead better adult lives than theirs. Schools did not exist in ᶜAmran when they were growing up, and very few are literate. The few women who can read the Quran at all are much respected for their special knowledge. Most women see literacy as a great asset, and some say their daughters will surely make something of themselves through the mastery of reading and writing.

When questioned further, however, most women express skepticism as to the future employability of women in Yemen. They expect there will be few jobs for women in Sanᶜa and virtually none in ᶜAmran. There is also the fear that to be employed in Sanᶜa, their daughters would have to forgo the veil, a price they would not have them pay.

For many women, the primary reason for schooling girls is the belief that any amount of elementary education will make their daughters more desirable as marriage partners and more competent as parents. The combined effect of these attitudes and of most women's keen desire to get out of their houses to enjoy the society of other women is to prevent most mothers from seeing regular school attendance as crucial for their daughters. Although a large proportion of ᶜAmrani girls now attend elementary school intermittently, there is nowhere near the seriousness of commitment that there is to the education of boys.

Schoolgirls see careers as inviting, but have little idea of the amount of education required. Of a class of twenty third-grade students, almost all expressed a desire to become teachers; another two intend to become doctors. Second-grade students hoped to become teachers or nurses. Only one girl in each class, however, said she intended to pursue her education beyond the elementary school diploma. Each of these has a sibling attending high school in Sanᶜa, and the second grader is one of the very few girls who attends the boys' morning school as well as the girls' afternoon one. To the others, the completion of sixth grade appears a great achievement. Their assumption that it is sufficient for their employability is understandable because the elementary certificate is such a rarity among ᶜAmrani females. It is the sole certificate held by the only native ᶜAmrani female teacher. The paucity of women employed in ᶜAmran's public sector undoubtedly contributes to the vagueness and lack of seriousness in the girls' attitudes toward school and career.

Girls' descriptions of their future goals deviate only slightly from the lives of their mothers. All expect to marry and have children (but only two or three); almost two-thirds hope to live in ᶜAmran rather than Sanᶜa after they marry, and over three-quarters would prefer to live in extended family households with their husbands' kin rather than alone with their husband and children. When asked, "If your husband were to travel abroad to study in Jordan or Lebanon or another foreign country, would you wish to go with him or stay home with his family?" all but two stated a preference for staying home with their in-laws.

There are only two female high-school graduates from ᶜAmran, compared to about thirty male graduates. Like the males, both began their education in ᶜAmran and moved to Sanᶜa to attend high school. Neighbors, they were among the few girls to attend ᶜAmran's first elementary school, a coeducational institution that was a gift from the government of Kuwait. Most of their female classmates were removed from school as they approached adolescence. Three of those removed spoke of their grief at having been forced to leave school by their fathers. One said she was reduced to tears every day by the sight of her two girl friends on their way to the school she could no longer attend.

The two girls moved to Sanᶜa in part because one of their fathers owned a house and had relatives there and because each had a brother in a Sanᶜa high school. They came and went from ᶜAmran frequently, their mothers supplying them with food. After completing their second year of high school, one became ill and returned to ᶜAmran, so the other did her last year alone. During that year she also became employed in a bank. She graduated in 1978 and intended to attend Sanᶜa University while working at the bank. Instead, her father arranged her marriage. She and her husband live in the capital, where she has been promoted in her work; but she does not study at the university. (A family friend claims that the husband allowed her to continue working at the bank only after being "paid off" by her family.) The other student returned to Sanᶜa after one year at home, stayed with a family originally from ᶜAmran, and completed high school in 1979. She then returned to ʿAmran, where, after many months of staying at home, she became employed in a newly established ʿAmran branch of a Sanʿa bank. She has not yet married and may attend college in the company of a brother who is also a high-school graduate.

By the end of our stay, no other ʿAmrani females were following in their footsteps. The two graduates seem to be viewed less as models to be emulated than as distinct anomalies. They have enhanced their own and to some extent their families' prestige, but this has not yet been sufficient to make the idea of female schooling as preparatory for outside employment catch on. The attitude for the moment remains that girls should acquire literacy to enhance their marriageability and for the sake of their future children. In contrast, many parents believe that the education of males is a key to upward mobility.

Before entering their teens, boys and girls have become increasingly separated. The former move further and further away from the interests and social life of their households and neighborhoods. Some begin to wear adult male headgear (the *samāṭa* or *shāl* or *kūfiya*) on occasion, and by the early teens chew *gāt* when they can afford it. When not in school, they spend great amounts of time in the *sūq*, in the tea shops in particular. Although they prefer the company of other youths, they also interact with adult men.

Some male teenagers move to Sanʿa to attend high school, which even more dramatically separates them from the physical and intellectual confinement imposed on their mothers and sisters. They spend as much time as possible with fellow students and other educated youth. This is in sharp contrast to female teenagers, who continue to interact regularly with women of all ages and with young children.[4]

As they become more proficient in women's work, girls gradually assume more of their mothers' duties. They and their mothers take particular pride in their improving skill at baking *malūj* (the dough of which must be spread by hand on the sides of the burning hot clay oven). In fact, the size of each growing daughter's *malūj* is often seen as a measure of her progress toward womanhood, or at least toward marriageability.

Girls rarely have opportunities for sustained play or conversation without interruptions from their younger charges. They play a game that is a variation on hopscotch, sing girls' chants, practice women's dances, and listen to adult conversation. They frequently play games of make-believe, sometimes enacting adult familial roles, at other times including the younger children in setting up pretend shops. On one occasion an elaborate make-believe kitchen was assembled from objects found on the street; a rag became a mat and several rocks were stacked to create an oven on which pretend tea and meat were prepared. These were served in various discarded cans to the small children, who clearly relished their imaginary repast.

Girls' movements become increasingly circumscribed as they move toward their teens. It becomes improper for them to enter the *sūq* or to be seen very much by outsiders in other contexts. Daughters of some poor families, however, have little choice but to appear often in public. If they veil properly and behave modestly, their marriage chances are not significantly impaired.

Informants do not relate the limitations on girls' movements to fears that they may behave unchastely. It is not said that unmarried daughters are a threat to family honor. One might infer, however, from the restrictive practices, that these concerns exist. The confinement of unmarried daughters and of wives can also indicate high economic status, as it does in many other peasant societies.

Few unmarried girls are totally confined to their homes. Most leave their neighborhoods occasionally to perform essential errands, to attend the public bath, to visit relatives, or to do the family laundry at one of several irrigation pumps outside of town. The pumps are a lively female space in the mornings, where girls are exposed to topics of conversation and gossip that may not reach them at home. Accompanied by friends and sometimes by younger charges, girls unquestionably enjoy laundry excursions, which give them a rare break from routine and an opportunity to observe girls and women from other parts of ᶜAmran.

On certain feast days, all unmarried girls are encouraged to congregate in the courtyards of a few large households. In new fine dresses, with decorated hands, and often sporting Sanᶜa-style veils, they come together for games, swinging, and songs. These are the only major social occasions for unmarried girls, and some exchange their usual controlled behavior for roughness and wild abandon.

96 / *Daughters and Sons*

Girls dressed up in the San'a-style *sharshaf* for the holiday. Note hand decorations.

Although most girls delight in these celebrations, a few are put off by the rowdiness of the crowd and prefer to stay home.

Regardless of family hereditary or economic status, all girls (the physically or mentally unfit aside) are moving together toward their inevitable roles as brides. At widely varying ages (roughly between six and ten), girls or their mothers decide that the *gargūsh* (the peaked bonnet worn by all unmarried females) is no longer sufficient head covering, and they begin draping large cloths over it. These are sometimes of different material and color than for the adult black *fūṭa*. They also begin to wear either the adult black *sarmiya* (head and face veil) or a brightly colored *shāsh* (also a head and face veil), but wrap them slightly differently from the married women's style. The transition to veiling, which begins with early childhood's enthusiastic playing at dress-up, is a gradual one in which considerable variation occurs. All girls converge, however, at the same ultimate point: the giving up of the *gargūsh* for good on the trip to the public bath preparatory for their wedding night.

98 / *Daughters and Sons*

Girls playing on swing specially erected for the holiday.

6

Marriage: Arrangements, Celebrations, and Consummation

> Girls should marry while young and ignorant. They should be timid and humble. (A thrice-married man, the father of three sons and three daughters)

> Early marriage is no good. A girl should be educated first, so she'll have a degree of independence from her husband. Otherwise, she'll be stuck, like me. (A mother of two daughters and one son)

> Is it really true that in America they marry for love? Here, if a girl told her parents she loved a certain man, they would call her *wasakha* [dirty], and quickly marry her off to someone else. (A teenaged bride, separated from her husband since one month after their wedding).

In ʿAmran parents or guardians arrange all marriages, almost always selecting a spouse from within their own social stratum and sometimes preferring alliances with kin or close friends. According to many informants, parents are most concerned about the family reputation of a prospective son- or daughter-in-law: "If they are honorable and agreeable people, their child probably will be too. If they are garbage, how could their child be different?" In actual practice, however, economic, political, and personal considerations often take precedence over the criterion of family reputation.

Informants agree that men dominate in the arrangement of marriages, although women play important advisory and supportive roles. As in other sexually segregated societies, women have access to information unavailable to men. They also can engage in preliminary inquiries, sparing men the social embarrassment of being rebuffed.[1]

Some men hope to marry their sons into families with which they already have or hope to establish economic or political ties. They know, however, that they have to consult their wives and kinswomen about the girls and women of those families. Only women can gather information about potential brides and mothers-in-law. As Makhlouf (1979:42) points out for San^{c}a, because women control the circulation of information about other women, they are in a position to influence their brothers' and sons' marriage choices.

Most parents of sons seek a young bride, usually between fourteen and seventeen, but sometimes only twelve or thirteen years old. Although they say this is because it is best for women to raise their children while still very young themselves, there are other factors contributing to the preference. Men consider females in their early or middle teens more attractive than "older women," and their mothers hope that a childbride will be a more tractable daughter-in-law than a mature one.

While virgins are preferred, many families marry sons to a widow or a divorcée. There is no stigma even to unions between a never married male and a previously married female. The motive for some but not all of these marriages is economic: the bride-price for a woman who has borne a child is one-fourth to one-half less than that of a virgin.

There are other important criteria in selecting a bride. Most informants rank health and temperament as primary factors, followed by competence at female tasks (which is expected to improve rapidly after marriage if insufficient beforehand) and beauty. There is no doubt that beauty is valued, but most women consider it less critical than robustness and good nature.

The perspective of parents of daughters is, of course, different from that of parents of sons. Fathers of marriageable daughters are often eager to receive as large a bride-price as possible. Women say that in many cases men's avarice supersedes any concern about the character of the daughter's prospective in-laws. Mothers try to persuade their husbands to think first of their daughter's future well-being, but no woman can make her husband act upon her advice if he chooses not to do so.

In theory, both the daughter and son have the right to refuse a particular match; however, there exist cultural factors that support the son's right and thwart the daughter's. Bybee's generalization (1978:53-54) about Middle Eastern marriage arrangements is only partially substantiated by the ʿAmran case:

> The husband-to-be is as much manipulated as the bride-to-be.... In terms of power and powerlessness, it is the parents, *both* husband and wife, who have more power than do the potential spouses, *both* groom and bride. We are dealing here with a differential in power between generations, not between men and women.

In ʿAmran there are power differentials between *and within* generations. Husbands have more power than do wives in marriage arrangements, and sons have greater influence over parental decisions than do daughters. It is acceptable for a son to convey to his parents an eagerness for marriage and, later, his attitudes toward a particular girl or woman. A daughter must always act as if she wishes never to marry and must sob miserably when any match (even one she privately desires) is proposed. Informants say that a girl's true feelings can be inferred from the duration and intensity of her crying. If she assents after a suitable amount of time, she falls into total silence. For her, muteness is the only proper indication of acceptance, but a young man can speak his mind freely. Furthermore, of the two, only the prospective groom is present when the marriage contract is written. The bride's father or a male guardian, who is trusted to have established her consent, represents her. Sons are not exempt from parental pressure, but there can be little doubt that their part in the decision-making process far exceeds that allowed most never married daughters. Only widows and divorcées have rights that approach those of even never married young males.[2]

A man who marries his daughter against her will is likely to suffer inconvenience, aggravation, and sometimes financial losses if she refuses to stay with her husband and in-laws. On the grounds of self-interest alone, one would expect men to take their daughters' feelings into account. Yet, informants say that more than a few fathers are precipitate in their marriage negotiations. Whether out of greed (for a large bride-price or a desirable connection), gullibility, ignorance, or coldheartedness, they are all too likely to rush headlong into commitments despite the objections of their daughters and of their wives as well. Neither female nor male informants speak of similar victimizations of sons, men being more likely to mention alliances they had wanted to establish that were foiled by the refusal of their sons (Thomas Stevenson, personal communication).

Although some marriage arrangements proceed smoothly, more often conflict and confusion develop. If the problems that arise are considerable, either side may back out. There is a risk of appearing somewhat dishonorable, however, if either withdraws at an advanced stage in the negotiations, as in the following example:

> H lived in a large extended household with his mother, two married brothers, their wives and children, his own two small children, and younger brothers and sisters. He and his wife were separated, and he planned to divorce her.
>
> H's mother and sisters-in-law approached their neighbor F, who was a member of their endogamous stratum, told her of the impending divorce, and expressed interest in arranging H's marriage to F's husband's half brother's daughter. F told them she would look into the possibilities for them.
>
> F told her husband of the neighbors' interest, and he spoke to his half brother, who appeared receptive to the match. F's husband told her to suggest to the neighbors that they could proceed.
>
> H's mother and sisters-in-law had already interrogated F about her niece's health, temperament, and work skills. Now they asked her to arrange for them to observe her secretly. F agreed, and on a specified morning sent a message to her niece that she needed her help with housework. When the two of them went out on F's roof to shake out blankets together, the girl had no idea that she was being watched by her prospective mother-in-law and sisters-in-law from the adjoining roof.
>
> As the women were satisfied with what they saw, H's brother then consulted with F and her husband. He asked them how much they thought should be offered as bride-price. F's husband then arranged for both sides to meet in one week's time at his house to discuss a settlement.
>
> F mentioned the offer to her niece, who cried and appeared extremely upset. F ignored her protests that she was too young to marry, and was convinced that the girl was lying when she insisted that she hadn't yet begun to menstruate [although it is not considered wrong for prepubescent girls to marry in any case]. F repeated to her niece over and over that the family who wanted her were all good people

and that they had extensive property. Finally, the girl's sobs subsided and she fell silent, a clear indication, according to F, that she acquiesced.

At this point F had no doubts that the marriage would come off. She said that once word has been passed to the prospective groom's family that the match is acceptable, even if there has not yet been a face-to-face meeting, it is ʿ*ayb* [disgraceful, shameful] for either side to back out.

However, on the very day of the proposed meeting, F's brother-in-law told her and his half brother that he had changed his mind. He said that his full sister had researched the family and learned that they were bad-tempered and violent people. One of the men, possibly the prospective groom, had even beaten his old mother. He was angry with his half brother and sister-in-law for having tried to arrange such a terrible match for his daughter. They, in turn, were furious with him for withdrawing at an embarrassingly late stage in the negotiations. Finally, H and his family were piqued to learn they had been rejected and would have to recommence the pursuit of a new wife all over again from scratch.

Although not a factor in the case just described, disagreements about money are the most common problems in marriage arrangements. Frequently, a bride-price is agreed upon well in advance of the actual wedding. The prospective groom may then go to Saudi Arabia to earn the necessary money or his father may sell land or other property. With the delay, local bride-prices become further inflated, and the bride's family are no longer willing to accept the amount to which they had previously agreed. If the groom and his father are unable or unwilling to meet the new demand, the marriage is called off.

Not all broken engagements derive from financial disagreements. Conflict between the parties can develop during the prolonged negotiations, or one side might be swayed by the possibility of a better opportunity elsewhere. Townswomen say that it has become increasingly common for engagements to be broken, whereas formerly it was a disgrace. Most women are sharply critical of those who withdraw from a match and triumphant when such machinations backfire, as in the following case of "just deserts":

> A was one of the highest ranking tribal families, and had attended high school in the capital. He was engaged to an ʿAmran girl who was good-natured, plump, respectable, and the daughter of a highly

respected man. After one year's engagement (while A completed his schooling), A objected to the match because his fiancée was illiterate. He told his parents he had to have an educated, modern Sanʿani wife. His father accepted his wishes, broke the original engagement, and arranged a new match to his son's liking. This engagement, however, also was broken, but this time by A's fiancée, who told her parents she refused to live in dirty, provincial ʿAmran. ʿAmrani women chortle that "before A had two fiancées, and now he has none!"

It should be noted that A is related to both his former fiancées. Kinship ties are not always sufficient to prevent dishonorable conduct in marriage negotiations. Most people believe, however, that a man can usually trust his own brother, particularly when they occupy a single house. In such cases, exchange (*badl*) marriages are common. (X and Y are brothers; X's daughter marries Y's son, and Y's daughter marries X's son.) Although both marriages take place at the same time in most cases, the second marriage may be delayed several years. Either no bride-prices or identical ones are paid; the brides receive identical gifts and trousseaux. Not all marriages between patrilateral parallel cousins are exchanges. Those that don't take the exchange form involve much lower bride-prices than marriages between nonkin.

Bybee (1978:69) points out that Middle Eastern women often favor patrilateral parallel cousin marriage and cites Hilal (1970) and Khuri (1970) on the advantages of this marriage form for women. A daughter of the retired *shaykh* of ʿAmran explains:

> We marry our *ʿayāl ʿamm* [father's brothers' sons] because doing so keeps our family united and strong. We women like this kind of marriage because we don't have to go and live our lives with strangers. We have known our father's brother and his wife and their children all our lives, and so feel comfortable with them. Because they are our family, we can feel confident they will treat us well. In some of our cases, we never have to leave our parents' house, and so remain always close to our mothers and fathers.

This informant's foreign-educated, older *ibn ʿamm* (father's brother's son), a government employee who resides in Sanʿa, takes the opposite, modernist view. Strength, he says, comes from intermarriage with other families. He claims that endogamous marriage has practically disappeared from the more developed countries of the Middle East and that Yemen should follow suit. He, nonetheless, is married to his *bint ʿamm* (father's brother's daughter). Whether his objections to patrilateral parallel cousin marriage are purely political or partially personal cannot be said. It is worth mentioning suggestions from Hilal (1970:83) and Fischer (1978:198-99) that this marriage form may be less appealing to males when wives feel so secure and comfortable that they do not defer to their husbands' wishes.

When brothers occupy separate houses and live their own lives, the chances of conflict-free marriages are considerably less than when they live together. The mother of a teenager separated from her *ibn ʿamm* gives this bitter account:

> We married our fourteen-year-old daughter to her sixteen-year-old *ibn ʿamm* for only 25,000 riyals, whereas we could have gotten much more than that from any other family. She is now six months pregnant, and back home with us because of abuse from my husband's brother.
>
> One day he got mad at her for no good reason, and called her a whore and other terrible names. She maintained her composure, but came home that afternoon to tell me of the insults. My friend and I calmed her down and told her to forget all about it.
>
> That night I told my husband what his brother had said to our daughter, and he became furious. He told me to send her a message first thing in the morning, telling her to come home, and to leave all her belongings behind, except the sewing machine and the gold that we had given to her.
>
> My husband himself went to complain to his brother, and informed him that until our daughter and her husband are provided with a house of their own, she will stay home with us. My husband's brother continues to refuse to rent a house for them, so our daughter must stay with us. Not only that, but my husband is so angry at his brother that he insists he won't take any money from him toward her postbirth expenses. As you know, those are always paid by the husband's family unless they intend to terminate the marriage.
>
> My daughter and her husband are both so young and immature that they don't really care at all for each other yet. Since her father-in-law is so terrible, she is better off for now at home with us.

When there is a divorce between cousins (as may happen for the couple described above), it can be just as acrimonious as one between strangers. As in almost all divorces, the children stay with their father; their mother may be denied contact with them, despite the extremely close kinship connection. In short, the protection of patrilateral parallel cousin marriage often is no greater than that provided in marriages between relative or absolute strangers.

Informants are almost unanimous in viewing the exchange marriage as the least desirable marital form, except in the case of cousins. Special problems of exchange marriages are reported in other parts of the Middle East (Granqvist 1931; Salim 1962; Cohen 1965; Antoun 1972; Bybee 1978). As in ʿAmran, the exchange marriage is practiced most often for economic reasons. Its main advantage is that no bride-price need be raised. The primary problem is that

> exchange marriages are interdependent, for each couple is affected by the actions of the other couple. . . . If one of the exchanged women returns home in protest against mistreatment of some kind, the other woman will also be obliged to return to her home and stay there until the problem has been solved. (Bybee 1978:71)

Some ʿAmran families try to avoid these disruptions by stipulating in the marriage contract that a woman must stay on with her husband even after the return of her exchanged sister-in-law, unless fetched by her own father. Informants claim, however, that such stipulations (like most of the special provisions of marriage contracts) are rarely honored. No woman, they say, will stay in her husband's house once her own brother's wife has returned there.

Sometimes each wife gets along well with her husband and in-laws from the start, but more often problems abound for the first few years. As in conventional marriages, young wives are quick to return to their parents' home when they feel ill-used. With exchange marriages, obviously, the problems multiply. After children have been born, however, whatever the marital form, women are much less likely to leave their husbands' home.

In conventional marriages, large bride-prices are the rule. Although townspeople concur that it is *ḥarām* (sinful) to demand exorbitant amounts of money, very few fathers are so righteous as to let their daughters go cheaply. Bride-prices ranged between 20,000 and 30,000 riyals ($4,400 to $6,600) in spring 1978; one year later, the range had risen to between 40,000 and 60,000 riyals ($8,800 to $13,200). As mentioned earlier, conflict over bride-price and other marital expenses are common, in part because of the high rate of inflation and people's escalating expectations. Informants say many townspeople exaggerate the amounts paid to negotiate their sons' marriages as well as the amounts received for their daughters. Sometimes the lies are obvious, but in other cases it is difficult (for townspeople and researcher alike) to assess the truth of parents' claims. There is no question, however, that the size of the payments has increased rapidly over the last decade.

The portion of the bride-price that goes to the bride (*mahr*), is much smaller than the portion (*shart*) that goes to her father or her brother(s). A typical *mahr* is 1,000 to 2,000 riyals worth of gold (the bride receives a trousseau and engagement gifts as well, costing between 2,000 and 5,000 riyals); a typical *shart* is 50,000 riyals. Many townswomen are aware that in Sanᶜa the bride's share is at least half and sometimes equal to that of her father. Some of them see the discrepancy as unjust, and are vociferous in their praise of the occasional ᶜAmran father who converts a sizeable portion of the *shart* into gold for his daughter.

There is, however, extremely strong female support for the institution of bride-price in general. Few ᶜAmrani women would disagree with Bybee's claim that bride-price "represents a definite acknowledgment of the value of a woman" (1978:58). Myntti (1978:58) is correct in stating that

> Yemeni women are proud of their bridewealth. It is a statement of their honorable, chaste state and the value of their labor. Indeed, they feel pity for Western women who do not have such a cash security and statement of worth.

One young divorcée blames the failure of her marriage on the low bride-price paid for her. Her match had been arranged by Sanᶜa relatives who disapprove of high bride-prices; they convinced her parents to forgo financial gain for the prestige of marrying their daughter to a foreign-educated government employee. The marriage was a dismal failure from the start, and the divorcée is convinced that her former husband would have treated her better had he paid properly to marry her in the first place. Many married women claim, only half humorously, that their husbands would take a new wife every week were it not for the high costs involved.[3]

The parents of marriageable sons express their opposition to the high cost of getting married. Many must sell some or all of their property or require that their sons raise part of the money themselves, often by working in Saudi Arabia. Those who delay the marriage may discover that the terms of the earlier settlement are no longer acceptable; they then must meet the heightened demand, negotiate a compromise, or break the engagement:

My husband and I have eight children; only the two oldest are married. Six or seven years ago we married the eldest girl to her *ibn ʿamm* for only 400 riyals because there was a local agreement limiting the bride-price to that amount at that time. We immediately used the 400 riyals to provide a wife for our firstborn son. With all our additional wedding expenses, we ended up spending 1,000 riyals. As our daughter received no gold from her *ibn ʿamm*, we figure his family's expenses totaled only 700 riyals.

Now we are about to marry our second son. After all the negotiations, the *sharṭ* is settled at 50,000 riyals; the bride's trousseau could cost us another 5,000, and there's all the other wedding gifts too, and the *muzayyina*'s fee as well. We had to pay 200 riyals for a calf to serve at the wedding feast, and it is the size of a cat! There are other expenses too.

We've had to sell lots of land to X for only 800 riyals a *libna* [one *libna* equals .01 acre]. Eight hundred riyals for that land is highway robbery, but we have no choice, as we need the money now. The whole wedding may end up costing us close to 100,000 riyals [$22,000]. The parents of our prospective daughter-in-law have simply cleaned us out.

This estimate of total wedding costs may be exaggerated, but it is true that there are major expenses in addition to the *sharṭ*; the bride must be given engagement gifts (usually a watch and a gold ring), a large trousseau, a small *mahr* of gold (rarely worth more than 2,000 riyals), and approximately 1,000 riyals more on the wedding night. Her mother and her mother's brothers normally receive 1,000 riyals each. There are also the costs of the feasts and the fees the *muzayyin*, *muzayyina*, *dawshān*, and, in some cases, the *ʿūd* (lute) player charge.

The engagement presents are given shortly after marriage negotiations have been finalized. The trousseau, which is given several weeks prior to the wedding, is the most exciting aspect of the arrangements for the bride-to-be. As with bride-prices, there has been rapid and dramatic inflation in the composition of the trousseau, so that recently married women are infinitely better dressed than all but the wealthiest of "older women." Just as a virgin receives a significantly larger bride-price than does a previously married woman, so too is her trousseau bigger. It contains cloth for fifteen to twenty dresses and for a *sharshaf*, shoes, slacks, fine scarves, and many lesser items.

Occasionally a female relative of the bride is asked to pick the cloth for her trousseau, although this is more common to San'a and seen as improper by 'Amran traditionalists. If the bride dislikes any items of the trousseau, she may send them back to her future husband's household with instructions as to how they should be replaced. After the neighbors, relatives, and friends have all admired the trousseau, the cloth is sent to one of the town's many seamstresses, except in the case of a few brides who do their own dressmaking. In either instance, she is well supplied with at least fifteen new dresses by the time of her wedding.

Usually several weeks before the wedding, both the bride's and the groom's households purchase new supplies of grain and firewood for the wedding feasts. The women become very busy cleaning and processing the grain and, in some cases, chopping the wood. They also whitewash one or several rooms of the house; arrange to borrow floor coverings, cushions, and cookware; and recruit relatives, neighbors, and friends to help prepare the wedding feasts. Although one or two women may be hired to help with the cooking in some cases, women in reciprocal support relationships with women of the bride's and groom's households donate almost all the labor. These relations are especially common between neighbors, but sometimes obtain between women with neither residential nor kin ties. They crosscut traditional status and present economic divisions. When the bride's or groom's house is too small to hold the expected guests, it is common for one or more of their neighbors' houses to be borrowed for the occasion.

The women of the bride's and groom's household also need to enlist the services of a *muzayyina*. The *muzayyina* performs (drums, sings, and jokes) at prewedding women's parties at each house, and prepares the bride on her wedding night and escorts her to the groom. While the role of the *muzayyina* has shrunk in other parts of Yemen, it is still the case that marriage cannot take place in 'Amran without one. Townspeople object to their inflated fees, but know that eventually they have little choice but to submit.

Of the town's many women of *muzayyin* descent, only a few do traditional *muzayyina* work. There are two who perform the primary *muzayyina* role, and several others who work in supportive, secondary roles regularly or occasionally. The term *muzayyina* is confusing because in some contexts it is applied to all women of *muzayyin* descent and in other contexts only to those who perform at weddings. The most popular ͑Amrani *muzayyina* tries to maintain a monopoly over local weddings by threatening those who employ an outside *muzayyina* (from San͑a or elsewhere) that she will never work for them in the future. Fear of such a refusal keeps most ͑Amran families in line.

Men of the bride's and the groom's households have far fewer wedding preparations than the women do, once they have come to terms with each other. Each side must draw up a guest list and make sure that invitations are conveyed. The father of the groom also has to engage a *muzayyin* to announce the groom's gifts and perform other tasks on the wedding day. He may also engage an *͑ūd* player, but this is not essential. A few days before the wedding, there is a secret meeting of the groom and his father-in-law for the purpose of writing the marriage contract. Also present are the groom's father and one or two close male relatives or friends, who witness the signing of the contract. The bride does not appear.

Minimally, the marriage contract states that authority (*mulk*) over the bride is transferred from her father to her husband (although her father and brothers retain certain rights over her throughout her life). Sometimes, additional stipulations are included in the contract at the request of the bride's father or other guardian. Bybee (1978:62) believes that, because the marriage contract in Islamic societies is legal rather than religious, conditions specified by the bride's representative are "legally guaranteed." ͑Amrani informants, however, are extremely dubious of the efficacy of special provisions in the marriage contract. They say that most husbands simply ignore them because there is little risk of reprisal for doing so.

After the contract is written, it is ritually sealed by a third party, who pours raisins over the joined hands of the groom and his father-in-law. The first verse of the Quran is recited as a kind of sanctification of the agreement.

Because the groom is in a supernaturally vulnerable state for a week or two prior to his wedding, he avoids most social situations. He is particularly susceptible at the time that the marriage contract is solemnized. Its time and location are kept secret to prevent evil-wishers from playing tricks that can cause him impotence. Although he remains vulnerable on his wedding day, the groom is then in the company of large numbers of guests. His head is always covered, however, and his demeanor withdrawn. Close, trustworthy relatives or friends flank him at all times.

The bride is expected to stay inside her house and do little or no work for the week prior to her wedding. Actually, the period of seclusion ranges from three days to two weeks. Women say that the purpose of the seclusion is to lighten and soften the bride's skin for her wedding night. During her days at home, it is customary for the bride to receive afternoon visits from neighborhood girls.

Usually, three days before the wedding, the bride, accompanied by married and unmarried relatives, neighbors, and friends, washes at either the ʿAmran public bath or the one in Sanʿa. This excursion is at the expense of the groom's family and is almost always at a private party. Once she returns from the public bath, the bride should not leave her house again until the wedding night, unless her prewedding party is held in another house.

If the bride is to marry for the first time, this trip to the public bath is the occasion for giving up her virgin's peaked bonnet (*gargūsh*). As such it can be seen as a demarcation between girlhood and womanhood, although she, of course, retains her status as *ʿazaba* (virgin) and *bint* (maiden, girl) until the marriage is actually consummated.

The next day the bride stays at home and has her hands and forearms decorated by a *muzayyina* or a friend. A few young girls or women may have their hands done also, but most, knowing that the designs would quickly fade as a result of preparing the wedding feasts, do not.

On this same day, a very large and lively women's party takes place at the groom's house. This all-day affair, called *mashjab*, is never attended by the bride herself, although her mother and sisters or other close relatives are obligated to appear. The bride does attend a similar large party, also called *mashjab*, held the following day at her own house.

MASHJAB AT THE GROOM'S HOUSE

The first few women begin to arrive before eight in the morning. One hour later, when the *muzayyina* and her assistant should arrive, the room is usually full. Firstcomers sit with their backs against the wall (usually wall cushions are provided for part if not all of the room) or climb into small niches created by raised window sills. The latter seats are particularly desirable because they are slightly above and apart from the multitudes packed together on the floor. After all the choice seats have been taken, the room fills gradually from the periphery inward. Only a small space is left in front of the *muzayyina*, where women dance, one pair at a time, for five riyals apiece.

The *muzayyina* performs until shortly before noon, when most women leave to prepare lunch for their families. The women of the groom's household stop those they wish to stay for lunch (close friends or women of particular prestige or popularity), pressing them either to stay or to cook their families' meals quickly and return to lunch with them. Even if she has no intention of accepting the invitation, the guest must act as if she will do her best to finish her work and make it back. A few especially close friends were invited several days earlier to the *mashjab* lunch to allow them ample opportunity to free themselves from obligations at home.

Relatives, neighbors, and close friends of the groom's household prepare and serve lunch. It is a lavish and costly meal, but usually somewhat less so than the one served to male guests on the wedding day. At least twenty, often as many as fifty, women (many of whom were involved in the preparation) share the *mashjab* feast. They then drink *gishr* or tea and relax quietly until the guests for the afternoon session begin to arrive.

No woman ever wears the same dress in the afternoon that she wore to the morning part of the party. At a *mashjab* and other wedding-related parties women wear their best clothes, finest scarves, and much of their gold and coral jewelry. As in the morning, the *muzayyina* plays, and women dance two by two. The noise and activity level is even higher than earlier, as more women are free after lunch. The afternoon party is considered the more exciting and socially significant part of the day.

Late in the afternoon the *mashjab* (a flowering plant, after which the celebration is named) is brought in to the musical accompaniment of the wedding specialists (*muzayyināt*). There is a lighted candle or two with the large plant, and other lighted candles are brought in on trays, with at least one egg among them. Occasionally a woman of the household dances while holding the very heavy plant, but more often everyone remains seated and the trays of candles are balanced on a few women's heads. By this time of day, the room is somewhat dark, so the effect of the candles and the lighted *mashjab* is extremely dramatic; all eyes are fixed on them for the duration of a long song. When the song is over, the *mashjab* and candles are removed from the room, the former to be set aside until the wedding night. The *muzayyina* distributes gifts of cloth from the groom to a number of his close kinswomen, after which the singing and dancing continue until approaching nightfall brings the *mashjab* at the groom's house to a close.

MASHJAB AT THE BRIDE'S HOUSE

The following day is the bride's *mashjab*, which is like the *mashjab* at the groom's house except that the bride is present and is given *rifd* (gifts). According to Chelhod (1973b:14), the presentation of gifts is the defining element of the Yemeni *mashjab*. Whereas the announcement of presents is undoubtedly the high point of the day, it is neither required nor expected that all those who attend the *mashjab* give *rifd*. However, each guest is expected to contribute one riyal ($.22) toward the fee of the *muzayyina*, which is not the case at the *mashjab* in the groom's household.

The bride is present but invisible through most of her *mashjab*. At half past seven or eight in the morning she is installed on a raised platform of cushions (*martaba*), with a colorful, patterned cloth (*tarha*) draped over her in a tentlike fashion. The *tarha* is sheer enough for her to see and yet prevents the guests from seeing her. In nearby villages, the *tarha* is not used, but in ᶜAmran it is considered essential to protect the bride from evil eye. Further protection is provided her by rue (an herb that is widely considered to have curative and protective powers) and by a *hirz* (amulet, in this case a Quran in a purselike holder) hanging on the wall above her head.

The bride is expected to stay perched on her platform in a cramped position from as early as half past seven until nearly noon, and then for another two or three hours in the afternoon. She gets inevitably very hot, stiff, and thirsty, but as the wedding cloth is tentlike, she can consume cans of fruit juice or soda and pieces of fruit that she keeps under it.[4]

Almost without exception, the bride has company on the little platform; this may make her hotter and more cramped, but gives her someone to whisper with and from whom to derive moral support. The companion is either a recent bride, a specially honored guest, or a close friend of the bride and her family. In some cases, there is a struggle between the bride and her companion over their limited space, mirroring the frequent territorial skirmishes among the masses of ordinary guests below them. (In one extreme case of disrespectful treatment, the bride's prospective sister-in-law [with whom she was to live in an extended household] tossed her cloak onto the platform so recklessly that it struck the bride in the face, and then lumbered up next to her, taking more than two thirds of the available space. The bride endured her future sister-in-law's assault passively, and may have interpreted it as a show of dominance, meaningful for her future. Only a handful of guests observed the performance, so the sister-in-law risked no censure.)

As with the *mashjab* at the groom's house, specially selected guests are invited for lunch. The bride, however, is expected to eat in seclusion or with a few trustworthy relatives and friends. The rare bride who is so unconcerned about evil eye that she insists on eating with the ordinary guests is sure to be criticized. Most brides are stiff and badly need the opportunity to stretch their limbs before returning to the platform in conditions even hotter and more crowded than in the morning.

The bride must be back on her special platform, concealed under her *ṭarḥa*, before the afternoon guests begin to arrive. The singers perform and women dance, and the *mashjab* and candles are displayed, just as on the previous day. Usually the bride's *mashjab* is even more crowded than the one at the groom's house; interaction is lively, despite the oppressive heat and crowding, which sometimes lead to bickering over space and cold water, both of which are always in short supply.

The high point of the bridal *mashjab*, the presentation of *rifd* (gifts), comes late in the afternoon. The many women who were cooling off in an adjacent hallway or another room fight their way back into the *mashjab* room to hear the *muzayyina* announce the bride's gifts. Some of the guests, those in reciprocal gift-exchange relations with the bride's family, and all of those who lunched at her house on this day give gifts. Others need not.

First, the most important gifts, usually items of gold jewelry from the bride's close kin, are announced and held up by the *muzayyina* for all to see. She bellows, "Behold! Two gold bracelets from the bride's brother Ahmad!" The gifts are not presented to the bride until after the party is over. She remains apart, usually at the far end of the room, on her platform and under her *tarha*.

The guests all display tremendous interest in the gold and large cash gifts from the bride's close relatives, but are often openly skeptical about their authenticity as presents. It is common practice for the family of a bride to borrow gold for the *mashjab*. The object of the deception is to enhance the family prestige, but this usually backfires when women, familiar with the bride's relatives and their holdings in gold, recognize a piece and announce its source to the company at large.

After the *muzayyina* finishes announcing the important presents, guests begin to hand her the lesser ones at a furious pace. Every single giver and the amount of her gift—usually between 5 and 50 riyals ($1 to $11)—must be proclaimed. As these announcements do not much interest the guests, they become increasingly noisy and disorderly. This angers the *muzayyina*, who threatens repeatedly to quit unless the women quiet down.

It is crucial that each announcement (of which there are usually over one hundred) be audible, so that the bride and her relatives will be able to reciprocate appropriately when an opportunity arises. A cassette tape recording is made to ensure that no gift is overlooked, and it is the responsibility of the *muzayyina* to keep the noise level low enough that all announcements can be heard on the tape.[5]

After the gift announcements are over, most brides retire to another room, but, as on the previous day, the singing, dancing, and socializing go on until almost dusk. The departure of the bride goes virtually unnoticed. As the time for the evening prayer call approaches, women tear themselves away from the *mashjab*, stopping briefly to cool off in another room or a hallway before exiting into the brisk air outdoors. In groups of twos and threes, they head homeward, rehashing the gifts of gold and the other important and amusing events of the day.

THE WEDDING EVE

With the completion of the second *mashjab*, the women's prewedding festivities are concluded, but informal visiting continues at the bride's house. A couple of hours after the end of the *mashjab*, neighbors return to help with advance preparations for the men's wedding feast the next day, and to keep the bride and her mother company. Neighborhood girls and never married women, who were excluded from the *mashjab*, are welcome at these more casual and intimate gatherings.

Since a primary purpose of the visit is to distract the bride and her kinswomen, their neighbors strive to maintain a lively atmosphere throughout the evening. Sometimes, a young woman dresses up in male clothes and does a comic imitation of a man. In one case, the crude and ridiculous "fellow" swept down upon one woman after another demanding a kiss from each. In effect, "he" put on a series of comic male-female duets, allowing each woman a turn to put "him" off by the wit and sting of her tongue. These support sessions rarely break up early, despite the fact that all are tired from the day's work and from the *mashjab* and know that the next day will be more taxing yet.

THE WEDDING DAY

On the wedding day, the women prepare a feast for the male guests and wait for the bride to be taken to her groom. While the wedding feast of the past was a relatively simple (although costly) evening meal, now many families serve an elaborate wedding lunch. Some families serve both lunch and dinner; others continue the traditional evening meal pattern.

The groom's household must have a wedding *ḥalāfa*; although the obligation of the bride's family is weaker, very few families have no guests at all and some invite as many or more guests than does the groom's family. Guest lists exceeding one hundred men are common. There also must be enough food for the women who help to prepare the food, their children, and for female relatives from out of town and their children. Over one hundred and fifty people may be served.

Most of the helpers are neighbors, who are asked to loan their houses (several may be used in which to prepare the meal and serve it and, for later, where the guests can chew *gāt*), their furnishings, and their cooking paraphernalia; they are asked to knead bread dough and bake hundreds of breads and to prepare as many as nine courses for over one hundred voracious appetites. On rare occasions a family will hire one or two women to cook the meat or do other food preparation, or a *muzayyin* might be hired to cook the meat outdoors. Still, the bulk of the work falls to the bride's neighbors and relatives. More often than not, the formidable task is accomplished splendidly with nothing more than the traditional Yemeni ovens and some primus stoves.

The bride remains inactive while her mother, kinswomen, neighbors, and family friends work. Usually she is kept company by old women or guests from out of town. While they wait, and the other women labor, the groom begins his preparations for the wedding day. Today is the groom's day; unlike his bride, who will be honored at numerous celebrations in the six weeks to come, his new status is celebrated on this day alone.

THE GROOM'S CELEBRATIONS

In the late morning, the groom is accompanied by a few close friends to the public bath. After bathing, he dresses (with the friends' help) in a fine, new *zanna* (Saudi-style long robe), and covers his head with a handsome, new *shāl* (shawl). With his friends close on either side, where they will remain all day, he returns to his home.

Wedding guests begin to arrive outside the groom's house after the noon prayer time. They fire their automatic rifles, set off firecrackers and dance with their daggers until lunch is served. When there is a shortage of space, the feast is served in shifts; those served first wait outside for the rest to finish. There may be more drumming and dancing until the entire assembly sets off in procession toward a mosque. Some pray along with the groom, while others head toward a teahouse in the *sūq* or home for a rest.

Many of the lunch guests return to chew *gāt* with him. (If, as in the past, only the evening meal is served, guests first appear at this time.) There may be drumming and dancing outdoors again before the men settle down for the afternoon indoors. Part of the *gāt* session is given over to the chanting of Quranic verses. Throughout the afternoon the groom is silent and appears withdrawn.

An evening meal may be served, either before the men depart for a mosque or after they return from praying. While appetites were keen at lunch, few men desire food after chewing *gāt*. (Ordinarily men eat very light late-evening meals.) The groom and his guests have to be pressed to partake of the abundant meat, rich broth and, *laḥūḥ* (a thin, pancakelike bread).

The groom performs the evening prayers at a mosque, still accompanied by a few close friends. Large numbers of wedding guests join them outside the mosque (sometimes other men join as well), forming a slow, intensely dramatic procession to escort the groom back to his house, where he must remain until his bride is brought to him later in the night.

For women, this procession is the high point of every wedding, thrilling even if they do not know the groom and his family. They and their children assemble on rooftops all along its route to watch and to joy-call as the groom passes by. Their ululations, heard by the men below, are a kind of indirect participation in the procession. Men are excited by a wedding procession, but, because they are a part of it, its aesthetic and dramatic effect is much less apparent to them than to its viewers from above. The wedding procession might thus be seen as a public male performance put on for female eyes.

Led by a paid singer, the men chant religious songs for the duration of the procession. Several youths carry lanterns, lighting the men's way and illuminating their faces. Also spotlighting the performers are plates of lighted candles and the candle-illuminated *mashjab* left from the prewedding party two days before. The groom, with a friend holding each arm, proceeds slowly and woodenly, showing no interest in what is going on around him.[6]

The intensity of the chanting builds as the procession approaches the groom's house. Sometimes, he is seated outside the entrance, while a musician plays the *ʿūd* or while others dance to a *muzayyin*'s drums. At other times, after almost frenzied repetitions of the refrain of a particular prayer, the groom is virtually thrust inside his front door.

Most of the men then follow him in and settle down again, as after lunch, in one or more comfortable reception rooms. Some resume chewing *gāt* (an extraordinary practice, for evening *gāt* consumption is limited to Ramadhan and weddings) and prayers are chanted. A musician sometimes plays the *ʿūd* and sings. The groom continues to appear withdrawn.

At some point in the evening, the *dawshān* (town crier or messenger-poet, according to Chelhod [1973b:19], arrives to greet and flatter the guests. His tone of voice is bizarre and distorted, his language obscure. The father of the groom is obligated to "tip" the *dawshān* (about 50 riyals) and give him *gāt* for his performance. after which he leaves or stays outside the house to chew his *gāt*.

Just before the presentation of gifts (*rifd*), the barber lathers the groom's cheeks, and gives each a token stroke with his razor. The guests virtually ignore this ritual, one Chelhod (1973b) believes to be a possible survival from an earlier period when the groom's entire head was shaved on the wedding night.

Then the gifts of cash are handed to the *muzayyin*, who announces each giver and the amount given in the same manner as that of the *muzayyina* at the bride's *mashjab*. In this case, however, the money is placed directly in the groom's lap. He appears oblivious to the money, which is collected by his friends on either side. Although over one hundred gifts are announced, there is not the commotion that makes the job of the *muzayyina* so difficult. As at the *mashjab*, the *rifd* announcements are tape-recorded so none will be forgotten. Balanced reciprocity underlies the giving of *rifd* by both sexes.

After the announcements are over, many of the guests leave since it is already between nine and ten o'clock. Only a few relatives and friends stay on with the groom until the bride arrives, an hour or two later.

THE WOMEN OF THE GROOM'S HOUSEHOLD

As at the bride's house, kinswomen, neighbors and friends help with the wedding feast (although the *muzayyin* often prepares the meat outside). After the men lunch, the women share a leisurely meal, relaxing after their arduous morning. Even though they have to wash dozens of dirty dishes and may have to bake more bread for the evening meal, they have time to recuperate and to perform their prayers. Most stay on to view the groom's procession and the men's dancing, when possible, to eavesdrop on the *dawshān*'s greetings and the *muzayyin*'s *rifd* announcements, and eventually to catch a glimpse of the bride. They linger until late at night to keep the groom's mother and sisters-in-law company and for the vicarious enjoyment of the wedding excitement.

THE WEDDING DAY AT THE BRIDE'S HOUSE

The bride's father hosts guests for lunch or dinner or sometimes for both. Guests usually stay on to chew *gāt*, and a few close relatives eventually accompany the bride and her father to the house of the groom. There is no dancing or presentation of *rifd* at the bride's house, and the guests do not participate in the groom's procession.

After the male guests finish their lunch, the bride and her relatives and the many female helpers eat together. As at the groom's house, there is usually an abundance of food left over, but occasionally the women do not eat as well as the men. Friends, relatives, and neighbors stay on throughout much of the day and evening to provide the bride and her mother moral support; they still have a long vigil ahead of them.

In the evening, whether or not they serve male guests, the women and children partake of rich broth and bread as well as meat when some is left. The bride eats with them.

Eventually the *muzayyina* arrives. She drinks *gishr* and chats for a while, distracting the company from the matter at hand. Between eight and nine o'clock she sends the bride off to wash and requests a room in which she can prepare the bride in privacy. More often than not, a few women invade the sanctity of the bridal dressing room, sometimes by the bride's invitation, more often by their own insistence. The preparation of a more than usually stylish ᶜAmran bride took place as follows:

> First she put on a brassiere and a white T-shirt over it, long white underpants, a white slip and white sheer knee-high socks. Heavy applications of perfume accompanied each layer of clothing. Her sheer white dress was knee-length and her high heels silvery. She wore several gold bracelets and necklaces.
> Her face was made up heavily with foundation, rouge, powder, lipstick, and eyeshadow (all worn by very few ᶜAmrani women, forbidden to the unmarried, but considered appropriate for wedding nights). The *muzayyina* sectioned the hair framing the bride's face, perfumed and rolled each section into a sausagelike curl, which she then fastened securely with bobbypins. She left the rest of her hair loose, and placed on top of the bride's head a stiff white gauze crown from which trailed a white veil, which partially concealed the bride's long hair.

While the *muzayyina* does her job, the women and children wait eagerly in another room to view the bride. All conversation halts when they are told that the *muzayyina* is about to usher her back among them.

The cosmetics, the curls, the crown, the fine white dress, and lavish jewels all combine to make the bride appear truly transfigured. A poor makeup job or a shabby rented crown will be remarked upon cattily in a few minutes, but for a single moment the dramatic alteration in the bride's appearance quite takes her viewers' breath away. In a way, the *muzayyina* has erased the girl's personal identity; she becomes, in the eyes of her audience, not herself, but ḤARIWA (a bride).

That the bride's fear shows through her glamorous facade only adds to the power of her effect. As she sits briefly among the women and girls, her tear-filled eyes cast down, a handkerchief clutched in her hand, no one can take her eyes off her. It appears that all thoughts are focused on what the bride is soon to undergo, the women with memories of their own wedding nights, the girls in anticipation of their own.

In the final moments of her girlhood, the bride may be given last-minute admonitions to behave creditably in her husband's house. One respected *sayyid* woman spoke urgently to her unmannerly young neighbor:

> You will have to be polite and agreeable all the time. You can't act there the way you do at home. You can't make a lot of noise and run around all over the place. No matter what happens, you have to act as if everything there is just fine!

By half past ten the groom's kinsmen (but never the groom) appear outside to claim the bride. She puts on her *sharshaf*, receives rushed kisses from the women and girls, and departs, accompanied by the *muzayyina*, her father, her mother's brother, and sometimes by other male relatives. If her husband's house is too far to walk, automobiles are used.

The groom's kinsmen head the procession, sometimes carrying the lighted *mashjab* from their prewedding women's celebration with them. The bride's *mashjab* is brought with her, and the two plants are placed inside the nuptial chamber. Behind the groom's relatives is the *muzayyina*, who burns frankincense to banish evil spirits from the bride's path. The bride is supported by her father on her right and her mother's brother on her left. Her kinsmen, like the groom's, are usually heavily armed. The men chant as they proceed, standing extremely close to the bride, almost as if supporting her weight.

Although it is considered improper for more than a few women or girls to trail after the bride, her neighbors, relatives, and friends often take matters into their own hands and come in large numbers. The bride's mother, however, never accompanies her and has no direct contact with her for one full week. If the groom's house is far enough away to require the use of a car, the bride's sole female companion may be the *muzayyina*.[7]

When the procession nears the groom's house, the *muzayyina* breaks at least three eggs, one on the street, one outside the entryway, and the other on the steps just inside the house to drive away devils (*shayāṭin*). For symbolic reasons no longer understood by ᶜAmrani women, one of the groom's kinsmen places a dagger or an automatic rifle in the doorway for the bride to walk over on her first steps inside her husband's house.[8]

These ritual actions quickly completed, the bride is rushed upstairs. The *muzayyina* accompanies her into the nuptial room, but her female followers must huddle together against the walls of a hall or a stairway if they are not offered a room in which to wait. Sometimes the groom and his entourage must push past them as he is hastened to his bride.

She is seated on a platform with her legs tucked under her. Her veiled face is cast downward when the groom comes in to her.[9] His brother or friends wait outside the door. More or less simultaneously, the groom presents his bride with the amount of money agreed upon for the unveiling (usually 500 to 1,000 riyals, $110 to $220) and lifts her veil to uncover her face. Even if he pushes her forehead back, she does not look up at him. He places his thumb and forefinger on her temples and recites the *fātḥa* (the opening verse of the Quran) and then removes the sprig of rue or basil from her crown or her veil. Most men place the sprig in the sheath of their dagger, but a few put it on the floor and step on it. The former act ensures the bride's affection and the couple's compatibility and the latter establishes the groom's power over his bride and prevents her from leaving him. At this time, the groom must also pay the *muzayyina* (usually about 100 riyals or $22) for having delivered him his bride.

Without speaking (aside from reciting the Quranic verse) and without having seen the bride's face clearly (because of her refusal to look up), the groom immediately leaves the room to rejoin the remaining male guests. They salute him with a morning greeting, a practice women considered highly amusing.[10] He drinks one cup of tea with them before returning to his wife, this time to spend the night.

In the meantime, all the women and girls (the groom's contingent as well as those who accompanied the bride) push their way into her room. For hours they have been saying they will shake their skirts at her, thereby sending her *baraka* (blessings); now many of them do, even though they view the custom as more humorous than serious. The bride continues to look down, partially covering her face with a handkerchief as she sniffles and trembles or, in some cases, actually sobs. After all the women and girls have packed in to stare at her and a few have kissed her a last time, they are rushed back out again as word reaches them that the groom is ready to come in. When they have left, the bride may receive a brief visit from a brother of the groom, who gives her a small gift of cash, and from her father. Then they too depart, and the groom enters.

Many women say they had no knowledge of what was to occur on their wedding night, and believe it is best for a woman to learn such things from her husband. Many mothers say they would be too embarrassed to tell their daughters what to expect. However, some women say that, in actuality, girls do learn about sex from an early age, although the knowledge may well fail to protect them from experiencing shock and shame at their first sexual experience.

Opinions differ as to the importance of an immediate consummation of the marriage. Most women believe that, as long as the bride is *nazifa* (literally "clean"; in this case, not menstruating), no matter how great her fear, how vigorous her resistance, she should be entered on the first night. Some women, however, speak very highly of men who demonstrate a willingness to wait for the wife's consent, and cite examples of those who allow very young wives as much as a year's postponement and others who do not press their wives until after they return from their postwedding visits with their own relatives. Most men are less patient and insist upon their conjugal rights on the wedding night; some use drugs to sedate an extremely resistant bride. (The marriage is *not* consummated on the first night if the father or other kinsmen of the bride stay the night in the groom's house. This is most likely to occur when the two houses are in separate towns or villages.)

Informants agree upon how the wedding night should unfold, although acknowledging that exceptions are far from uncommon. The groom should spend several hours in conversation with his bride before making any move sexually. Then he gets her flat on her back, spreads and raises her legs, and penetrates her once. He may not repeat the act that night. Following are descriptions given by several townswomen of what happened and how they felt on and after the wedding night:

Account A
I was sitting there shaking and gushing sweat when he came in and sat down at the other end of the cushions. Neither of us said a word for about an hour. Then he started telling me about his wedding gifts from the guests. I kept quiet, didn't even cry. Then he did it, but he didn't kiss me until the following night! It hurt terribly but he kept saying "That's all right, don't worry." What is really funny though is that, the next morning, I ran into my husband on the stairway, but pulled my face veil up since I did not recognize him. The room had been dark the night before and I hadn't yet seen his face! Within a few nights we were staying up talking and stuff until dawn. He is really very, very nice.

Account B
I was only fourteen and because of the kind of life we lived was even much more sheltered than other young girls. You would not believe how naïve I was! Or how plump I was! When they asked me if I wanted to marry A, I told them no. I'd heard nothing but bad things about that family, and cried for three days straight. My father said that A wasn't like the rest of the men in his family, that he was an industrious and good man, and, you know, my father pretty much neglected me in favor of his other wife's daughters, so he made me marry A.

All my mother had told me about marriage was that there *had* to be blood. Believe me, I hadn't the faintest idea of what she was talking about.

So on my wedding night, I sat there, veiled, on my platform, and he came in, gave me money, and uncovered my face. Then he went out and the women came in. Then we were alone together. He kissed me on the cheek, and I asked him why he did that. Then he chatted about all sorts of things, while I kept silent, but stole glances at him when he didn't see I was looking. Eventually, he said we should undress and go to sleep. I, of course, assumed he meant separately, and took off all my clothes except my underdress and underpants, just as I always did.

He told me to take off the underpants too. I asked why, but he didn't answer. I took them off anyway. Then I also agreed when he told me to sleep next to him, instead of separately. I said to him, not knowing what I was saying, "There has to be blood." I was simply repeating the one thing my mother had told me about the whole business. Well, he went to work, but it was very painful for me. It was only later that I learned to enjoy doing this with my husband.

Account C
That night I was so frightened I wouldn't stop crying and screaming and fighting. Ask his next door neighbors; they'll tell you how much noise I made that night and then all that month. Finally, my husband got tired of struggling with me and so he gave me a medicine. Of course, I didn't know what it was or that it would put me into a deep, deep sleep. Lots of men use it when their brides resist. After that I didn't know what happened to me, and when I woke up in the morning and saw the blood and felt my pain, I just couldn't believe he could have done that to me. I never stopped crying all that month, and I never want to live with him again.

Account D
He gave me 1,000 riyals to unveil me, and I sent that to my mother. Then he went away for a few minutes. When he came back in, he gave me a standard greeting, like you'd give to any casual acquaintance. I gave the obligatory response to his greeting and shut up. I refused to come down from my platform, so he lifted me down. I cried and cried for days, and the only words I spoke to him for the entire first three days were "I'll talk to you tomorrow." I said those words to him constantly. "I'll talk to you tomorrow. I'll talk to you tomorrow."

As the bride's mother in account B told her daughter, and as the daughter unwittingly repeated to her husband, there has to be blood. Lutfiyya (1966:141) points out that blood proves the groom's potency as much as it does the bride's virginity, and ʿAmrani women sometimes blame the husband when a bloody sheet is not produced. Much more often, however, an absence of blood after several days of marriage leads to suspicions about the bride.

A bride is expected to bleed on her wedding night or on the following night. The groom then pays a morning visit to his mother-in-law; he presents her with the bloody cloth (to which rue is attached) and gives her raisins and almonds. Household women, sometimes joined by neighbors and relatives, joy-call upon seeing the evidence of the bride's virginity, although there is not a general viewing or a public celebration.[11] Because it is not uncommon for a groom to visit his mother-in-law and present her with gifts on the first and/or second mornings after the wedding, even if the bride has not yet *ṣabaḥat* (figuratively, produced blood), his appearance at her house is not sufficient to prevent the spreading of doubts and gossip. In some cases, the speculations are not without basis, as in the following example (one of the rare occasions I was alone in the company of men):

> Ahmad and Tagiya had married their daughter Arwa to a man from Ahmad's natal village on Thursday. Arwa's husband ʿAbdu spent the night with Ahmad (after a brief meeting with his bride) because it was too late for Ahmad to return that night to ʿAmran and it is *ʿayb* for a man to consummate his marriage while his father-in-law remains in the house.
>
> On Friday morning Ahmad returns to ʿAmran. He and Tagiya anticipated that ʿAbdu would pay them the obligatory postwedding visit and present them with the evidence of Arwa's virginity within the next few days.
>
> Late Monday morning ʿAbdu and his father arrived at Ahmad's house. A child was sent to fetch Ahmad home, and the guests were ushered in to his best reception room. I was left alone with them while Tagiya assembled tea things and a plate of sweets and nuts. The men assured me that Arwa was *murtaḥa* [content], the term used for all brides regardless of their true emotional state.
>
> Very soon, Ahmad arrived, and greeted ʿAbdu and his father warmly. Tagiya burnt frankincense; the guests placed their faces near the fumes and directed them inside their head cloths. Tagiya then sprinkled all of us with perfume.
>
> After a few minutes of polite, general conversation, we heard female voices in the house. Neighbors and relatives had learned of Arwa's fiancé's arrival and come right over. In unison they joy-called just outside the room, after which a few of the bolder ones peeked in to catch a glimpse of the groom. Some departed quickly, but others lingered in the hallway in the hope of seeing the bloody cloth, and perhaps of getting a share of Tagiya's raisins and almonds as well.
>
> While the women waited outside the room, Ahmad and ʿAbdu's

father continued talking to each other. Tagiya then asked her son-in-law very quietly about the bloody cloth, and looked stricken when he replied that there was none. Fearful of being overheard (by me or by the women near the door), she went and sat right next to ʿAbdu. As they whispered in each other's ears, Tagiya looked more and more troubled.

Shortly, ʿAbdu and his father stood up and departed, even though it is customary for the groom's party, if they have come from a distant place, to stay for lunch. Their failure to do so might be taken as evidence of dissatisfaction with the bride.

Tagiya later told me how relieved she was to learn that Arwa was *murtaḥa* (despite the general belief that such assurances are meaningless), and asked me what ʿAbdu and his father had said to me when I was alone with them. Ahmad looked disspirited for the next several days, and spoke to me of his plans to move the entire family to America. Inevitably, I was asked by Tagiya's neighbors if I had seen the bloody cloth and why it had not been shown to them.

The failure of a bride to bleed is a grave disgrace in ʿAmran, but it is not seen as cause for her murder. Parents who have reason to believe their daughter's hymen was accidentally ruptured can obtain a legal document to that effect. If the bride does not bleed and there is no such document, the outcome varies depending on the reputation of the bride and her family and on their relationship with the groom's family. Informants state that when trust is strong, animal blood is used to fake the evidence. When it is not, the bride may be sent home to her parents, who, if convinced of her purity, seek the mediation of the *ḥākam* (Islamic judge). She is examined by the *ḥākam*'s wife, who claims that in her many years of experience, she has never seen evidence of prior sexual experience. Despite her report, many grooms and their parents refuse the *ḥākam*'s ruling in the bride's favor. In other cases, instead of sending the bride home, a message is sent to her father of the shame she has brought upon him, giving him the opportunity to offer a large bribe. While the in-laws are likely to accept a sufficiently generous offer (reportedly, as much as 50,000 riyals), they rarely keep the matter quiet, and may never forgive the woman or treat her decently.

There is no doubt that the absence of blood is a terrible disgrace for the bride and for her family.[12] In abstract discussions of the issue, townswomen almost invariably assert that it is quite possible for a sexually inexperienced female to lose her virginity without bleeding. They often fail to apply this contention, however, in their consideration of specific cases. At the least indication of a possible problem, malicious rumors develop, although relatives of the bride are not confronted directly. The following two examples illustrate the responses of townswomen to a bride's apparent failure to bleed:

> In one case of an exchange marriage between an ᶜAmran family and a village family, rumors spread through ᶜAmran that the bride from town had not bled. Although no one knew or was willing to reveal the original source of the information, townswomen quickly became convinced that the villagers had been paid off (20,000 to 30,000 riyals or $4,400 to $6,600, depending upon who told the story) to keep the sullied bride.
>
> A sister of the unfortunate bride launched a counterattack to the effect that it was the village bride who had failed to bleed, and whom they now assumed to have been married previously. She complained bitterly that the dirty villagers had falsely advertised their daughter as a virgin and that now, to add insult to injury, they were treating her poor sister badly for absolutely no reason at all. No one believed this story, although it was never contradicted in the sister's presence. [The sister and her "friends" all recognize in principle that a failure to bleed does not prove nonvirginity, and concur that it is terrible to blame a bride in such a predicament. However, when it came to her own sister, this woman was far too ashamed to speak out against the injustice of the accusations; and her friends and neighbors, whom she knew were acquainted with the rumors, and who knew that she knew that they were acquainted with them, kept silent. She spoke lies out of humiliation, thus giving credence to the gossip, and cutting herself and her sister off from any possible moral support.]
>
> In this case of a marriage between two old ᶜAmran families, opinion was sharply divided as to why the bloody cloth had not been presented to the mother of the bride. Friends of the bride's family maintained that she had refused to be entered; others said that she simply did not bleed. The majority opinion was that the groom was impotent. Eventually gossip ended, as it became clear that the groom had simply shown unusual patience with the fears of his very young and extremely shy wife.

POSTWEDDING CELEBRATIONS

If, as is usually the case, the bride's virginity is not at issue, the married couple spend their first week together in relative seclusion. She neither goes out nor receives callers, although her younger sister or an equally innocuous family representative may show up before the week is out.[13] He leaves home only to pray in a mosque or to visit the public bath. It is expected that the couple do no work during this week and that they eat alone together in their own room.

On the afternoon following the wedding day, the women of the groom's household (except of course for the bride) call on the bride's mother. Accompanied by relatives, friends, and neighbors, the women, who bring a large kettle of *gishr* with them, formally assure the mother of the bride that her daughter is content (*murtaḥa*). The women of the bride's household are similarly supported by their own relatives, neighbors, and friends. Their neighbors, in particular, see it as their duty to keep the mother of the bride company for several days after the wedding, just as they did for the few afternoons and evenings leading up to it.

Only after the week's seclusion of the bride and groom, can she be visited by her mother and other adult relatives and friends. He resumes his normal life, and she begins a long round of postwedding social events. The first event, called *sābʿa* (seventh, because it is held on the seventh day after the wedding), is the most dramatic of the female wedding-related celebrations.

YAWM AL SĀBʿA (THE SEVENTH DAY)

The celebration is held in the groom's house. Townswomen rush there after lunch to see the bride make her entrance. This is a coming-out party, the bride's initial foray into the town's female social world, from which, until her marriage, she has been excluded.

The bride waits in her room while the reception room fills up. Her relatives, neighbors, and friends stop in to greet her before claiming a spot in the extremely packed party room. Her entrance will take place as soon as the wedding specialists (*muzayyināt*) arrive with her trousseau, which they bring from her father's house. When their drumming and singing is heard outside the house, the women of the household begin to burn frankincense in the stairways. The wedding specialists accompanied by women from the bride's household, carry the bride's trunk upstairs to her room. Only after the ceremonial transfer of her property from her father's to her husband's house, can the bride be presented to the company.

The bride was invisible under a tentlike veil at her prewedding party, and inspired little or no interest from the guests. Her specialness did not begin until the wedding night, when her appearance was transformed by the *muzayyina*. Today for the *sābᶜa* celebration she is again prepared as a bride. She wears a white dress and veil and a lavish display of gold; her head is crowned, her hair curled and her face heavily made up. On the wedding night the effect was ostensibly for the groom; today it is for female society at large.

The wedding specialists sing and drum as they lead the bride, her face concealed behind the white veil, into the room of impatient guests. The musicians take their seats, leaving the bride alone to rotate slowly and rhythmically to their beat. It is only for this brief moment of tight and stylized movement that the faceless bride once again transcends her personal identity. During it, all eyes and all attention are riveted upon her.

The tension is soon broken when the bride's mother or maternal aunt steps forward and throws back the bride's veil. Now visible, the bride is joined by a partner to dance at a more normal, lively pace. Although guests still stare at her face and costume for a while, the intensity of their interest soon dissipates.[14]

After dancing, the bride must climb over and through the tightly packed women to ascend her platform at the opposite end of the room. It is customary for her mother or maternal aunt to dance the next dance, during which many, sometimes the great majority, of guests get up and depart. They have seen what they came to see and, unless they are closely tied to the family of either bride or groom, prefer to spend the rest of the afternoon at another house. Despite the departures, the dancing continues until shortly before the evening prayer call as at the prewedding parties. If the bride can dance, as most can, she does so one or more times. If she cannot, she stays the entire afternoon on her platform, with a close friend or honored guest as company, just as at her *mashjab* only eight days ago.

For three weeks following the *sābᶜa*, guests call in the afternoon on her, her mother-in-law, and sisters-in-law. They chat, drink tea and *gishr*, dance to cassette tapes, and watch television. Some families hold weekly large parties, for which they hire musicians to perform. Throughout this period the bride is not yet expected to work. Her first month of marriage ends with a large dancing party, after which she leaves her husband's house to visit her parents.

SHIKMA

The bride's stay with her parents and relatives (called *shikma*) usually lasts about eight days, considerably longer when there are many kinswomen who wish to honor her. At each house she visits, lunch is served to specially invited female guests, and parties are held for women at large. Sometimes musicians are employed. A distinctive aspect of the *shikma* is an early morning party at which guests, who do not dress up, are served special treats. Guests arrive about eight or half past eight in the morning and are home again to do their household work by half past nine or ten o'clock. Some of them return for lunch, others for afternoooon visiting.

Brides vary considerably in their attitudes toward the *shikma* and in their relations with their husbands during it. Although it is customary for the bride to sleep at her parents' house for the initial days of the *shikma* and to sleep at the houses of those relatives who fete her, a few return at night to sleep at their husbands' house. Of those brides who stay with parents and kin, some are visited by their husbands daily, others every few days, others do not see their husbands again until the *shikma* is over. Some brides are disturbed when their husbands don't visit them, but others are so happy to be with their families again that they appear to think little of them. Most brides love the attention lavished on them by family and guests; some appear sulky at their *shikma* celebrations. The range is broad indeed: one bride of about sixteen announced at her *shikma*, "I don't like my husband and I don't want to be married to him. I'm only thirteen and I'm not yet menstruating and I don't want to go back to him." Another bride of roughly the same age whispered gushingly to me, "Marriage is fantastic!!"

With few exceptions, the bride returns to the groom at the end of the *shikma*, despite whatever misgivings each may feel about the other. The bride retains special privileges at women's parties for one year, but few or none in her husband's home. She now begins to learn her new place and to build relations with her husband and his family.

132 / *Marriage: Arrangements, Celebrations, Consummation*

Tribesmen perform a traditional dance at a wedding.

7

Marriage: Relations and Conflict

I only left my husband one time. Our first son was two years old. My husband sometimes hit him in the head, which I thought was very wrong. What upset me most was that he yelled at his mother. I said to myself, "If he treats her badly now, any day he'll be the same with me." Without telling anyone why, I simply left. I went to stay with relatives in San ͨa. My father was away in Mecca.

My husband sent intermediaries to try to convince me to come back to him, but I stayed in San ͨa. When he learned that our son was ill, he had a relative take the boy away from me to stay with my mother-in-law. After a little while I confided in one of my relatives why I had left my husband.

Then my father returned from his pilgrimage, as did his brother, who was also my father-in-law. I went to my father-in-law and said, "You are my uncle (ͨ*amm*) and my father is my husband's uncle (ͨ*amm*). How, then, could my husband take his son away from me?" I told him the rest of my complaints about his son too.

He became very angry with his son when he heard what he had done, and left immediately for his place of work. He yelled at him and beat him right in front of his co-workers. When they could not help but hear my father-in-law's accusations, his co-workers joined in and yelled at him too. My husband began to cry in front of all of them, and then ran away.

I stayed on another few days before returning to live with my husband in ͨAmran. My first day back, we were both silent all day and all night, but by the next day, things became normal again between us. Since then, my husband has never yelled at his mother or at me, and he has never smacked the children in the head again.

The above account is an idealized version of marital relations. Its narrator told me the same story on two separate occasions, on neither of which were other women present. The idealized elements are: she left her husband only once, and then for the most respectable of reasons (his physical abuse of their son and verbal abuse of his mother); because her husband is her *ibn ʿamm* (father's brother's son), she could go to his father and remind him that he is her uncle as well as her father-in-law; her father-in-law took her side both because she was in the right and because he is her father's brother; too indignant to wait for his son's return home, he went to his place of work, where, too angry to spare him embarrassment, he berated and struck him in front of his colleagues; finally, the colleagues, choruslike, reiterated the condemnations; because they are outsiders, their judgment was morally unimpeachable. The wife is proven right; the husband is publicly humiliated for his errors. After they reunite, he never misbehaves again.

This story obviously glorifies its teller/heroine and exaggerates the ease of resolving marital conflict. It was no accident that it was told to me in private. Had other women heard it, they would have expressed amusement and skepticism. Its teller, of course, knew this, and so did not tell the story in company. In this chapter, the missing company will be given the opportunity to comment. Significant differences in perspective will be seen.

I begin with a discussion of conjugal sexual relationships, and then explore other aspects of married life. Women's conversations avoid the routine; they prefer to talk about conflict, separation, divorce, and other such dramatic topics. I follow their lead.

SEXUAL RELATIONS

Chelhod (1973a:60) reports that it is very common for Yemeni girls to marry prior to puberty. Of a sample of 147 married women (from Sanʿa and from Khamir, a small town slightly north of ʿAmran) whose ages could be ascertained, 22 had been married between the ages of eight and ten and 89 had been married between the ages of eleven and fifteen. Bornstein (1974), drawing from data on Sanʿa and villages in three different regions of Yemen, claims the average age at marriage for Yemeni females is between thirteen and fourteen. Makhlouf (1979), who conducted research in Sanʿa, thinks the average age at marriage is about thirteen. The average age at marriage for Yemeni males is significantly higher than that for females (Chelhod 1973a:60, Yemen Arab Republic 1978:pt. 1, 79).

It is extremely rare for ᶜAmrani women or men to know their own or others' exact age. Women do remember, however, whether they had reached menarche prior to their first marriage. Twenty-nine of fifty presently or formerly married women, to whom I administered a structured interview schedule, claim to have been premenarcheal at marriage. (Myntti [1979:27] found 65 percent of ever married women in a far northern village had married before puberty, a 7 percent higher proportion than in the ᶜAmran sample.) Despite the general claim in ᶜAmran that a few considerate men delay sexual relations until their wives are sexually mature, this was not the case for any of these twenty-nine informants. Although townswomen are sharply critical of "excessively early" marriages (but do not define excessive earliness precisely), they do not focus specifically on the attainment of menarche. Almost no women state directly that girls who do not menstruate are not ready for marriage. In fact, many claim that sexual activity hastens the onset of menstruation, although several say they themselves did not begin to menstruate until several years after marriage. A few months after her daughter's marriage, a woman announced proudly to me, "Arwa has gotten to be all right!" When I asked what she meant, she explained, "She has gotten her period (*al-ᶜāda*). It usually comes quickly once a girl gets married."

It is considered normal for a young bride to dislike sexual relations at first.[1] Not only is she usually younger and more timid than her husband, but she is also far less likely to have had previous sexual experiences. Women say that premarital sex is considered a great wrong for females, but not for males. A woman expects her husband to be sexually experienced; a man would be shocked and outraged to learn the same of his wife. "When my husband told me of his earlier sexual encounters, I wasn't angry or upset because it happened before we were married. But men are different!"

An informant describes her initial difficulties in adjusting to conjugal relations:

> I hated it the first few years, but you know, in a way I liked it at the same time too. I wore heavy cloth underpants to sleep. Every night I'd

fight to keep them on and he'd fight to get them off. It wasn't playing at all! I cried and really struggled hard. Then the following morning, I would run home to my mother, and my husband would fetch me back that night. Finally, we separated for a year. After that, we got along much better—most of the time.

Informants say that most women learn to enjoy sex, and are orgasmic at least some of the time. Women's part in sexual intercourse should be active rather than passive. Both the husband and the wife "work" (*ashtughil*). If the wife does not enjoy sex and does not "work," her husband will be displeased by her passivity. A man wants his wife to be sexually active. It enhances his own sexual pleasure. Some, perhaps most husbands are also desirous of enhancing their wives' sexual pleasure. They caress them before and during intercourse and at least occasionally leave the choice of position to the woman. Some wives indicate their desires only indirectly; others claim to be quite direct.[2]

Some women who have been married a number of years complain that their husbands are far less interested in sex and less considerate lovers than during the early years of marriage. "He used to take his time and try to please me, but now he is through in five minutes or less. It is lousy for me. He often tells me how sorry he is, but sometimes I get mad anyway. If it's going to be like that, it's better not to do it at all."

The practice of obtaining magical papers to enhance husbands' sexual interest has not completely died out. Most women realize, however, that magic cannot undo the potency-reducing effects of *gāt*, and settle for less frequent intercourse than they would like. This is a common subject for jokes among women. Quite possibly, having a shared and unthreatening explanation for sexual neglect is comforting.

No woman told me of having had sex outside of marriage, although some describe seduction and rape attempts they had to rebuff. When I asked an informant what her father or brothers would have done to the man had he succeeded in raping her, she replied that they would have been convinced that she had been willing (*rādhiya*), and would blame her, not the man. Other informants concur that a woman is held at least partially responsible for any sexual act in which she is involved.

Although no informant spoke to me of ever having taken a lover, several told me that other women do engage in extramarital sex. Some, they say, are seduced by offers of cloth and jewelry; others take lovers purely for the sexual pleasure. Most enjoy both the act itself and the material rewards. It is clear that a woman risks much more than a man by engaging in extramarital sex. According to one indignant informant:

> Adultery is equally sinful for women and men, but in the opinion of men (not in that of women), adultery is normal (ᶜadi) for them. If a woman returns home to her father and tells him she has left her husband because he has a friend (ṣadiqa), her father will tell her that that is just the way things are, and send her right back to her husband.
>
> An adulterous woman would be divorced, perhaps lose the support of her children, and perhaps be ostracized by others as well.

There is little disagreement that it is best for a woman to confine her sexual activity to the conjugal relationship. However, there is also a recognition that women's sexual appetites are not always satisfied by their husbands. Clitoral masturbation is practiced, but, because women are embarrassed to discuss masturbation, I have no idea to what extent. One old woman enjoys entertaining female gatherings by miming how the old-timers masturbated while grinding grain. "We dangled a heavy little bag from the waist in such a way that it bounced against the clitoris as we ground. Then [acting out the accelerating motion], we would grind faster and faster and faster!" The recounting always receives an enthusiastic response. When, on a few occasions, I followed it with questions about the clitoris, women assured me emphatically that it is never removed in ᶜAmran unless extremely oversized, and expressed strong disapproval of the routine removal of the clitoris in nearby villages.

Further indicators of the importance of sex to women are numerous and varied. Only a few will be mentioned here. First, there is a pattern of sexual joking at female parties held six weeks after birth. The new mother (who usually has had her hands decorated to enhance her attractiveness) is teased relentlessly about the fact that she will resume sexual relations on this night, after a six-week postpartum taboo period. Typically, guests offer in mock seriousness to take the new mother's children home with them so she and her husband will be spared interruptions in the night.

A second indicator of the importance of sex to women is the sexual jealousy that is commonly exhibited when a husband takes a second wife. Some women in these always unwelcome circumstances appear stoic and resigned until the husband and his new bride retire to spend their first night together. At this point, informants say, few women can maintain self-control. Most return immediately to their father's or brother's home; others go crazy on the spot.

There is a story, reputedly very old, about female sexual pleasure:

> In the old days, men and women were so tired from all the hard work they had to do that they had sex only once or twice a month. One time a farmer returned from his faraway fields and told his wife that the harvesting would begin in the morning, so she should be sure to get a good breakfast out to him and the other men *early* in the morning.
>
> His wife got angry at the request. She ranted at her husband about how much hard work she had to do all the time, and the next morning in particular.
>
> Then the two sat down to their small evening meal. When they finished eating, he made love to her. Then they slept.
>
> He rose and left for the fields before dawn. She too got up extra early, did all her work, and prepared an especially good breakfast for the men. She arrived at the fields with the breakfast bright and early, just as her husband had requested. She got a good lunch to them on time as well.

Informants made certain that I grasped that the wife's promptness was a direct result of her having had sexual relations the previous evening. They were less explicit in explaining the also allegedly ancient saying: "Men are like bumping your crazy bone." The meaning, I was told, is: "If you bump any other part of your body it isn't too bad, but the crazy bone really hurts a lot, just like a man can."

In short, evidence is plentiful that sexuality plays an important role in many ᶜAmrani women's lives. Many complain of their husband's waning sexual appetites or of their inability to maintain erections as a result of heavy *gāt* usage. One still young woman with an aged husband complained, even in his presence, that he was too old and that she was going to get herself a new, young husband. Whereas such jokes are strongly disapproved, "older" women have a clear understanding of the sexual frustration that underlies them.

Newly married women, in contrast, are more likely to find sexual relations frightening and, in some cases, to consider their husbands' sexual demands excessive. Their marital problems take a different form.

EARLY YEARS OF MARRIAGE

After a bride completes her postwedding visits to her own family, she returns to her husband's home and begins to learn the realities of her new position. A few brides refuse to return to the husband, in which case a separation agreement of approximately six months' duration is written. Some recent brides speak glowingly of their husbands; others complain either of husbandly neglect or mistreatment. There are also complaints of stinginess. "He never gives me money to pay the musicians to dance at wedding parties, and all the other brides get to dance. If my family won't give me the money, I just don't get to dance ever." One extremely timid young woman complained that her husband is cruel as well as stingy. Fervently she expressed the hope that he would never return from Saudi Arabia, where he was working at the time.

Young wives are sometimes stoic, if not happy, about their husbands and married life in general. Seated near a very recent bride at a prewedding party, I asked her if she was reminded of her own recent *mashjab* and wedding. "Only slightly," she replied expressionlessly. Then, noticing my look of surprise, she added, "My husband is never at home. He comes for lunch and then leaves immediately." I said, "But he is with you in the evenings?" She answered woodenly that he was. "Is he nice?" I persisted. Eager to satisfy me and to be done with the subject, the bride replied in a hollow but exaggeratedly polite tone that y-e-e-s-s, her husband was nice.

There are other recently married women who express satisfaction with and great affection for their husbands. They are more likely to be in conflict with the mother-in-law than those who are unhappy with the husband. Problems between a young wife and her mother-in-law are at least as common as those between the wife and her husband.

Indeed, many informants say that the mother-in-law is the

reason for most separations. Relations with the mother-in-law are both more intensive and extensive than those with the husband. If they are troubled, life is likely to be considered insupportable by the young wife, who is unquestionably subordinate to her husband's mother. If the husband intervenes on his wife's behalf, the problems may be ameliorated. If he is unwilling or is not apprised by his wife of her dissatisfactions, the discord may intensify, in which case his wife is likely to return to her natal home.

Older informants say that the daughter-in-law sometimes takes extreme measures in her attempts to oust her mother-in-law and to have her husband to herself. The following account, which is said to be true, shows just how far a woman might go to achieve this end:

> A villager went to work in Saudi Arabia, leaving his wife and mother together in his house. After about seven months, his wife returned to her father's house to get away from her mother-in-law.
>
> When her husband returned from Saudi Arabia, he went to his father-in-law's house to get his wife. This is normal.
>
> She told her husband she would not return to his house until he killed his mother. He argued with her and left.
>
> The next day he went to try to take his wife back again. She repeated her demand.
>
> Finally, he told his mother what his wife had said. Eventually, she agreed and, one morning after she had prayed, she and her son went off up the mountain together. He carried two rifles.
>
> When they had gotten far away from their village, his mother told the man to pray. After doing so, he picked up a rifle and aimed it at his mother. Before he could kill her, however, Allah caused his hands to be paralyzed. His hands have remained gnarled forever.

Even though informants insist upon the veracity of this story, they comment that the man, his mother, and his wife are all crazy. "The man simply could have had separate houses for his mother and his wife, or he could have divorced his wife for her refusal to live with his mother." The story, then, is lacking in verisimilitude, but, in emotional terms, rings true.

Conversely, the mother-in-law can teach the young wife a great deal and provide her with invaluable emotional support if the relationship is a good one. As in Morocco (Mernissi 1975:72), the mother-in-law–daughter-in-law relationship is characterized by both cooperation and competition.

It is noteworthy that in ʿAmran parentless girls are much sought after in marriage. Quite possibly, the primary appeal of a motherless girl is the likelihood that she will form a strong emotional bond to her mother-in-law, thereby reducing the chances of discord and household division. (Dywer points out that in Taroudannt, Morocco, mothers are often thought to be evil influences on their married daughters [1978:82–85]. This is sometimes the case in ʿAmran as well.) If the young wife is fatherless and brotherless, there may be no men willing to protect her from her affines' maltreatment.

Interestingly, schoolgirls are unanimous in expressing a desire to live in extended rather than nuclear households. Despite hearing about, if not directly observing, conflict between the women in extended households, they believe that being alone (for husbands are essentially absent from the house) is a far worse fate than having to cope with a mother-in-law and sisters-in-law.

SEPARATION

Most women return to their own kin at least once during the early years of marriage (thirty-four of my sample of fifty claimed to have done so at least one time, but most informants say that the practice is more common than that). Many continue to leave their husbands periodically even after the birth of one or two children, but disapproval increases as the women and her children grow older. A young, childless wife is *ʿādi ghāwiyya* (still immature); it is understood that she has not yet learned how to get along with her husband and in-laws. Within a few years, however, she is expected to have developed enough *ʿāgal* (reason, maturity) to stay in her husband's home unless forced to depart by extreme maltreatment. This is not to suggest that "older" women do not return to their natal homes when in conflict situations, only that they risk greater censure for repeated departures than do younger, and particularly childless, women.

In ʿAmran a wife who has returned to her father or to her brother is said to have *ḥanagat* (literally means "to become very angry," but in ordinary usage refers to leaving one's husband's home). Much conversation revolves around who has *ḥanagat* and why. Most women recall and savor the details of their own departures. Almost all know, without pausing to think, how many times they *ḥanagat*; exceptions are those whose number is unusually high, as in the case of one woman who told me "one hundred times" and another who offered "one million."

Throughout the Islamic Middle East, women return home when they feel abused by husbands or in-laws. Bybee (1978:63–65) writes:

> It cannot be repeated too often that a woman continues to have the protection of her father and brothers after marriage. . . . Protection of a daughter or a sister is not simply a cultural ideal; it *is* something that is invoked in practice.
>
> There have always been stories of Middle Eastern women being beaten by their husbands, but the stories have often left out the aftermath in which the woman goes home to her father. It is generally only through negotiations with him that her husband, through promises and even a payment . . . can ensure her return. . . . A woman can, in fact, manipulate her husband through the fact that she has the right to return to her father's house if she is unhappy with her marital situation.

While Bybee's assertions generally hold true in ʿAmran, certain qualifications must be noted. As Bybee herself discusses in an earlier section of her dissertation, in many parts of the Islamic Middle East, female children forgo all or a part of their legal inheritance in exchange for future fraternal support (Bybee 1978:35). Both Maher (1974:158) and Dwyer (1978:25) discuss this phenomenon for Morocco. Although few, if any, ʿAmrani females forgo their inheritance, they state that they are often constrained by the need to stay in the good graces of their brothers and other male kin:

> It is true that our brothers do not have the absolute authority over us that our fathers do. But, really, the most important thing in a woman's life, after her father has died, is her relationship with her brothers and with her father's brothers. We cannot afford to alienate our brothers because it is only they that we can really bank on to take us in and to care for us in times of duress. If we *ḥanag* or are divorced, or if our husband dies, and our father and uncles are no longer alive, we have no one to turn to but our brothers.
>
> It is true that if my father is dead, I have the right to choose my second husband myself, but if my brothers disapprove of my choice they may refuse to help me in the future if I need them. This is a risk I cannot afford to take.

A further limitation on women's access to paternal and fraternal support is that not all fathers and brothers take the claims of the *ḥanagat* daughter or sister seriously. Fathers vary considerably in their treatment of daughters who *ḥanag*, depending upon the explanation given for returning home, whether or not it is believed, the father's relationship with his daughter's in-laws, as well as other factors. It was mentioned earlier that if a woman leaves her husband because he is adulterous, her father or brother will, most likely, send her right back.

Maternal support for a *ḥanagat* daughter is usually strong, but does not always suffice to win the father's and brother's support as well. Occasionally, a mother will herself *ḥanag* when her husband forces their daughter to return to her husband. In the case of exchange marriages, as discussed previously, conflicts over separation are most likely to occur. If a man's wife leaves him when his sister returns home, he has an obvious vested interest in keeping his sister in her husband's house and out of his own. If his father and mother are alive, they are torn between considerations of their son's wellbeing and that of their daughter.

When the *ḥanagat* woman's complaints are recognized as both real and serious by her guardian, she is allowed to stay on at home, sometimes indefinitely. If the husband and his parents want her back, and fail in their direct attempts to have her returned to them, they seek out a middleman to negotiate on their behalf. If he, too, is unsuccessful, there is one more option available to them, which is an application of the traditional tribal demand for action.

The in-laws buy a calf and hire a butcher to slaughter it in front of the guardian's house. The meat then belongs to the guardian, but is distributed to his kin and friends, including the in-laws who paid for it. If the husband admits to having abused his wife, physically or verbally, he gives his father-in-law (or other guardian) money as compensation for the maltreatment. (Even though it was the wife who was maltreated, she receives a share of the money only if her father is particularly generous. The money belongs to him.)

The slaughtering of the calf forces the father (or other guardian) to take action. He must return his daughter to her husband or begin negotiating her release from the marriage. In the past, even the very recent past, informants say, the amount of money needed to obtain a woman's divorce was small. Recently, with the dramatic increases in the cost of getting married, the amount has escalated enormously.

The husband's family wants to receive enough money to replace the divorced daughter-in-law with a new one. Usually, the amount required to free a woman from an unhappy marriage is at least twice what was paid for her in bride-price. Few men can afford to pay such a high price, and fewer still are willing to do so.

Whereas the husband's family may attempt to effect his wife's return through tribal law, her family is likely to rely instead on the government specialist in Islamic law, the *ḥākam*, if they wish to keep her home for an extended period of time. Her father (or other guardian) seeks to arrange a meeting with his daughter's father-in-law in the office of the *ḥākam*, so that a legal separation contract can be written. The separation agreement (*altizām*) stipulates the duration of the separation (between six months and five years) and the portion of her trousseau and other possessions that the estranged wife may remove from her husband's house. During the period of the separation agreement, it is strictly forbidden that the husband call on his wife. When the agreement expires, it is expected that the woman will return to her husband or that divorce proceedings will begin. In actuality, further delays and struggles are not uncommon.

Separation agreements are particularly common in the case of young brides. If the husband is also quite young, the chances of a legal separation appear to be even greater. When either spouse is viewed as still immature, few people are surprised to learn that the wife has returned home for six months or longer. After that period, however, it is expected, or at least hoped by most of the parties involved, that she and her husband will adjust to each other and to their new roles in life.

A man who is seriously dissatisfied with his wife or whose wife refused to return to him is likely to contemplate polygyny or divorce. Islamic law allows him to divorce his wife with ease and to have as many as four wives at one time. A woman on the other hand can obtain a divorce in most cases only by paying her husband (or, as is more likely, having a father or brother who is willing and able to pay the husband) a large amount of money. She cannot have more than one husband at a time.

All that a man need do to begin divorce proceedings is to state his intent before witnesses in unambiguous terms. He need not declare his reasons. Many Westerners are aware that a Muslim man can divorce his wife by stating, "I divorce you." There is less familiarity with subsequent steps. A three-month waiting period follows, during which the man may revoke the divorce. The three months are stipulated so it may be known whether pregnancy has occurred. No formal action is necessary if the man decides to continue the marriage before the waiting period closes. However, if the man goes through this divorce procedure on three successive occasions, the marriage is absolutely terminated at the end of the third waiting period. He can remarry his former wife only if she has since been married to another man, and he must compensate her or her family for the remarriage.

It is also possible for a man to repeat his statement of repudiation three times in immediate succession. This is generally considered less desirable because it does not permit the husband to reconsider his decision.

Women receive full financial support from their husbands during the three-month waiting period. They are less likely to be finally divorced if pregnant. Many marriages are continued even without pregnancy, the husbands having either gotten over their anger or never having seriously intended to terminate the marriage in the first place. A statement of divorce can serve as a warning to a woman that she had better modify her behavior or face serious consequences. (Islamic marriage and divorce laws are discussed in greater detail in Coulson and Hinchcliffe [1978], Pearl [1979], and Haddad [1980].)

POLYGYNY

Polygyny is legal in the Yemen Arab Republic, as it remains in most Islamic nations. Governmental attempts to impose mild economic sanctions on polygynous men have never been implemented. Bybee (1978:78) estimates that the rate of polygyny for the Middle East in general is between 5 and 10 percent, but much lower in some areas. The national figure for the Yemen Arab Republic is 4.3 percent (Yemen Arab Republic 1978:pt. 1, 80). The results of the structured interview schedule I administered in ʿAmran show that seven of fifty husbands (14 percent) have at one time in their lives practiced polygyny, but only three (6 percent) lived with more than one wife at the time of the research.

ᶜAmrani women object strenuously to polygyny. Approximately half say they would have to accept a co-wife (especially if infertile, ill, or incompetent) but find the prospect very distressing, whereas the remainder insist they would return to their kinsmen or kill their husbands first.[3] Schoolgirls are unanimous in saying that they would never tolerate a co-wife.

In contrast, one still young mother of four claims that she suggests her husband take a second wife whenever they have an argument. "Of course, I know he doesn't want to or I would never suggest it." Undeniably, like the great majority of ᶜAmrani men, her husband could not afford a second marriage even if desirous of one. The high cost of getting married is women's greatest protection against polygyny. Among the educated youth, acceptance of modern ideas adds to the unlikelihood of multiple marriages.

While polygyny seems to run in families and is more common among the affluent and influential, others sometimes practice it as well. Some polygynous unions arise out of the levirate; others out of the husband's desire for a new affinal connection, property, children, or sexual pleasure. Economic gain is the primary motive in the following highly unusual and strongly disapproved case:

> M fled to Saudi Arabia several years ago after murdering his brother. After returning to ᶜAmran and paying his brother's widow a settlement for the benefit of the children of the marriage, he decided to marry her. Public opinion was that he sought to regain control of the settlement and to increase his control of family land. Although both the widow and M's first wife opposed the marriage, he eventually achieved his end.

While M was successful in the above case, sometimes women manage to have their way. One rich old woman of a high-ranking family frequently recounts the following story of how she achieved lifelong monogamy. Stories like hers may serve as a partial deterrent for men and even as an inspiration to some women:

> One day, when I was still young and childless, I heard that my husband had gotten engaged. When he came home that evening, I just sat there silently. After it had gotten late, he asked about dinner. Then I spoke up: "So you're engaged! Let your fiancée get your dinner!" He denied the engagement but I knew he was lying. Eventually he gave up on dinner and sat down to write, but I snatched the pen and paper out of his hands. After he went to sleep, I pulled all

the blankets off of him. Through all this I was not in my right senses, and I remained like a crazy person for a month. Once I saw my husband's fiancée and I attacked her. Most of the time, I just crawled around the house, seeing things that weren't there at all, like an airplane in the big reception room. It wasn't until about four weeks later that I regained my senses. By then my husband had broken the engagement, and never became engaged again.

The above informant successfully averted the co-wife problem in advance, although whether by contrivance we cannot know. Other women take much longer to oust the rival. It is common for a first wife to return to her kinsmen when faced with the reality of a co-wife. In many cases, the husband eventually is compelled (because of social pressure if the first wife has borne children or because he misses her) to divorce the second wife. In one example, a man married a second time largely because his first wife, although still young, had not conceived following the birth of her youngest child for five or six years. The first wife returned to her relatives even before the arrival of her co-wife, where she stayed for two full years. During this period her co-wife conceived and bore a daughter, but did not please the husband as much as the first wife. He decided to divorce the second wife so the preferred first one would return. Several years later, the first wife still had not conceived, but there was no indication that her husband was considering a second marriage again. She is raising her former co-wife's daughter along with her own older children.

Sometimes the problems resulting from a second marriage are complex. Women took great interest in the following case, which had not yet been fully resolved when I left ʿAmran:

In a fit of pique, Ahmad divorced his wife, Lutfiyya. She had asked his permission to take the children to lunch at her brother's house, since he would be out of town until evening. He said she could go but the children could not. She then went to his parents and told them that Ahmad had threatened to divorce her if she took the children to her brother's house. They told her not to worry and to just take them along for lunch. When he returned home, however, he was furious at her disobedience and did in fact divorce her. She had no choice but to return to her brother's house. As the women tell the story: "So she had dinner with her brother as well as lunch." She was four months pregnant at the time. When she gave birth, Ahmad paid all the customary expenses. In the meantime, he had married Hindia. Hindia soon became pregnant and had a daughter, and is now pregnant again.

Lutfiyya's brother wanted her to marry again (presumably for the sake of the bridewealth), but she refused. Her reason was that Ahmad had up to this time allowed her to keep their children with her, and she of course would have to give them up were she to remarry. When her brother insisted on a match, she fled his house, and moved into an empty house belonging to their father. While she stayed there, Ahmad paid all of her and their children's expenses, even though this is in no way required of a man after divorce. He, however, could afford it and was on very friendly terms with Lutfiyya's kinsmen. Eventually, for a modest bridewealth, Ahmad married Lutfiyya again.

As soon as Ahmad remarried Lutfiyya, Hindia returned to her kinsmen. She took her young daughter with her and is soon to give birth. Women concur that if she demands a house to herself as the condition for her return, Ahmad will have to give it to her. Otherwise, he will have no choice but to divorce her.

If a first wife does not try to keep her husband to herself or if her efforts fail, her husband has certainly scored a victory. However, he may yet find himself entrenched in a long and bitter war. Polygynous households are often disharmonious, and maintaining separate residences is expensive. Furthermore, it does not eliminate all conflict.

While co-wives are expected to make a public show of camaraderie, people assume their private relations are poor. Women with co-wives corroborate the general view when they reveal to their kinswomen and friends their profound dislike for each other. The following folktale portrays the baseness to which a jealous co-wife may descend:

Hizam had two wives, Fatima and ʿAbdiyya; each wife had two sons and two daughters. One night Hizam came home from work in his fields and told his wives to slaughter a calf the next day.

In the morning ʿAbdiyya's son Hamud left early for the fields. A little later ʿAbdiyya called Fatima's son Hussayn into the kitchen to take the breakfast she had prepared to Hamud. When Hussayn entered the kitchen, however, his *khāla* [mother's co-wife] ʿAbdiyya killed him and added his meat to that of the calf that she had just slaughtered.

That evening when Hamud came home from the fields, ʿAbdiyya said to her son, "Where is your brother Hussayn? I sent him after you in the morning." Of course, Hamud replied that he had not seen Hussayn. Their father Hizam became concerned immediately, so he and the rest of the family went out to search for Hussayn. When they returned home from their futile search, the entire household ate their evening meal, which contained the meat of Hussayn mixed with that of the calf. After they had finished eating, ʿAbdiyya took all the bones up to the rooftop. As soon as she had laid the bones down, a bird lighted and took them away.

From that time on, whenever Hussayn's full sister Karima left the village, whether to fetch water, collect wood, or to take the animals to graze, that same bird came to her. He gave her the finest of breakfast foods, and so she grew plumper and plumper.

ʿAbdiyya began to wonder, "Why is it that my co-wife's daughter does more hard work, like grazing the animals and fetching wood and water, than my daughter does, but my daughter stays skinny and Karima gets plumper and plumper?" She decided to send her son Hamud along with Karima one morning in order to investigate. As usual, the bird brought delicacies to Karima, but Karima convinced her half brother to keep the bird a secret. Hamud told his mother nothing. Still not satisfied, ʿAbdiyya sent her daughter Nuria along with Karima the next day. Unlike her brother Hamud, Nuria was unwilling to keep the bird a secret from her mother. When ʿAbdiyya learned from Nuria about the food-giving bird, she decided to take the animals out to graze herself the next day.

In the meantime, Hizam had fallen ill from the grief of his son's disappearance. On the day that ʿAbdiyya took the animals to graze, he was at home, too weak to labor. His daughter Karima decided to tell him about the bird that came to her with delicacies every day. They went up on the rooftop together where the father called out for the gift-bearing bird to appear before them.

The bird did so. He told Hizam that he was his son Hussayn, who had taken the form of a bird after having been slaughtered by his mother's co-wife ʿAbdiyya and consumed by the entire family. He then demanded that his father present him with the murderess's liver.

That night it was with difficulty that Hizam convinced ʿAbdiyya to sleep in his room with him. After she had fallen asleep, he executed his son's request; he killed her and cut out her liver. In the morning, when he presented the liver to the bird, the bird transformed immediately into a handsome young man.

Had it not been for supernatural intervention, Hizam would have lost his son. In another folktale (this one told me by a man), a wealthy man comes equally close to losing all his land when he marries a second wife. Although she had not objected when her husband said he was going to marry, the first wife went insane on his wedding night and destroyed all his deeds and contracts. Only through the clever duplicity of the local agent of the imam does the husband retain all of his holdings.

In both tales disaster is only narrowly averted. The message for men is that the advantages of polygyny may be outweighed by the risks, although these may be considerably less dramatic and severe in real life. Still, even the recurring inconveniences and stress that result from co-wife conflict are sufficient deterrent for many men, and, as mentioned earlier, the high cost of getting married makes polygyny impossible for most men, should they wish to hazard its perils.

DIVORCE

Twelve of fifty respondents (24 percent) to the structured interview schedule had been divorced by their first husbands. Thirteen of the fifty respondents' husbands (26 percent) had divorced one or more wives prior to their present marriage. Some men divorce their wives in a moment of anger, as in the case of Ahmad and Lutfiyya. Like Ahmad, many such men marry the divorced wife again. Divorces preceded by a long separation are less likely to be followed by remarriage. Infertility and incompatibility between husband and wife or between mother-in-law and daughter-in-law are the primary reasons for permanent divorce.

Because some degree of incompatibility is so common and because Islamic law makes it so easy for men to divorce their wives, one might expect divorce to be more prevalent. As in much of the Islamic Middle East (Bybee 1978:93–95), informal constraints operate to keep most marriages intact. First, many women avoid divorce through psychological manipulation. If they cannot make their husbands love them, they can implant in them a fear of revenge through magic or damaging gossip. Second, few men can afford to replace the divorced wife with a new one. Third, men as well as women think it very wrong to deprive children of their natural mother, and very few men are willing to allow the children to depart along with the divorced wife. Shi^{c}ite doctrine holds that children should stay with their mother at least until weaned; sons are to be returned to their fathers at age two, daughters by age seven (Levy 1957:140). In ^{c}Amran the practice is somewhat variable, but most men reclaim daughters as well as sons after they are weaned, and some divorcées are not allowed to take their small children with them at all.

If, despite these considerations, a man decides to divorce his wife, he is completely unhindered by the law; whereas a woman who wishes her marriage terminated must get her husband to divorce her.[4] A main tactic is to pay the husband enough money so that he can afford to take a new wife. As very few women have resources worth the 50,000 riyals the husband might demand, most rely upon their father or brothers. When a kinsman finances the divorce, however, he is likely to pressure the woman to marry again so he can recoup his loss. Because of her dependence upon her kinsmen, she will feel pressured to accept the match even if she has great misgivings about the man or his family. There are only a few men who allow their still young divorced (or widowed) daughters or sisters to remain at home with them.

In many cases, men do not help a daughter or sister who wants to be divorced. Some cannot afford to purchase her release, and others are unwilling to do so. A woman in such a plight can try to turn her husband against her by mistreating him, by leaving him repeatedly, or through magic. She may resort to desperate measures. When one young woman who had been separated from her husband (whom she loathed) for over a year learned that her father intended to send her back any day, she comforted herself (and amused others) with fantasies of how she was going to force her husband to divorce her:

> If I have to go back to him, I am going to grab his penis and twist it back and forth, back and forth, back and forth as hard as I can, and I won't let go no matter how much he pleads with me. As I twist it with all my might, I'm going to keep saying to him, "And now will you divorce me?"

The scenario was an expression of anger rather than a plan to be enacted. On a more practical level, she asked me to get her birth-control pills so she could prevent conception. She knew that her chances of yet being divorced would diminish greatly were she to become pregnant.

If she successfully maneuvers her husband to terminate the marriage, this woman, like almost all young divorcées, will remarry, probably within a year's time. This is due in part to the Quranic view of marriage as a religious duty (ᶜAbd al-Ati 1977:52) and to the fact that divorce is little stigmatized in ᶜAmran. The failure to conceive or to please (or to be pleased by) the husband or the mother-in-law of a first marriage is rarely seen as predictive of similar difficulties in the next. It is understood that infertility may as well have been the fault of the husband and that conflict could have resulted from incompatible temperaments or from one or both having been married too young.

Although some divorcées say they wish to remain husbandless, few are thought to mean what they say. This is because it is considered only slightly less becoming for a divorcée or a widow to express interest in a matrimonial prospect than it is for a virgin. Probably most women wish to remarry, but few have a real choice in the matter. Their kinsmen are usually eager to obtain bride-price for them, especially if they have paid off the ex-husband to secure the divorce. When their houses are overcrowded or their wives resentful of their sister-in-law's presence, they are even more anxious to get the divorcée married off. However, there are a few divorced women who are allowed to stay permanently with their relatives and even a few instances of informal arrangements allowing the divorcée to raise one of her children. Women of independent means are, of course, much freer than others are to insist upon remaining unmarried. For the great majority of women who lack such economic resources, a second marriage is almost inevitable.

8

Pregnancy, Birth, and Motherhood

When a woman conceives for the first time, whether in her first or second marriage, she, her relatives, her husband, and her in-laws are almost always relieved and delighted. The pregnancy does not, however, prevent problems between the woman and her husband or his family. Many pregnant women quit their husbands' homes in anger and give birth in their parents' homes. Because husbands and in-laws are always pleased by the first few pregnancies, they may show slightly heightened consideration of "their wife" than previously. This consideration, however, rarely extends to reducing the pregnant woman's work load. Except in extremely unusual instances, she does all her normal work and has sexual relations until she gives birth. Furthermore, she is not exempt from fasting during Ramadhan.

Although pregnant women are not thought to have increased nutritional needs, it is believed that food cravings must be satisfied. A male informant says that because these cravings come from Allah, not from the woman herself, it would be sinful to ignore them, and female informants insist that it would be sinful for a pregnant woman *not* to ask any neighbor or friend for any food she craves. Her child's skin may be discolored if she does not eat the food(s) she desires.[1]

Large numbers of women attend the German antenatal clinic, where they politely accept free vitamins and advice about diet during pregnancy. Once out of the clinic, however, many say they disregard the advice and skip the vitamins to prevent the fetus from growing too fat. They do what they consider necessary to avoid a difficult birth, one dangerous to mother and fetus alike.

Pregnancy involves one particular danger: the growth within the womb of a bizarre animal (ʿaūgari, perhaps from ʿugr, "barrenness" or ʿagur, "voracious"). It is described variously as looking like a small chick, a mouse, a hunk of flesh all covered with eyes, or a large worm. (The hydatidiform mole, a rare abnormal uterine growth, may be the empirical source of the belief.)

The ʿaūgari is caused by emotional upset, primarily distress caused by the husband, most specifically, when he forces his wife to have sex against her will. According to some informants, other mammals may suffer from the ʿaūgari as well as humans. I was told of a cow who gave birth to a calf and to an ʿaūgari; the ʿaūgari immediately reentered her womb and killed her. Women can avoid this danger by closing their legs immediately after giving birth.

In some cases the ʿaūgari harms both the fetus and the woman; in others it leaves one or both alone. Stillborn births, deformed fetuses, and spontaneous abortions are often blamed on the presence of an ʿaūgari. To an outsider, it seems clear that the ʿaūgari beliefs can be used to displace blame for a failed pregnancy from the woman to the person who upset her, almost always her husband.

Very few women claim to have seen an ʿaūgari themselves, but all are convinced of its reality. My claim that they do not exist in America was dismissed as ignorance of such matters, resulting from my not yet having borne a child. A high-school graduate (one of the town's two female graduates) told me the ʿaūgari is like a giant worm that afflicts approximately one of every one hundred pregnant women. Most commonly, she added, it kills the fetus by eating its head, and leaves the woman unharmed.

If one suspects she has an ʿaūgari in her womb, she can try to kill it by consuming raw onions (local variety) daily. For women suffering from indigestion, this remedy is a trial. One informant, who was not convinced she had an ʿaūgari, but whose mother, fearing the presence of one and insisting upon her daily consumption of onions, said, "I don't know which is worse, to have pain and terrible gas every day or to just let the ʿaūgari stay inside me, if I even have one anyway." There is a stronger, surer potion used to purge an ʿaūgari. This, a mixture of vinegar and ashes, is rarely administered during pregnancy; it is given when a woman suspects that an ʿaūgari remains inside her womb after childbirth.

There are a few women who are said to have had ʿaūgari problems with each pregnancy, more who had an ʿaūgari in only one or two pregnancies. The latter can recall the upsetting circumstances that precipitated its growth. Other women say they experienced strange sensations during pregnancy and right after parturition, but are not sure whether these were caused by an ʿaūgari. The great majority of women say they never had one, but know that the possibility exists that they might in the future. There is no doubt that they are real.

CHILDBIRTH

Whereas there are a few elderly midwives (who receive no payment for their services, because, as they say, it is a blessing to assist in the birth of a child), most women are assisted by relatives or in-laws. Usually, these are older women with considerable childbirth experience. In difficult cases, a pharmacist is brought in or, much more rarely, the woman is taken to the town clinic or to a Sanʿa hospital. The majority of women, however, believe that there are few fates worse than having to give birth in a hospital. Some aver they would far prefer death in childbirth to a hospital delivery.

Women distinguish between two stages of labor; the first is called *lahīb* (literally, burn or flame); the second, *zahīr* (literally, to groan or to moan). During *lahīb*, a woman is likely to continue her normal work. As the contractions become stronger and more regular, she notifies the woman who will assist her and begins to prepare for the birth.

The woman strives to keep her labor a secret from "outsiders."[2] It is believed that their knowledge of the labor can cause it to be protracted. Consequently, many women are assisted by someone from their own household or a nearby one. (This is in striking contrast to the situation described for Buarij, Lebanon [Fuller 1961:55], where village women and their children attend each others' births. "Female voices recite in exaltation the stories of their own deliveries. In a chorus at appropriate intervals they encourage the woman in labor by cries of 'Heave! Heave!'")

When it appears that the birth will occur soon, the laboring woman seats herself on old blankets laid down on the floor for the birth. She is fully dressed, except for slacks and underpants. A lighted charcoal grill is put in the room to keep it warm; to heat the heavy cloaks placed alternately on the stomach and the small of the back; and to melt *samn* (clarified butter) for the baby and, in some cases, for the mother as well. Everything needed for the birth is placed in the room. When possible, the laboring woman's children may be removed to a relative's house.

Once the labor has advanced to a certain point, women say, they have a keen aversion to being left alone, even briefly. They know, they say, that the birth is not yet due, but are frightened nonetheless. Between contractions, the women engage in normal conversation.

When contractions increase in frequency and intensity, the woman usually sits with back straight, weight on one hip and legs bent to the opposite side, or she may squat. Her assistant sits behind or next to her. For the duration of each contraction the assistant simultaneously pushes the flat of one hand against the small of the woman's back and pulls back with the other hand on the woman's knee. She pushes as hard as she can and, according to many women, is often more exhausted than the mother by the time the baby is born.

Throughout the labor, the woman's skirt covers her legs, although the assistant may occasionally peek underneath to see if the baby's head has become visible. In some cases, the husband, children, and other household members may come in and out of the room. Rarely do husbands assist in the birth. (Women say that if a man sees the blood of his wife's childbirth, he may lose sexual interest in her.) One man, however, assisted his wife in both of her births and would not allow any woman present.

If labor appears to have gone on too long, or if complications are foreseen, consideration may be given to calling in a pharmacist or removing the woman to the town clinic or to a San^{c}a hospital. Men are usually more inclined than women to seek outside help, although female opinions about the pharmacists are mixed. Generally, women's trepidations about being visited by a pharmacist are slight compared to their terror of a clinic or hospital delivery. Some women even ask that the pharmacist be called if labor is particularly difficult. Others, afterwards, appear proud and delighted that their husbands were so concerned about their well-being as to insist upon "professional" help. What this help consists of is injecting the woman with a hormone (to intensify contractions and hasten the birth) and a pain-killer or tranquilizer. Most women fear the potency of the former injection endangers both mother and fetus. In fact, according to a physician employed in the ᶜAmran clinic, there is a real possibility of fetal damage if the hormone is administered at an inappropriate point in the labor.

Most times, the decision is to let the labor follow its natural course. When, at last, the baby is born and its sex remarked, there is usually a momentary delay before the umbilical cord is cut. Next, the infant's nose and mouth are cleared of mucus, its body coated with a special oil (made locally and used only for infants and new mothers) and swaddled. Then the baby is finger-fed melted butter, purportedly to prevent later speech impediments. Some women say they breast-feed almost immediately; most say they give boiled water or nothing for several hours.

The new mother is helped to her feet. If she has not already passed the placenta, she sucks and blows on her upper arm to facilitate its expulsion. After it is expelled, she is supposed to stand briefly (if sufficiently strong) over frankincense fumes. Then she is expected to rest, while a special meal (usually a freshly killed chick) is prepared for her, regardless of the hour.

Most women say that it is important that the placenta be allowed to cool off (*abrid*) before being discarded. This refreshes and warms the husband's heart—more exactly, his feelings toward his wife. Some women insist that the placenta must be washed and thrown in a remote well or buried far from town. The key element, however, is the cooling, the neglect of which can have disastrous effects on the husband-wife relationship:

> Bishira and her husband got along fine and he always treated her well. Then, she was assisted in childbirth by her mother-in-law Fatima. As soon as Bishira expelled the placenta, Fatima threw it, still warm and bloody, to a dog, who ate it right up. From the day of that birth, Bishira's husband turned against her. He mistreated her for two years. Then Bishira got pregnant again, and this time arranged for her relative to assist her childbirth. This time, the placenta was allowed to cool and was disposed of properly. From the day of this childbirth, Bishira's husband was warm and considerate toward her again.

When the stump of the umbilical cord dries up and falls off, it is disposed of in the same manner as the afterbirth, although some women hide it in a trunk until the next laundry excursion, and forget all about it. Both the placenta and the umbilical cord are treated in the same way whether a son or a daughter has been born.

THE FORTY DAYS AFTER CHILDBIRTH

A woman who gives birth is called *walada* (from the verb meaning "to give birth"). She experiences marked privileges and restrictions for forty days. These restrictions and privileges are enforced even if she gives birth to a stillborn or if her live-born baby subsequently dies. In the case of births more than a month premature, some families treat the *walada* in the same fashion as if she had had a successful birth; others (who may be less generous, or poorer with respect to female labor and/or money) limit her postpartum recovery to a month or less. Most women and men believe the *walada* requires special treatment because of the weakening effects of childbirth, and do not see it as in any way contingent upon successful breeding.

"The *walada* does not work," say ʿAmrani women speaking in general terms. The ideal, however, is rarely attained in nuclear family households, unless there is a woman willing and able to move in and take over for the six-week period. In some cases, a *walada* is assisted for as many as two to three weeks by her mother, sister, co-wife, or in-law, but she still does much of the domestic work herself. Even in extended households, the *walada* is often expected or required to do light work, the amount gradually increasing as the weeks pass and her strength returns.

The *walada* does not pray during this forty-day period. Due to afterbirth blood, she is in a ritually impure state, as during menstruation. Neither does she fast if it is Ramadhan, although she is required to make up the missed days later. Her husband is bound to abstain from sexual intercourse with her until the forty-day confinement is terminated, believing that if he does not abstain, she may become insane and the newborn infant may fall ill.

The *walada* is thought to have special dietary needs, which men and women alike take extremely seriously. Her diet must be rich in protein, animal fat, and sugar. For the first few days to a full week after childbirth, the new mother eats local chicks. She consumes lamb for the duration of her confinement, as well as locally produced clarified butter, honey, a special grain dish, and canned fruit (pineapple in particular). Her *gishr* should be prepared with sugar crystals rather than the ordinary loose sugar and brewed with special spices considered to have healing effects. The *walada*'s food is prepared separately from that of the rest of the household and she usually eats alone.

The *walada*'s husband is absolutely obliged to provide her with the very costly special foods for one month. It is her father's or brothers' duty to provide them for the final week of the confinement. When the men are unable to make the actual purchases for the *walada*, they may give her sufficient money and have her send someone to the market for her. In such cases, some women decide to forgo part of the expensive *walada* diet (substituting canned butter for local butter after the first week, for example) to save enough money to buy items they consider more important.

As soon as she is strong enough, the *walada* is expected to squat daily over boiling water and then over hot coals. The initial object is for her to sweat profusely and expel all impurities from her body, thus restoring her health (*ᶜāfiyya*). Some women continue squatting over hot coals daily throughout their confinement, believing the heat restores the tightness of the vagina. One advocate of the practice said she was in such good shape by the end of the six weeks, that her husband exclaimed, "How did our son's head ever fit through here?!"

Not all women squat over the boiling water or hot coals. Dissenters (most of whom are relatively young) say that health comes from Allah, not from sweating oneself into a near faint. They also joke that they are afraid of burning their clitoris, and enjoy telling of a woman, no longer alive, who inadvertently urinated while squatting over hot coals and was badly burned by the steam.

The first few days after childbirth, the *walada* rests and receives brief visits from neighbors, relatives, and close friends. It is customary for her father and brothers to call on her on the third morning after the birth. They usually bring gifts of canned fruit and juice. The *walada*'s sisters are expected to call on the third afternoon, sometimes bringing canned fruit as well. When relations are strained, however, the visits may be paid late or not at all.

Usually at the end of the first week, a large reception room is furnished and decorated in an opulent style, unique to the celebration of a *walada*. Floors are covered with thick mats and carpets (only along the walls of the room, for women seat themselves around the periphery, supported by firm back cushions); walls are hung with brightly colored cloth and decorated with carpets, pictures, photographs, and an overwhelmingly cluttered display of additional ornamentation.

Although many households have to borrow some items, most appear to view a birth as a singular opportunity to show off their wealth and their ability to create a comfortable and visually dazzling reception room. Over the month's visiting, hundreds of women may enter the house. They can be expected to describe what they see to their husbands and kinsmen as well as to other women. The men and women of the *walada*'s household are often intent on making as good an impression as they possibly can. Some men put in electricity, buy a few dozen new tea cups, or travel to San'a to purchase plush new blankets for their wives or bouquets of brightly colored plastic flowers. A few prepare and hang a display of photographs of themselves, their kinsmen, and friends. A common and very popular enhancement of a *walada* reception room is an operating television. Many men buy a battery so the female guests can watch the afternoon programs, mainly soap operas from other Middle Eastern countries. The owner of a generator may provide power to his own house while his wife or daughter-in-law is a *walada*, but other houses must wait until evening for electrical power.

If, as is usually the case, no bed is available, cushions are assembled to form a facsimile of one. The *walada* lies atop this secure, if not always comfortable, construction for the duration of the daily visiting hours. The swaddled infant lies between her and the cushion-lined wall, completely concealed under a thin white cloth, or sleeps in a separate room. The baby is thought to be extremely vulnerable to evil eye, as is the *walada* herself. Both are partially protected by application of a local ointment and sprigs of rue on their persons, containers of rue nearby, amulets hanging over their heads (and worn by the infant), and the burning of frankincense. The *walada*'s head is covered by an exquisite cloth, worn only by new mothers and by brides. Her body is covered by blankets up to her armpits. She must be especially careful to keep her breasts covered because of their particular vulnerability. (It takes considerable coordination for a woman to nurse her baby without allowing it or her breasts to be seen.) Coral beads, worn by almost all new mothers, provide further protection; gold jewelry and other finery make the *walada* more attractive, but serve no supernatural purpose.

The main, and most socially significant time slot for visiting new mothers is late afternoon to early evening, roughly between half past three and half past six. Some new mothers also receive guests on a more informal basis briefly in the morning and (more commonly) in the early afternoon. Some social patterns are fairly uniform for all three visiting periods, but more accentuated in the late afternoon.

Each guest removes her shoes before entering the reception room and deposits her kettle or thermos of *gishr* or tea at the brazier. If it is her first visit, she approaches the *walada* immediately and places her right hand on the *walada*'s head before greeting her in the normal way (which is a swift exchange of hand-kissing repeated at least twice, sometimes three or four times). If the guest is polite, and especially if she is not in regular contact with the women present, she then circles the room, greeting each in turn with the same hand-kissing salutation. She drops to the floor and kisses the knees of any woman to whom she owes particular respect (mother, older female relative, mother-in-law, and sometimes other older women) and even greets each child with a light touch on the head. A few young modernists kiss the cheeks of their intimate friends, but give traditional greetings to all others.

After she has greeted everyone, the guest must quickly decide where to sit. As women are seated one-deep along the walls of the room, guests are often obligated to seat themselves next to the last woman of a row, whoever she may be. Some avoid this by squeezing in next to a friend or relative. Interestingly, women who pay a visit together often disperse to different parts of the room and may ignore each other until time to depart. This enables them to revive old ties, cultivate new ones, and gather or dispense information useful to themselves and their families. (See Aswad [1967, 1974, 1978] on the information-gathering functions of female visiting networks.)

Shortly after she is seated, if not before, each guest is chastized spiritedly by the *walada* or a member of the household for not coming more often. She must offer a plausible excuse as appeasement before settling down to enjoy the company.

The *walada* is not ordinarily the social focus of the group. As at wedding celebrations, an honored guest or special friend of the *walada* often shares her platform and converses with her. Other guests chat with the *walada* sporadically or ignore her almost entirely. Individual personality differences are, of course, a factor. An extroverted *walada* may address the company frequently and try to monopolize the attention.

In some households, one or more in-laws or relatives of the *walada* are counted on not just to pour and serve beverages, but to amuse the guests as well. As mentioned earlier, verbal skills are very highly valued. Certain houses are always rich in guests after a birth because of the comedic reputation of one of its women. Others are popular because of a member's skillful recounting of folktales. (Television watching, although undeniably a preferred leisure activity among many young women, has not yet eradicated women's pleasure in their own and each others' performances.) In some households, a young woman enlivens the mood by doing the *majnūna* (crazy woman) dance, an extravagant imitation of possessed frenzy, or by dressing up as a man or a serpentine beast, who burlesques aggression upon the sitting-duck guests. On some occasions individual guests dominate the group for part or all of a visiting session. At a very few large *walada* parties a *muzayyina* is hired to entertain the guests. This is done occasionally by traditionally powerful families, such as the *shaykh*'s, but of late it is also done by some newly rich ones, who allocate part of their wealth for image building by means of female opinion.

Besides the musicians, who are thought to "make" any social event at which they perform, an old *muzayyina* performs as a comedienne in a few select households. She acts out and tells long, involved, racy stories that her audience receives with great enthusiasm. Her career is almost over and there does not appear to be anyone to replace her.

Other houses sponsor an altogether different performance. This is a *mawlid*, a fixed set of Quranic readings with frequent opportunities for chorused audience participation.

Most often, however, the mood for much of the afternoon is

low-key, and the conversations dispersed or localized. Especially at large gatherings, two women can engage in protracted private talk, their whispering covered by the high noise level in the room. They are interrupted periodically by hostesses passing refills of *gishr* or tea or burning frankincense, but essentially are left alone. Guests are free to chat; do needlework; even try selling a variety of goods[3] or sit silent, listening to more talkative neighbors, as they choose.

Each *walada* has at least two large parties: one (at her father's or brothers' expense) is held one month after the birth,[4] and the other (at her husband's expense) is on the final day of her confinement. Women who have visited the *walada* frequently are specially invited to these parties. Guests bring nothing, since the hostesses provide highly sweetened *gishr* and treats, usually popcorn and sweets.

Many women have an additional party or two given in their honor by a female relative, in-law, or close friend. As at the month-ending and confinement-ending parties, guests (those close to the *walada* and to the hostess, as well as anyone else who wants to come) bring no *gishr* or tea. The *walada*'s friend prepares *gishr* and treats at her own home and, helped by her neighbors, transports them to the *walada*'s house. The *walada* who is so feted is strongly obligated to reciprocate in kind when her friend next gives birth. The party is financed by husbands only when the wife's friend is his own brother's wife or other close affine; otherwise the woman must pay for it herself.

Female visiting routines in general follow a pattern of balanced reciprocity.[5] Because most women have numerous visiting relationships, they often get behind in their social calls. Consequently, it is typical for a *walada*'s reception room to be crowded during the last week or so of her confinement. Her close friends, neighbors, and relatives continue to visit her, but are joined by remoter associates who are fulfilling their reciprocal obligations to the *walada* or to other women of her household. Women are conscious of this pattern and sometimes express amusement at the last-minute crowds.

A woman who has failed to visit a *walada* prior to her fortieth-day party cannot attend that party. It would be shameful for her to do so. Similarly, it is shameful to attend the one-month party if she has not called previously. It is better to risk alienating the *walada* by missing the birth entirely than to visit her only on the day of one of these major events. There is a strong likelihood that if the woman visits her after her next birth and makes believable excuses for having failed to do so after the last, no social breach will ensue.

The *walada* period usually ends on the fortieth day after childbirth, although some husbands and fathers indulge a *walada* with an extra few days or weeks. The party on the final day is the largest and most socially important event of the six weeks. It is at this party that the *walada* wears the dress made of the cloth she received as a postchildbirth gift from her husband. Women say that, in the past, husbands did not give cloth if a daughter was born, but this is no longer the case. Most new mothers also have had their hands decorated on this morning. They receive special last-day salutations from each guest and, more informally, jest about the resumption of sexual relations with their husbands on this night. Most women who visited the *walada* more than a couple of times are specially invited to attend this final party and often feel obligated to do so. The size and composition of the company on this day comprise a statement, I believe, of the support and connections of the *walada* and, to an only slightly lesser extent, of her household as a whole.

Some women have a final gathering on the day after the party that marked the end of the postpartum confinement. Only intimates are invited, and nobody attends who has not been invited. In contrast to the heat and commotion of the previous day, this gathering is comfortable, relaxed, and very informal.

RETURN TO NORMAL LIFE

Aside from the additional time and energy she must allocate to the new infant, a woman's life returns to a large degree to prechildbirth patterns. The change in her status is far from dramatic. A mother is not referred to by her child's name (except in the reciprocal practice whereby both husband and wife address each other by the name of the oldest male child when nonintimates may overhear them). Neither is she eligible to engage in any social or ceremonial activities formerly closed to her. However, she is likely to feel more secure and self-confident in her relationship with her husband and in-laws. This usually carries over to her relations with other women as well, and there is no doubt that mothers are much more fully integrated into the female community than are childless women.

With subsequent births, the same *walada* restrictions and privileges are repeated, although many women say they are too tired and pressed by the demands of their older children to much enjoy the later *walada* confinements. Women concur that the mother of several young children is at the busiest and, in many ways, most trying period of her life.

By the age of twenty, most women have borne at least one child and continue to give birth and to nurture young for another two decades or longer. Most aspire to be good mothers, but the best of intentions are undercut frequently by limits of time and temperament. As mentioned earlier, infants are locked in a room alone while their mothers pay afternoon visits. Toddlers are sometimes frightened into submission by maternal references to lurking madmen or boogeymen; at other times they are allowed to follow yet irresponsible older siblings out to the street. Most women succumb to one or more of these temptations regularly and criticism is reserved for those who seriously overdo it.

Childrearing practices were discussed in some detail in chapter 5. Here, I will only reiterate the intensity and importance of women's relations with their children. This is most apparent when an infant or toddler is sick. Women who nurse their children through serious illness are exceedingly proud of the extent to which they sacrifice themselves. They tell others, "I never put her down for two and a half days straight." "Except to use the bathroom, I never left his room until the fever broke." It is only in crisis that such self-denial is viewed as essential and that a mother is given the opportunity to show her true worth. If she is thought to have been negligent and her child dies from the illness, women will blame her for the death.

A woman who has shown herself to be a "good mother" is more secure in her relations with her husband and in-laws, more highly regarded by other women, and surer of her children's loyalty than those who have not.[6] She can reasonably (although not with certainty) expect her children to repay her devotion when they themselves become adults. The form and extent of the anticipated returns are, of course, not the same for sons as they are for daughters.

RELATIONS WITH SONS AND DAUGHTERS

Most women make greater demands upon and more frequently punish daughters than they do sons. This is partly due to the belief that it is more appropriate for girls to do housework and care for younger siblings, but it also may stem from differences in what women expect from their sons and daughters after they grow up. No matter how she is treated at home, a daughter will leave when she marries and is unlikely to provide her mother with a permanent home or substantial financial assistance. It is the ideal norm, however, for a son to remain always at home and to take care of his mother's needs. Consequently, by pampering a son, a woman is investing in her future material well-being.

This does *not* mean that women love their daughters less than their sons, only that they feel a greater need to ensure that their sons will love *them*. If there is a crack in a son's devotion to his mother, his wife might find it and chip away at it. Even without daughter-in-law interference, an adult son may turn against his mother. The physical abuse by an adult son of his mother is, significantly, one of the commonest causes of insanity in older women. Differential treatment of male and female children is understandable when it is realized that mothers are always aware of the power their sons will have over their lives in the future.

Few women can resist the temptation to rely increasingly on their older daughters for child care and housework, even though most are frequently dissatisfied with the results. Some acknowledge that they expect too much and blame themselves for striking their daughters in anger. They say, however, that it would be impossible to stop themselves from venting their rage in this way, that it is inevitable that they will lose control of themselves again. Although most daughters appear stoic about their heavy work load, many are resentful of having to take so much abuse. Some are sullen and others nervously watchful for signs of impending explosions.

Negative feelings between mother and daughter usually fade with the approach of the daughter's marriage. Most women begin to dread the daughter's departure well in advance of the wedding. One woman, unable to stop sobbing on a neighbor's wedding night, explained that since her own daughter's engagement she could not bear such occasions. Even when another daughter at home is old enough to assume her sister's duties, the sense of loss is usually keen. As mentioned earlier, neighbors continue to pass their afternoons and evenings comforting and distracting the mother for several days after her daughter's wedding. The first week of marriage, when contact between mother and daughter is forbidden, is extremely hard on both.

Unless their houses are too far apart, the bride is likely to visit her mother frequently once the postwedding festivities are over. Her mother is often her main source of emotional support and advice for dealing with husband and in-laws. Mothers and daughters often visit privately but also arrange to pay their afternoon social calls together.

A woman looks forward to the security her daughter will gain with her first pregnancy. She advises her on how to care for herself and, in a few cases, assists with the birth. Most, unless ill or tied down by small children of their own, visit the daughter almost daily during postbirth confinement.

Most women are supportive of a daughter who wishes to return home in protest against husband or mother-in-law. As mentioned earlier, there are cases of women so incensed by their husbands' refusal to allow a daughter to remain at home that they have returned to their own kinsmen in protest. Some women even have been divorced for intransigent support of their daughters.

It is expected and approved for a mother and daughter to be emotionally close. I, like Fernea (1969:35–36) in Iraq, was pitied for the long separation from my mother; I received no sympathy at all for the equally long separation from my father, brothers, and friends; and my husband was offered none for being apart from any of his family.

Older women claim to derive great comfort from their daughters. Some pity their contemporaries who have only sons. "Who will there be to wipe her brow for her when she is ill?" they ask. One independently wealthy mother of adult daughters and sons repeatedly contrasts the virtues of the former with the failings of the latter and their wives. Perhaps more women would voice similar sentiments were they not economically dependent upon their sons; few women have the means to live alone comfortably. Solitary older women, in any case, are thought to suffer loneliness and run the grave risk of being left alone when ill.

Solitary older women are not a rarity in ᶜAmran. Some have no kin and live off charity. Others have adult offspring in town. Sons-in-law are not expected to take them in, although some do provide temporary care. (When one older woman's sudden illness made moving her impossible, a daughter and son-in-law moved into her house to care for her. The son-in-law stayed home some afternoons so his wife could pay pressing social calls. His conduct was strongly approved but not regarded as extraordinary.)

Ideally, if a woman has an adult son, she should never have to live alone. In reality, women say that neolocal residence is on the increase. Many express considerable apprehension about their future. The pampering of sons is an almost universal strategy of protection against desertion, and it is often equally important for a woman to find the right sort of wives for her sons (ones that she can count on not to work against her) and to "sell" her choices to her husband and sons.

A desirable daughter-in-law is loyal, compliant, industrious, and cheerful. A perfect daughter-in-law always obeys her mother-in-law and identifies with her more than with her husband or own kin. As mentioned earlier, an unprotected orphan is ideal. If fatherless and brotherless, she cannot risk rebelling against her mother-in-law's authority; if motherless, she is more likely to learn to love her.

The closest mother-in-law–daughter-in-law relationship I observed was between a motherless daughter-in-law and a daughterless mother-in-law. When the former's first husband died, even though her children had also died, she was married to her husband's younger brother. She and her mother-in-law are consistently loyal and affectionate, each seeming more bonded to the other than to the man through whom they are linked.

Self-centeredness, defiance, and laziness are qualities to be avoided in a daughter-in-law. All women, regardless of age, agree that a daughter-in-law must be hardworking and dutiful. Universal criticism fell upon one young woman who claimed to be too ill with her first pregnancy to perform household tasks. Her mother-in-law had to endure the bad situation because her son was deeply fond of his wife. She did use female networks, however, to manipulate public opinion against her. Although this had no immediate effect, it shored up support for possible future confrontations.

As long as differences remain minor, neither mother-in-law nor daughter-in-law is likely to involve the son or husband directly, although some women involve either of them indirectly on a routine basis. Most women reevaluate their relations with their sons and their sons' wives and adjust their behavior accordingly. A woman feeling particularly threatened by a daughter-in-law may behave with greater than usual generosity and docility toward her son. At other times, she may show him no special consideration at all.

Some women who feel very secure in their position contradict their sons frequently, while others barely bother to conceal the fact that they are humoring them. In some cases, harmonious mother-in-law–daughter-in-law relations allow both to be more assertive toward the son or husband. In one such household, the brothers who returned late from harvesting found a tepid, dry lunch on a charcoal grill. Their mother and wives had decided against waiting lunch for their return because they had two social calls to pay that afternoon. This kind of behavior is less likely in households where women compete with each other through the men.

When mother-in-law and daughter-in-law get along well, they pay more of their afternoon visits together. Even when relations become slightly strained, they continue the pattern for the sake of public opinion. Only close friends or women with exceptional powers of observation can detect mother-in-law–daughter-in-law conflict at this stage.

Usually conflicts are defused without creating an actual breach, but occasionally one of the two women decides she can no longer tolerate the other. Then all-out assaults and counterattacks come into play, each struggling to gain the support of her son or husband. Some women's tactics are direct (recall the story of the estranged wife whose condition for returning to her husband was the death of the mother-in-law); others utilize the services of specialists in magic. Many women also strive to rally public opinion in their favor. They tell friends their side of the story and count on them to spread the word. The son or husband is less likely to behave unfairly when he knows that reports of his conduct are widely circulated.

If a mother of two or more sons loses the battle to her first daughter-in-law, she can try again with another. She may try to find the other sons more malleable wives, modify her behavior toward the other daughters-in-law, or improve her technique at influencing her sons. All three methods might be combined. (Similarly, the divorcée ousted by her first mother-in-law almost always has a second chance. She can try harder to please her new mother-in-law or to win her husband over to the idea of a separate residence.)

It may be that in pre-republican Yemen widespread economic hardship made neolocal residence impossible for most ʿAmranis. If so, the mother-in-law was secure more or less by default. Expanded economic opportunities and the diffusion of "modern ideas" combine to make separate residences a real possibility. The mother-in-law must protect herself or risk being left alone.

9

Neighbors and Friendships

Despite an ideology of neighborly loyalty and solidarity, most men have little to do with their neighbors except at weddings, funerals, and other irregular and infrequent occasions. Residential proximity is, in reality, of slight social significance to men—not surprising since neighborhoods are heterogeneous with respect to traditional status, wealth, and place of origin. Most men prefer interactions with relatives, in-laws, and others who occupy statuses close to their own. Spending most of their free time in the *sūq*, in tea shops, or in or near mosques, men can fraternize with whomever they wish.

Women have an ideology of neighborly loyalty borne out in practice. Their social roles obligate them to stay close to home most of the day, and they must rely on co-resident women (if there are any) and neighbors for company, moral support, and material assistance. Economic, social, and age differences are less significant than they are for men.

Among the many practical bases to the maintenance of close, reciprocal ties between neighbors are the following: (1) Households vary in what they have, so neighbors need each other for water, electricity, grinding stones, sewing machines, television watching, eggs, *laban* (buttermilk), and other items. (2) Kinswomen may be too far away to help when goods or services are needed in a hurry. (3) It is rarely possible to prepare and serve feasts associated with life crises without the labor, kitchens, and furnishings of nearby women. (4) It is considered wrong for a woman taken ill, in mourning, or pained by her daughter's recent marriage to spend too much time alone. Consequently, neighbors spend considerable time comforting and distracting women in these situations. (5) Many women do not leave their neighborhood alone, either because husbands, kinsmen, or in-laws do not allow them to or because they fear gossip. When they wish to go out, they arrange joint excursions with one or more neighbors, whether to do laundry at a pump outside of town; to bathe at the public bath; to pay a social call; or to obtain treatment for themselves or their children from the clinic, a pharmacist, or a traditional healer. (6) Neighborhood children play—and sometimes fight—together. By staying on good terms with neighbors, a woman improves the chances that her children will receive adult protection and fair treatment. (7) Most women are gregarious and find constant confinement at home oppressive. In many households (thirty-seven out of seventy-one in my neighborhood, for example) there is only one adult female; in many expanded households, co-resident women are not always compatible. If women are friendly with their neighbors, they have an ever-available respite from boredom and isolation, as well as access to wide-ranging news and gossip. Neighborhood disputes alleviate boredom and allow women safe outlets for frustration and hostility. (8) Neighbors sometimes take collective action against a man who has abused his wife, as in the following example:

> One morning, after being beaten over a trifling matter by her husband and his younger, still unmarried brother, Maymuna decided to leave. Her sister-in-law, the only other woman residing in the house, decided to leave in protest too. Her husband was in Saudi Arabia at the time. Both women went to stay with relatives in Sanᶜa; neither could arrange to travel to her remote village at such short notice.
> Maymuna's husband and his younger brother were left alone in the house. Like the two women, the men have no relatives in ᶜAmran. Ordinarily, when men have neither wives nor kin to feed them, neighbors give them lunch. In this case, however, the neighbors decided that the men would receive no food from any of them. They explained that neither Maymuna nor her sister-in-law could go anywhere without the men's permission and that both were beaten frequently without cause. None of the neighbors were particularly close to either of the women, but they felt sorry for them and were convinced they in no way deserved the physical abuse they received. They decided that the men would have to eat lunch in the *sūq*. As lunching there is strongly stigmatized (because the food is thought to be dirty and inferior, but also, I think, because it demonstrates social isolation and a loss of independence), the neighbors' decision was significant punishment indeed.

The neighbors stood up for Maymuna and her sister-in-law at least in part because there was no one else to do so. Most likely, their action also reminded their husbands of female retaliatory power. In general, women feel obligated to help a neighbor who is in need, even if they have been feuding with her or expect that their actions will never be reciprocated. Examples follow:

> Salma and her next-door neighbors had not spoken for seven years. Townswomen agree that Salma is a disagreeable person who had behaved shamefully toward these neighbors. When Salma's third son was married, however, the neighbors buried the hatchet (at least temporarily); they loaned their house, helped to prepare the feasts, attended the parties, and kept Salma company. Their conduct was such that no one who did not know of the long feud would suspect anything amiss between the two households.

> Khadija is a very poor older woman who lives alone. Much of the time she relies on the charity of neighbors for food. When she was brushed by an automobile, her next-door neighbors took her into their house. For two weeks they prepared special, restorative dishes and cared for her, even though she appeared to them (and to me) to have recovered before the first week ended and was a singularly tiresome person to have about.

> Dulai, a villager, lives alone with her blind, old husband. She has no relatives in ʿAmran, only the weakest ties to her husband's female relatives and his daughters by his first marriage, and no really strong friendships. When she gave birth to her third child, she was alone, and during all but the first three days of her recuperation was on her own. One of her neighbors, Fuzia, a woman with almost nothing in common with Dulai, took it upon herself to visit Dulai every afternoon of her *walada* confinement. She served tea and *gishr* and helped entertain the few guests who came. She herself prepared the special, overly sweet *gishr* served on the final day of every *walada*'s confinement, and another neighbor painted the customary designs on Dulai's hands.

Cases such as the preceding one are common. Some women send lunch every day to a *walada* who is on her own. Usually they call no attention to their generosity and expect nothing in return.

Women's attitudes toward the obligations of neighbors and the importance of friendship are illuminated by the following example:

> Fatima, an unsociable, older divorcée, died inside the house where she had lived alone for years. What was unusual and extremely disturbing

about Fatima's death was that it went unnoticed for several days. When her decomposing remains were found (and buried at night, without having been washed or carried in procession), all the women of ʿAmran were in an uproar. Fatima's tragedy was of more universal concern than almost any other event during my stay. It was blamed not so much on Fatima's son and daughter-in-law (whose house is far from Fatima's), but on her neighbors. Even though Fatima had kept aloof from them, women insisted that it was *ʿayb* (shameful) of the neighbors not to have been concerned about her. Carried away by their indignation and pity, women began to wonder whether Fatima's death would even be mourned. They lamented, "Those without friends in life—who is there to be their friends after death?"

There was one household in my immediate neighborhood considered particularly needy. This household and my neighbors' relations with it are described below:

When I arrived in ʿAmran, the household consisted of Atigha, a widow of *muzayyin* descent, her two sons and her two younger daughters. People say that the family had lived comfortably until Atigha's husband's death, but since then, has been exceedingly poor. The family lives in a tiny and very shabby house. Atigha bakes bread, which her children sell in the *sūq*, much of the year; she also does occasional odd jobs inside other people's homes. Atigha has no presentable clothes and no jewelry; she does not participate in the formal female visiting system, but is on intimate terms with most of her neighbors upon whom she relies for assistance and company. One neighbor prepares extra food almost every day to contribute to Atigha's family's lunch. Others allow Atigha's daughters to take water from their taps.

Three of Atigha's children were married within the span of one year. The neighbors' contributions to these events included the following: they helped prepare the wedding feasts; they gave their houses for the preparation and serving of the feasts and the celebrations and informal visiting that preceded and followed the actual weddings; they gave substantial gifts to the daughters, and spent several afternoons and evenings before and after the girls' weddings comforting and distracting Atigha.

All three weddings were dependent upon the neighbors' material assistance, but that of the son evoked a particular display of neighborly loyalty. He was slightly crippled and very timid; people had assumed he would never marry. Atigha amazed us all, however, by arranging his engagement to his sister's mother-in-law, a widow thought to be twice his age and in all likelihood no longer able to bear children. At first no one could believe it. Once rumors of this bizarre match began spreading to other neighborhoods, we, Atigha's neighbors, were tapped for information constantly. Was it really true that he was going to marry his sister's husband's mother? Had we seen her? Was she really an old lady? What was his sister going to call her after the wedding—"mother-in-law" or "sister-in-law?" Although the neighbors had laughed over these same questions among themselves, they appeared to see it as their duty to answer "outsiders" with sober dignity. As long as no one was being hurt by the marriage, they were obligated, as they saw it, to stand behind Atigha and her family.

The neighbors who did so much for Atigha all feel morally superior to her. They see her as a chronic liar who manipulates the norm of helping neighbors to her own advantage. She embodies traditional negative stereotypes of *muzayyin* nature by her poverty, her dependence, her casualness about veiling, and her lack of concern about her own and her children's honor. The more traditional neighbors, especially poor tribal women, are comforted to have their moral evaluations of traditional Yemeni social strata affirmed by her. Poor women of all strata are pleased that they, at least, maintain their modesty and honor. Interestingly, an unimpeachable *muzayyina* can earn respect, but is not always liked; a wealthy *muzayyina* (like the wedding specialist described in chapter 2) is resented. Atigha is looked down upon, but liked. Women may recognize that extreme dependency breeds excessive manipulativeness; and many enjoy the company of someone whose coarseness and lack of position free them of the burden of impression management.

Because of the social and economic heterogeneity of ʿAmran neighborhoods, reciprocal relations do not equalize the social strata of those involved.[1] That is, wealth and traditional status differences do not keep neighbors apart and they appear to be de-emphasized in routine interactions, but they are not obliterated. Women remain aware of status differences, despite the veil of politeness cast over them.

There are times when women deliberately lift or inadvertently let slip the veil. A woman interrupts a joking conversation about marriage arrangements for infants and toddlers by pointing out the impossibility of a particular arrangement: "Your baby girl can't marry her son; you're a *muzayyina* and she's a *gabīliya* [tribeswoman]." If her adversary protests, the issue is usually dropped quickly. In one such interchange, a *muzayyina* retorted: "*Muzayyin, muzayyin*, what's all this *muzayyin* business?! Anywhere else in Yemen, a *muzayyin* can be a judge, a government official, anything! Only in ᶜAmran are people so crazy!"

After a neighborhood death, those of the same social stratum as the deceased are expected to show greater respect than are other households. The difference is real but, like so many status-related differences, rarely articulated. Below, a *gabīliya* explains why there will be a festive party in her house on the same day her neighbors (with whom she is intimate) are holding a *mawlid* (religious ceremony) to conclude the period of mourning for their family patriarch:

> When Hussayn [a merchant] died, we decided to have no singing or dancing at my granddaughter's wedding parties. We went ahead and held them, but without having a *muzayyina* [singer]; this is what you do when there is a death. Now, it's almost a month later so we decided to give my granddaughter at least one dancing party. The women of Hussayn's house said it was all right for us to have the party on Wednesday because they were holding their *mawlid* on Monday. We can't help it that they changed their mind or Atigha [the *mawlid* reader] changed her mind or I don't know what happened. It is too late for us to change. Besides, you know, they are one thing and we are another thing. For some other families to have the dancing would be shameful, but for us it is all right. [The women of Hussayn's house complained mildly, as it turned out, but there was no breach.]

Although status differences do not prevent close friendships between women of separate strata, they can create additional strains. There are, however, "mixed" friendships which have endured for years and which are tolerated, if not actually approved, by the relatives and associates of both friends.

Friendships vary in intensity and longevity. Neighbors who are casual friends rarely enter each others' houses except in cases of illness or life-crisis celebrations, whereas neighbors who are on intimate terms come and go constantly. Some intimate friendships endure after one friend has moved away; they visit informally in one or the other's house and sit together at formal gatherings. Even if they see each other rarely, they feel confident of the other's loyalty, as illustrated in the following example:

> Karima was in a bind. She had just given birth and, like almost all women, looked forward to having a lavishly decorated reception room

and a daily stream of visitors. However, she had sold her coral necklace several months earlier to loan her mother money, and insisted she could not receive guests without coral beads. (As coral is only one of many defenses against evil eye, its importance to the *walada* is probably as much social as supernatural.) She hoped that a relative or sister-in-law would offer to loan her coral, but she was too prideful to ask directly. They all knew, she said, that she had had to sell her own, and if they wanted to help her they would do so without being asked. When it became clear that no relative would do so, she sent her daughter to ask a former neighbor for hers. The two had been the closest of friends, but because each was tied down by numerous small children they saw each other rarely. Karima's friend sent her coral necklace and called on her repeatedly during her postbirth confinement. [Two pertinent facts should be added: (1) Karima's friend was considerably better off financially than Karima, and, although Karima wore her friend's new, large coral beads, her friend had her old set to fall back on. (2) Karima is a female *sayyid*, her friend of *sūq* family origin; Karima's confidence in her friend, and her willingness to ask the favor directly might be linked as much to an expectation of deference to her status as to the bonds of old friendship.]

Often friendships that have waned or faded entirely are reactivated during a crisis. Betrayals of confidence, competition, petty conflicts set friends apart frequently, but if one falls seriously ill, a former friend can be expected to reappear, almost as if nothing had happened between them. As in women's interaction with their small children, friends are called upon to transcend ordinary roles in the face of life-threatening disease.

The brittleness of many friendships is an effect of their great emotional importance to women. Intimacy is scarce and highly valued. As a consequence, one's friend's friend may be considered threatening, and the slightest hint of withdrawal taken for wholesale rejections. The love felt for a female friend, then, is often a jealous, possessive love, as shown in the following example:

> While Fuzia and Arwa both remained single, they were the closest of friends. Fuzia spent every afternoon at Arwa's house until her marriage to a house in another part of town. Then, she was expected to attend dancing parties and pay formal visits like all other brides. Most girls and young women regard entry into the female social world as one of the main benefits of married life. However, Fuzia was uncomfortable at the few gatherings she attended and decided to resume daily visits to Arwa. By this time, her husband had gone to Saudi Arabia, leaving her under his mother's control. Fuzia's mother-in-law opposed her visits to Arwa and dealt harshly with other manifestations

of what she saw as rebelliousness. In protest, Fuzia began spending more and more time in her family home; living there, of course, made it easier for her to visit Arwa.

About a year later Fuzia's husband returned from Saudi Arabia and reclaimed his wife. She finally began attending wedding parties and other social events that young women especially enjoy. Arwa, who had encouraged Fuzia's mutiny and treasured her company, gave her a desperate ultimatum: "Choose me or 'all that'; you can't have both." When Fuzia chose "all that" and never returned, Arwa was despondent; she almost never spoke Fuzia's name. I ran into Fuzia more frequently at major social occasions and grew to expect to hear her light, carefree, "How's Arwa?"

Like other respectable, unmarried young women, Arwa rarely leaves home. The intensity of her feelings toward Fuzia is related to her isolation and confinement; but, married women with active social lives also care deeply about their friendships. They say, however, that their friendships are fragile:

> It's no good. Women fight over their children; or when a woman gets sick or has to prepare a feast, she expects so much from her friends, and they don't always come through. A woman gets mad at her friends in a flash. If a woman is good, she gets over her anger quickly, but sometimes I can't. About six months ago my neighbor Nuria and I had an argument over street cleaning. It was the day the government came around with their loudspeaker telling us to clean up. I haven't spoken to her since that day, but, you know, now she is a *walada* and Ahmad [the informant's husband] says its *ʿayb* [shameful] if I don't call on her. She is my neighbor, he says. [The informant did call on her neighbor as her husband urged her to do. A few months later, when the informant's two small children had measles, her former friend brought her food every day, knowing the informant would not leave her children's side to cook.]

> Once Fatima bint Hizam was my friend; once Maymuna bint Ahmad was my friend; once Lutfiyya bint ʿAli was my friend; but they all let me down. You know, Salma and I were best friends long ago, back when she was very poor. I did everything for her, and, you know [whispering now], she is a *muzayyina* and I'm a *gabīliya*, and it was *ʿayb* for me to do so much for her. [Reverting to normal speech level] Now, she is doing very well and I hardly see her. When I need her, she doesn't come. My heart is good. I am quick to forgive, but others are different. Some people just want to take and never give anything in return.

Women say it is not good to be quick to anger and far worse to be unforgiving. One informant enlarged:

> Men are better than women. They don't get mad at each other all the time, and when they do they make it up right away. My husband never stays mad at his friends, but I sometimes stay mad at mine.

If her evaluation is correct, it may be linked to the fact that while a woman's behavior toward men must often be guarded, she deals with other women more directly and immediately, especially when upset; for men, the pattern is reversed. A fight between women only jeopardizes their friendship; one between men might endanger shared economic or political concerns. Furthermore, women's arguments occasionally end up in brawls, but no one really gets hurt. Men carry daggers and guns and value their honor very highly; if their disagreements escalate, grave, even mortal wounds might result. Other informants, in any case, did not offer the same evaluation. Women do not generally see male character as morally superior to female. Whenever I asked about the relative goodness of the sexes, the question was dismissed as foolish. Only individual variations exist; some men are good, some bad, some in between; and the same holds for women.

There are two dimensions in which individual women are seen as commendable: one is based on temperament and sociability and the other on honor and virtue. Women ranked high on the first dimension are popular, whereas those topping the second scale are respected. A neighbor (a middle-aged *sayyid* woman) told me, "All our neighbors are *wasakh* [trash], all of them; the only one who isn't is Amina [an elderly tribeswoman]." This informant's evaluation was honest, although overstated. Unlike the others, Amina does not lie, fight, or manipulate. She is not sanctimonious, and, if she judges others, she usually keeps her opinions to herself. What is of significance is that the informant who pointed out Amina's special virtue has almost nothing to do with her. She prefers the company of other neighbors, the ones she described as trash.

The word *wasakh* literally means "dirty." When applied to women, it has a range of meanings, the harshest of which refers to adulterousness. ("Nuria is a *wasakha*; she meets men on the road.") The term can allude to quarrelsomeness or lack of respect.

One of the oldest and most popular women in ʿAmran.

("Maymouna has to do all the cooking and cleaning because her daughter-in-law, that *wasakha*, says she's sick and won't do it.") Most often it describes meanness and vulgarity. ("Forget about her! She's *wasakha*. Don't cry." "Wait until you hear the way Fatima's sister-in-law talks. She's *wasakha*!") It may also refer neutrally or half-admiringly to any deviation from the norms of female conduct.

Generally, to be *wasakha* is the opposite of being *sharifa* (honorable). Although women of the *sayyid* stratum are addressed and referred to as the *sharifa* and are expected to be more circumspect than other women, no one would argue that all *sayyid* women are in fact *sharifa*. Women of all strata acknowledge that any woman can become *sharifa* or *wasakha*, although many *sayyid* and tribal women believe that those of lower rank are more predisposed to behave dishonorably than they. There are lower-rank women who accept this evaluation; some show extreme respect and gratitude to *sayyid* women and to women of important tribal families, and others are prone to extremely coarse and sometimes rowdy displays in female public settings. Most women appear to enjoy watching such buffoonery, but some from the lower strata see the performances as demeaning.

There is no doubt that some women of the higher strata behave dishonorably. A number of tribeswomen (although no *sayyid* women) reputedly have committed adultery. Some *sayyid* and tribal women speak loudly when passing through the *sūq*, and others allow their veils to droop or fall when they shouldn't. There are also chronic liars, manipulators, and untrustworthy gossipmongers.[2]

Because extroverts add life to women's gatherings, they are particularly popular. This includes women considered as *wasakha*, whose sexual jokes and gossip are disapproved of but enjoyed. Women who listen attentively and laugh with the others are considered likeable, too. Aloof silence, however, is thought to indicate a bad temperament. Only if a woman is in unfamiliar surroundings, at a Sanʿa party for example, might one attribute her reticence to shyness or self-consciousness. Those consistently reserved at home in ʿAmran are, quite simply, ill-natured.

My *sayyid* neighbor, it will be recalled, prefers the company she refers to as *wasakha* to that of the honorable woman. The latter is aloof in that she rarely visits households other than those of her relatives and immediate neighbors. The women categorized as *wasakha*, in contrast, are exceedingly gregarious. They spend free moments in each others' company and pay formal visits almost daily. In their own informal gatherings they frequently exchange gossip and ribaldries. Several smoke the water pipe regularly and a few chew *gāt* on occasion. At least two are said to have tainted pasts, and one is openly disrespectful to her timid, old husband. They are, in short, a lively group.

Most of them are also occasionally untrustworthy. Fights and betrayals occur frequently, making lines of affiliation unstable. Unlike the stay-at-home Amina, some of these women are socially ambitious. Although they probably do not wish to hurt an old friend, the temptation to forge new, prestige-enhancing connections is sometimes irresistible. An old friendship is put on the back burner. My neighbor's condemnation of her friends, I think, stems much more from their disloyalty than from their lack of refinement or dubious histories. They are so much fun, however, that most of the time, at least for this informant, the risk is worth taking. Additionally, as might be expected, my neighbor is much like them. When carried away, she and they are capable of saying almost anything, true or untrue, about anyone, including each other. In most cases, the truth comes out and no one is hurt; almost everyone plays by the same rules. Sometimes, however, reputations are damaged and feelings badly bruised.

There are a few women who stay out of female society almost entirely. Reciprocal ties with nonkin are less important to them than avoiding pettiness and vulgarity. The wife of a major government official is an extreme example. She says that when she was young she wanted to attend women's gatherings, but her husband wouldn't let her. Now, he would let her go, but she has lost interest. The content of her criticisms of ʿAmrani women is unoriginal, but the acidity and contempt with which she voices them are completely unparalleled:

> Yesterday I was on my way from my house to my mother's house when a woman I didn't know called to me, "Where are you coming from?" I didn't answer, but she went on, "Are you coming from the *mashjab?*" I said, "Yes." Then the woman told me that my *tarīq* [route, way] was not the best one. I told her, "It's my *tarīq.*"

Quite apart from the double meaning of *ṭarīq*, this informant's account was savage. Whereas many women imitate the way in which even total strangers ask them where they are coming from and where they are going, the intent is at least partly humorous. Their complaints are, if not completely indulgent, at least moderated. In contrast, when this informant parodied her interrogator, it was with cold cruelty.

She is not humorless, however, having once asked me, for example, if I had heard that her third daughter was engaged to a Sanʿani student for 100,000 riyals. This joke was meant to remind me that she and her husband are both so honorable that they had declined more than a nominal bride-price for their elder daughters and have no intention of marrying the third until she is a young woman. They are not like the hoi polloi who marry their daughters before menarche for as much money as they can get.

Other informants, perceiving themselves above ʿAmrani women's society, are much more ambivalent. Some are women from powerful families who spend some of their time in Sanʿa and periodically call on the household of the head of the Hashid tribal confederation in Khamir. They are active in the ʿAmrani female social world, visit frequently if not widely, and, in many cases, aspire to popularity. But they let it be known that they are accustomed to superior settings and company. Others are women who believe that maintaining a *sharīfa* (honorable) image is more important than having fun. They enjoy female society, but think it unseemly to gad about too much or to become intimate with those who might tarnish a reputation. Women with this perspective—a high proportion of whom are *sayyid*—interact a great deal with their own kinswomen. However, for the great majority of ʿAmrani women, formal and informal visits are the highlight of the day, and friendships are the core of their emotional lives.

10

Women's Perceptions

ᶜAmrani women live both with men and in their own separate female social domain. Having a distinct, private sphere of interaction allows them to question and criticize the androcentric Islamic and tribal constructs of the dominant cultural ideology. Their values and aspirations only partially overlap with men's.

One way in which women "define and comment upon or criticize their situation" is through verbal art (Webber 1985:310–11). This chapter begins with a discussion of selected women's folktales, traditional stories told exclusively at women's gatherings. Narrators, usually older women, use dramatic delivery; listeners also serve as chorus, thus participating in the performance:

Tale 1

Two childless co-wives pray to Allah, one for a daughter like the moon, the other for a daughter like a monkey. Each woman gets her wish. It isn't long before their husband dies, then the two co-wives in rapid succession. The moon-sister and the monkey-sister are on their own.

Monkey-sister decides they must travel to town. When they arrive she hides her beautiful moon-sister in a hole in a room and sets off to find them food. Soon she finds a house in which wedding celebrations are being held; she steals food and takes it back to her sister. Then she returns to the wedding house, sneaks into the room where the newly married couple sleep, and steals the bride's gold. She returns to her sister and gives her the bride's jewelry.

When the bride and groom awake and discover that the gold has been taken, the groom becomes furious. He decides to comb the town for it. Eventually he arrives at the house of the two sisters. Monkey-sister opens the door to him, having first bedecked moon-sister in the bride's gold. The groom sees moon-sister's beauty and decides he must have her for his bride. He divorces his wife of one day and marries moon-sister. Monkey-sister lives with them forever.

Moon-sister is beautiful and passive; she must be secluded and protected. Monkey-sister is ugly and clever; she acts to protect herself and her dependent. As a female, she cannot do this in a normal, ethical way, so she steals, first food and then gold. Her sins are not punished but rewarded. Moon-sister gains a husband and she, monkey-sister, gains a place in her sister's home.

In other folktales women tell, sin is punished and innocence rewarded, but monkey-sister's transgressions are glossed over, as is the injustice done the ousted wife. According to the dominant cultural model, monkey-sister's antisocial and immoral actions are inexcusable, but the outcome of this story shows that for women the standards of the dominant cultural model must sometimes be ignored. Although it is possible to interpret monkey-sister's character as symbolic of women's natural inclination to disrupt the social order, it makes more sense to view her as representing women's ability to cope despite the enormity of the restrictions imposed upon them. Further, the tale dramatizes the truth that there are at least as many females who *must* take aggressive action to survive (monkey-sister) as there are ones who can count on being protected (moon-sister). Lastly, it is monkey-sister, not passively beautiful moon-sister, who is the "heroine" of the story.

In contrast to the mothers of monkey- and moon-sisters, most childless women in folktales desire, and get, sons, albeit irregular ones. The following is such a story:

Tale 2

Atigha had never been pregnant in her life. One day there was a snake in her kitchen. She told him of her troubles. Then she conceived. She gave birth to a snake, a long one, almost a foot long. Knowing her husband might be upset and harm her son, she hid the snake in a cupboard. When her husband came home that night, she told him she had borne a son, but he was dead and had already been buried. She kept the snake hidden in the cupboard when her husband was home, but took him out, fed him and washed him, the minute her husband left the house. She nursed the snake from her breast.

The snake grew big. One day he told his mother, "Teach me to read."

At first she was stunned. She answered, "Teach you to read! Are you crazy? Are you drunk? How can I find someone to teach *you* to read?" Her son, however, remained firm in his resolve to read, so Atigha went off in search of a teacher for him. Not only did she get him a teacher, but she brought him two Qurans.

Later on he told his mother to arrange his marriage. Once again, she was shocked, and answered him, "Get you married? Are you crazy? Are you drunk? How could I find someone to marry *you*?" As previously, her son could not be dissuaded, so she went off in search of a match.

Atigha went to the house of a man whose daughter she knew to be of marriageable age. She said to him, "My son is a big officer in the army. We want him to marry your daughter." The man agreed.

When Atigha told her son of his engagement, he was pleased, but said that he wanted a wedding outfit. "Wedding clothes for *you*?!" she asked incredulously, but went to her husband and asked him to provide the appropriate garments. [He had discovered his wife's secret long ago, but, despite his shock, had taken no action against the snake.] At first he refused, but eventually Atigha convinced him to buy the clothes.

Finally the day of the wedding came, and Atigha and her husband gave the snake his wedding clothes. He then removed his snake skin, and inside was the body of a fine young man! When his parents saw him, they rejoiced. He kissed their knees [a sign of filial devotion]. Then his father slaughtered a sheep and they made the largest, grandest wedding celebration that has ever been seen.

Atigha's devotion inspires her to take effective action for her snake-son, but, unlike monkey-sister in the preceding tale, she does not seriously transgress the moral code of the dominant cultural model. As in other tales dealing with women's relations with their sons, the heroine more or less abides by male rules. In the following, similar story, the focus is on the mother's enduring love. Her role is much more passive than Atigha's:

Tale 3

Khadija, who had never been pregnant, envied her co-wife's fertility. She begged Allah that she might conceive by means of a squash. The child she bore was, like its genitor, a squash. When her husband came to her and asked her what they had [meaning, what sex was the baby], it was with great distress that she replied "A squash."

Her husband too was stricken but responded conventionally that the important thing was Khadija's health. Then the squash said, "Praise be to God." He asked to be placed in water on a window sill. He grew and grew.

Many years later, Khadija's husband arranged the marriage of his daughter by Khadija's co-wife. When the squash learned of the engagement, he asked his father to arrange his marriage too. His father became angry and drove the squash-son from the house. From that day, Khadija was inconsolable.

Allah guided the squash to a distant town. He led him into a house where a fortune in gold was hidden. The squash used the gold to arrange his marriage. On his wedding day, he was transformed into a handsome young man.

On the eighth day after the wedding, Khadija's son and his bride traveled to her village. When he knocked on the door of his father's house, Khadija was upstairs crying in her room, as was her wont since her son's banishment. Her son demanded that Khadija descend. When she appeared, he embraced her and then kissed her knees, and told her that he was her son who had been a squash.

It is implicit that Khadija will never again be separated from her son. Her devotion will be repaid. The enormous appeal of the stories of Khadija and Atigha is related to women's anxiety, previously discussed, about their relationships with their sons.

Just as folktales are recounted at women's gatherings, so too are the dramas of real life. No matter how tragic a woman's story, she is very unlikely to tell it in a somber way. Her pain is converted to drama, usually replete with abundant comic relief. Even though the story probably describes her victimization, she tells it heroically. Making the tragedy entertaining is doubly therapeutic; it helps the teller to feel some distance from her plight and ensures her a sympathetic hearing.

Nuria, a guest in the reception room of a new mother, told the following story. Nuria has only one living child, a son; her other five children died in infancy. When I entered the reception room and saw all the women laughing at Nuria's flamboyant performance, I (unlike the others) had no idea that the comic opening was only a prelude to tragedy:

> I was washing clothes at the Hadhig well when all of a sudden a bad feeling came over me. I knew it was crazy but I was afraid something had happened, so I threw the clothes into a bundle and hurried home. When I approached my house, the neighbors called to me that my house had been robbed while I was away. "Yu! Yu! Yu!" I gasped. "Robbed my house? Who did it?" When they said it was my son

ᶜAbdu that they had seen removing things from the house, I said, "Oh well, that's all right then."

Then [gesturing dramatically] I opened the door and saw that ᶜAbdu had taken all of his things and some of ours too. Without a word to me or to his father, he and his wife had just packed up and gone off to a house of their own. I was so upset that I was crazy. [As she says this, Nuria's eyes fill with tears; the audience, who had been laughing up to this point, immediately become teary-eyed with her. The dramatic part of the recounting over, our complete sympathy elicited, she fills us in on the circumstances that led up to this ultimate betrayal.]

When ᶜAbdu refused to continue his schooling, we got him a job as a clerk, but after a year or so he quit that. We didn't know what to do with him. Then we decided to marry him to Amina bint al Hulaym. We thought he would settle down once he had a wife, but instead, shortly after the wedding, he decided to go find work in Saudi Arabia. We didn't want him to go but he went anyway. Amina refused to stay with us, so she lived with her parents the entire time he was away. After a year and a half, ᶜAbdu came back. We gave Amina's father 1,300 riyals [to compensate them for her upkeep], and he sent her back to us. Then there was fighting among us for a month or two, until the day I came home and found ᶜAbdu and his wife and the furnishings gone. It wasn't too long until Amina left ᶜAbdu and returned once again to her father's house, so now ᶜAbdu is back home with us. All he does is nag us to buy him a car, or at the very least, a motorbike, but we can't afford one. I urge him to go out and find work. I tell him that these days it is no disgrace for a *gabīlī* to be a hired worker, but he just sits around all day. He keeps telling us, "Everyone has a car or a motorbike but me!"

All the women present listened attentively and sympathetically to Nuria's story; some added specific or general comments about the terrible deficiencies of the young men of the day. Nuria still had her problem, but the telling of it appeared to make her feel, for the moment, much better.

Nuria was not driven insane (*majnūna*) by her son, but some women are. As mentioned earlier, many cases of female insanity are blamed on abusive (usually physically abusive) sons. Other causes of female insanity include being forced to have sexual relations prior to the fortieth day after childbirth, evil eye, brain fever, punishment for past sins, and becoming immobilized by grief instead of going out and answering back those who are responsible for the misery. Whatever the cause of female insanity, the behavior associated with it is extreme shamelessness. The language and conduct of the *majnūna* are the antithesis of the dominant cultural norm of virtuous, modest womanhood. The full-fledged *majnūna* is quintessentially *wasakha* (dirty). One, for example, improvises on women's constant incantation, "Pray to the Prophet of God," sometimes saying, "Pray to the penis of the Prophet of God," at other times, "Pray to my cunt." Another passes time in men's tea shops and sometimes drapes a man's cloth around her. Others scream at and physically attack their relatives and undress in public.

Given that female insanity manifests itself through shameless, *wasakh* behavior, it is interesting that one *majnūna* is said to have achieved a temporary remission by avoiding contact with anything considered *wasakh* (women making dung cakes, menstruating women, recent mothers, and the like). A local curer had prescribed avoidance, apparently believing that the *majnūna* absorbed the *wasakh* that grew wildly, cancerlike, inside her. Other temporary remissions were achieved by the wearing of special Quranic amulets (reminding one of Ortner's model of Culture, here Islam, battling to control the chaos that is Nature), but sooner or later the amulets were lost and the insanity returned.

Although few of the insane (this includes men) are dangerous, women are fearful of insanity and teach children to share their fears. Adherence to the norms of modesty and decorum is, to a degree, related to the fear and horror of madness. If license is madness, then propriety is safety.

When women deviate from the dominant cultural norm (or even when falsely perceived as having done so), they often pay dearly. Some are divorced and lose their children; others lose the support of fathers and brothers. Folktales illustrate such dangers. Although things eventually work out for the antagonist of the following tale, she must first be humbled for excessive pride and stubborn disobedience:

Tale 4

Every match her father proposed for her, Hindia refused outright. Then the son of a sultan in Sanʿa asked to marry Hindia, but she still refused. When the sultan's son offered to cover every inch of his house and courtyard with raisins if she would marry him, she agreed.

However, she watched through a tiny hole in the sultan's courtyard wall, and when she saw her fiancé eat one of the raisins, she said she would not marry him. Her father pressured her to go on with the marriage, and told her there was no one left for her to marry (since she had already refused all the other men), but she refused. Her father said, "I'm going to marry her to the first stranger who shows his face here. I swear to it."

The next morning the sultan's son approached a stranger and asked him to change clothes with him. Dressed in the stranger's outfit, he went to Hindia's house, knocked on the front door and called out to be given breakfast. Hindia's father called to her to answer the front door with him.

"What should I come down for?" she asked.

He answered, "I swore I'd marry you to the first stranger who came along." Immediately he transferred control of his daughter to the "stranger." He was quite fed up with her since he had had to pay the sultan's son enough money to cover the cost of all the raisins to secure her release.

After the wedding, the "stranger" took Hindia to a horrible, filthy house, and installed her in a dreadful room designed to store grain, firewood or livestock. Every day he gave her nothing but a little bread and *gishr*, while eating well by himself in another room. Eventually Hindia became pregnant.

One day her husband told her that they had been offered a job in the sultan's house and were going to live there. She agreed readily in the hope that she might be given more food there. Once again, she was installed in a dirty little storage room. This was on the first floor of the giant house. Her husband spent most of his time upstairs with his parents and his first wife; Hindia continued to live in privation.

When she gave birth, her mother-in-law took the infant upstairs to be raised in cleanliness and comfort. Every day the mother-in-law prepared special *walada* dishes for Hindia, but Hindia's husband took all of it away. He continued to give her only crusts of bread. Hindia was miserable with hunger and begged him for mercy.

A week later, the first wife of the sultan's son went down to Hindia and invited her to accompany her and her mother-in-law to the public bath. Hindia at first declined but the sultan's son's wife insisted.

When they finished bathing, the two women told Hindia not to put on her old clothes. They gave her a fine dress of theirs to wear. As soon as they left the bath house, musicians appeared to escort them home in a procession. Hindia assumed they were showing deference to the wife and mother of the sultan's son, but while they had been away from the house, a fine reception room had been decorated for Hindia on an upper floor of the house. They took her up the stairs for the first time and installed her in the *walada* room. At last Hindia discovered she was the sultan's son's second wife, and was allowed to assume the position due her in that status.

Hindia is spoiled and excessively proud, qualities strongly disapproved by ᶜAmrani women. She is neither her father's nor her husband's victim. The former forebore her as she refused every offer in marriage; only when she rejected the son of the sultan over a single raisin *after* agreeing to the match did his patience give out. Backing out of a match at this point seriously tarnishes a man's reputation, and, in this case, the financial loss was severe as well. The penance imposed on Hindia by her husband is seen as a rendering of justice for her "sin" of pride. As each privation is told, women chorus satisfiedly: "Pay back for the raisin." "Pay back for the raisin." Only after Hindia has suffered, become thoroughly "de-spoiled," does she ask her husband (whom she still believes to be a lowly, dependent man) for pity. Necessity breaks her pride and forces her to acknowledge her dependency, after which she is rewarded by being allowed to assume her proper place as the second wife of the sultan's son. She becomes eligible for the gratifications of womanhood (a fine dress, a rich reception room in which to celebrate her having given birth, and the company of other women). The listeners to the tale have forgiven Hindia, see her deliverance as just, and are happy for her.

It is usual for the righteous in folktales to show generosity (sooner or later) to those who have wronged them. Only in cases of the gravest of transgressions (for example, the women who murdered her co-wife's son in the tale recounted in chapter 7) is forgiveness withheld. The focus, however, is usually on the virtue of the righteous rather than on the redemption of the wrongdoers. In one tale a wife and husband of the highest moral fiber find it in their hearts to rescue from poverty the wife's two sisters, who had, when wealthy, refused them assistance when they were in the direst of need.

Some righteous victims are saved by divine intervention, but others must take aggressive action to rectify their situations. Although the action may violate dominant cultural norms, it is seen as morally positive. One such tale describes a widow's vengeance on the butcher who cheated her young son out of a calf. She arranges her own marriage to the thief, collects all of his gifts, and then, on the wedding night, beats him to a pulp. With every blow, she tells him she is paying him back for the calf.

This heroine, like monkey-sister (tale 1) and many ʿAmrani women, has no protector. The exigencies of her situation force her to take intelligent, drastic action, and like monkey-sister, she achieves her desired end. Each heroine saves herself and her dependent. However, monkey-sister's solution involved theft and led to the dissolution of a marriage (the breaking of a serious law and hurting an innocent woman), and the widow solved her problem without damaging anyone but the butcher who had wronged her in the first place. She is more a moral heroine. The difference is linked to a perception of sanctity in the maternal role. Recall that Hindia (tale 4) repented her excessive pride and was forgiven only after having become a mother, and that the mothers of the snake-child (tale 2) and the squash-child (tale 3) had their exemplary maternal conduct rewarded in the end by the supernatural transformation of their sons.

The Quran and the Hadiths dwell on the mother-son bond; they emphasize maternal devotion and its rewards. Haddad (1980:75–77) claims that in traditional Arab society the only man a woman can develop a "free love relationship" with is her son. She reviews the writings of recent Islamic apologists, which, like the Yemeni folktales present an idealized picture of the mother-son relationship. Muhammad ʿAtiyyah al-Abrāshī (Haddad 1980:75) for example, writes:

> For the mother has suffered a great deal for her son. Long has she stayed up so he can sleep, and labored and become tired that he may rest, and suffered so he can be happy, gone hungry so he can eat, she put him above herself. Her happiest moment is when she sees him happy, smiling, healthy, intelligent. She is always ready to ransom him with whatever she possesses—no matter what the price. Can the son forget her good deeds?

Most writers on traditional Arab Muslim societies emphasize the power and authority that women gain when their sons become adults and marry (Bybee 1978:226), but, as has been discussed, ʿAmrani women cannot count on their sons to remember and reward their "good deeds." Like mothers in Taroudannt, Morocco (Dwyer 1978:114–15), they use indirection in disciplining their children so as not to jeopardize the image of themselves as "loving, caring, and protective beings." They make profound sacrifices in order to ensure their sons' allegiance, but are constantly plagued with the fear of losing it.

Haddad (1980:76) points out that while Islamic apologists of the past emphasized the superiority of men over women, more recent writers describe the sex roles as complementary—different but equal. They focus on the importance and value of motherhood, and, as in the quote from al-Abrāshī above, offer assurance that maternal virtue will not go unrewarded. Those who advocate increased social and political rights for women are described as going against Islam. Maqdād Yālgin (Haddad 1980:77), for example, argues that "the decrease in the woman's responsibility does not mean a decrease in her worth. Justice means that each should do what is best for him and this is what Islam has decreed." Haddad (1980:76) ponders the motives of the modern apologists:

> One wonders whether the shift in emphasis in contemporary literature from the superiority of the male per se to an analysis of differences and an affirmation of religious models for the roles of women is an attempt to maintain a status quo in the society that is changing rapidly, or whether it is a traditionally Islamic attempt at recapturing an "idealized reality" in a situation of flux.

Whereas some of ʿAmrani women's folktales are "conservative" in the sense that they perpetuate an idealization of the mother-son relationship (devotion repaid by devotion), few of the heroines are passive. They are women who assess their dilemmas and find effective solutions. Even when the solutions involve serious transgressions of moral and social codes, they are evaluated positively.

The "justice" of the Islamic sexual code requires that men, who earn money and control public affairs, provide for and protect women, whose dominion is the home. ʿAmrani women, however, know that even the most virtuous among them risk unjust treatment from their fathers, brothers, husbands, and sons. The Islamic model, whatever its appeal, does not always obtain in real life. As women remain cut off from all but a few minimally remunerative economic opportunities and are excluded entirely from public, political activities, they are obliged to do all within their power to protect their relationships with those on whom they count for support.

Dependency sometimes leads them to act against other women (most often their mother-in-law, daughter-in-law, or co-wife), but it does not cause a perception of weakness. Relations with women who do not threaten their security tend to be supportive.

As discussed, women have reciprocal relations and a female public domain that crosscut economic and traditional status divisions. These ties with other women are valued extremely highly. The ensuing female solidarity (which I define, following Llewelyn-Davies [1978:206], as "a commitment to some kind of mutual aid or support, based upon the perception, by those who are solidary, that they share certain significant characteristics, or that they are equal with respect to some social principle") is invaluable to women on both practical and emotional levels. It allows women to learn each others' strategies, share countervaluations, and acquire and disseminate useful information; but ʿAmrani women's solidarity does not challenge the existing social order. Women do not unite in an attempt to increase their rights, but rather to voice their distinctive concerns, to feel understood and "at one," and to gain the emotional support that enables them to carry on in their disadvantaged situations at home. However, by watching television programs from Egypt and Syria, the women of ʿAmran have learned that in more modern Arab Muslim countries women go unveiled, experience romantic love, receive an education, and work along with men. Some are beginning to think of the restrictions upon their lives as not so much "natural" or "Islamic," but as due to the backwardness of Yemen. Whether the female solidarity they now enjoy will be utilized to alter the social institutions that sustain their dependence upon men remains to be seen.

11

Conclusions

> [The fieldworker] believes in cross-cultural communion (he calls it "rapport") as his subjects believe in tomorrow. It is no wonder that so many anthropologists leave the field seeing tears in the eyes of their informants that I feel quite sure, are not really there. (Geertz 1968:151)

> When I came to Selma, . . . she smiled politely in a set way and then as I smiled back, her face changed and she threw her arms around me and cried aloud. At this my own reserve broke and I found myself weeping, passing from one abayah-clad figure to another in a welter of embraces and tears. (Fernea 1969:331)

Geertz calls our attention to the enormous cultural gap between anthropologist and informant. Jay (1974:371–72) argues that a primary obstacle to real rapport is the intent of traditional anthropological research. He discusses the research of Ruben Reina (1954) in Guatemala:

> In the field, Reina and his wife, by his report, did what they could to discourage the Indians they got to know from forming close friendships with them in order to avoid the difficulties, personal and professional, of their demands and jealousies, and succeeded by and large in keeping themselves neutral. They struggled to overcome the pressure for an exclusive relationship that some of their informants put on them by trying to explain their position, but managed mostly only to mystify and alienate those would-be friends. I might very well have been driven to the same means, with probably no better success, but I have come to think that the aloofness so achieved for the sake of efficient field work carries as its price a loss of knowledge which anthropologists generally do not seem willing to admit.

Few readers of Fernea's *Guests of the Sheikh* would doubt that there was rapport and intimacy between her and her close friends and informants. Fernea claims that her original object in wanting to get to know women was to help her husband with his research, but the relationships she formed came to be of emotional importance to her and to her informant-friends. Although the cultural gap was not obliterated, there is a sense in which it was transcended. When the Ferneas returned briefly to El Nahra after three months in the capital, she found that the room her hostesses had prepared for her was full of Western furnishings:

> For a moment I did not know what to say. I was moved by the women's thoughtfulness and concern for my comfort. I was also struck, for some reason, by the armchair. How I had fought, long ago, to sit on the floor with the women rather than in that lonely armchair in Haji's room. My friends, in trying to provide for my needs, had again pointed up the basic dissimilarities in habits which would always exist between us. But now it no longer mattered. I felt they had prepared the room and made it comfortable for me out of mutual respect and affection, and beside that reality, our differences seemed unimportant. (Fernea 1969:319–20)

It may be that a woman, studying women who are little accustomed to social distance, has no choice but to approach her subject in a personal way. It may also be true that some female researchers, if not fully resocialized into neutrality and objectivity by their training, are themselves more inclined than male researchers are to value rapport and intimacy. As with any choice, whether conscious or inadvertent, there are gains and losses. Jay (1974:372) writes, "the relationship we form with the subjects of our work—for whatever reasons we settle upon those relationships—controls the kind of knowledge that the material we gain will yield." The rapport-seeking researcher gains more personal knowledge, but often must sacrifice other, equally important kinds of data that are available to others who keep their distance.

Geertz (1976:224) claims that although ethnographers cannot hope to perceive what their subjects perceive, they should aspire to understand the systems of meaning *with* which or *through* which they perceive. When the subjects are members of a subordinate group, the researchers have to adjust their methods to the special problem of discovering muted or counterpart models (see chapter 1). Bujra (1975:553), who apparently did not, states that she had much less success eliciting information from women than from men. If, as she claims, her female informants "were less articulate, less straightforward, and less coherent," this probably reflects women's disadvantage at expressing themselves through the dominant cultural model. S. Ardener (1978:21) suggests that members of muted groups often have to "re-encode their thoughts to make them understood in the public domain." If the researcher removes herself from the public domain and identifies herself with the muted group, she may find her subjects to be forthcoming, lucid, and amply articulate. The suggestion made by a member of the London Women's Anthropology Group that "in most societies women were simply not trained to express themselves in speech or to concentrate on topics other than repetitive domestic ones" (Bujra 1975:553) is as absurd as it is offensive.

Narrowing our focus, we can safely assume that the endurance of the image of Arab Muslim women as being totally victimized results from most researchers' exclusive attention to dominant cultural models. There is no doubt that Arab Muslim societies are characterized by marked sexual stratification, but a delineation of the restrictions upon women tells us only part of the story of their lives. By looking at women's own perspectives and discovering their muted and counterpart models, we gain both a more realistic sense of them as persons and a fuller understanding of the societies of which they are an active, vital part.

As Fernea and Bezirgan (1977:xviii) point out, false western stereotypes will not be overcome unless we stop projecting and start listening to what Arab Muslim women have to say about themselves and their lives. They write that

> the Middle Eastern woman might well agree with Marcel Proust, who wrote more than a half century ago that "the image that other people form of our actions and behavior is no more like that which we form ourselves than an original drawing is like a spoiled copy, in which, at one point, for a blank line, we find an empty gap, and for a blank space, an unaccountable contour."

Even the writings of Arab feminists often present a distorted picture of the women whose lives they strive to improve. As highly educated women and men, they may be as blind (perhaps in some cases deliberately) as Westerners to the ways in which less-privileged women experience their lives. For example, in Nabawiyya Musa's argument (Mikhail 1979:31) for the education of Egyptian townswomen, she describes the latters' lives as "closer to non-life (death)," their minds corroded by the rust of "idleness and lethargy." While Musa's good intentions are clear, her depiction of uneducated townswomen is condescending and unfair.

Nawal al-Saadawy (Mikhail 1979:45) offers an illuminating analysis of the ways in which Islamic ideology supports sexual inequality, but the tactics she advises women to utilize are totally unrealistic for the majority of Arab Muslim women. Like Musa, she feels that women must be allowed to enter the work force. A woman, in al-Saadawy's opinion, is better off giving up her marriage than her work outside the house if she is forced to choose between the two:

> Any of the sacrifices made by a woman to continue working outside the home are, in my opinion, much less than the ones made by staying at home and resigning herself to the same fate as that of her mother and grandmothers. These sacrifices will not go beyond the husband's wrath, which may lead to a failure in the married life. This failure is less harmful to a woman than the failure in life in general, and losing herself between the walls of home.

The difficulty with this solution is that few nonelite women can find adequately remunerative employment, and fewer still would value their jobs higher than their roles as wives and mothers. (See Mohsen [1985] and Rugh [1985] for discussions of Egyptian working women's evaluations of their family and extradomestic roles.) At least, this is the case for the Yemen Arab Republic. Makhlouf (1979:57–59), whose research was on upper- and middle-class Sanʿani women, found her subjects to have little or no interest in the Yemeni Women's Association, an organization dedicated to advancing female literacy and ameliorating women's position in marriage and the family. She suggests that the value of the association's goals might appear "basic and obvious" from the point of view of society at large, but this is "not self-evident to the individual uneducated woman." The organization was floundering when Makhlouf did her original research in 1974 and was closed down when she returned to Sanʿa in 1976. Sanʿani women, especially those of the higher classes, are infinitely more modern and sophisticated than the women of ʿAmran. Yet most see the structure

Their paths crossing, a fully veiled woman walks toward town while a man rides his donkey in the opposite direction to a nearby village.

and objectives of the Yemeni Women's Association as unnecessary or irrelevant to their primary concerns. As Makhlouf suggests, Yemeni women's noninvolvement in reformist action is partly explained by the satisfaction they derive from their traditional social groupings, but it is also due to their evaluation of at least some of the restrictions upon them as benevolent in intent. S. Ardener (1978:29) notes that "among all the different mechanisms which 'keep women in their place' perhaps the most effective is the notion that the place is designed for their own good and that of their families."

ᶜAmrani women's values derive both from Islamic and tribal ethos and from their separate female domain and distinctive concerns. As discussed in the preceding chapter the strategies and self-definitions related to the latter domain only partially overlap with those derived from the former.

ᶜAmrani women would like to count on the support and protection of men. They have ample reason to fear, however, that the men in their lives may not support and protect them as the idealized code prescribes. Women are not so much critical of the code itself but, rather, are skeptical about men's adherence to it. Given men's tendency to deviate (and the absence of enforceable formal sanctions), it is expected that women must do so as well. Women generally disapprove of wholesale gratuitous violation of the female code of conduct, but they support and celebrate morally justified deviation. The laudable deviant's goal is not to overthrow the code or engender chaos in men's affairs but simply to protect herself and her dependents.

ᶜAmran is in an in-between and conflicted position vis-à-vis tradition and modernization in Yemen. Not unlike small towns elsewhere, it is in many ways more conservative than Yemen's large cities and her villages. In the latter, veiling is more casual, often forgone altogether; chewing *gāt* and smoking the water pipe are acceptable female activities. Whereas village women's physical mobility is necessitated by their chores and unproblematic because of the close ties between households, many women in Yemen's large cities enjoy greater mobility because of the anonymity of big-city life. They can make their own purchases, use public transportation, and speak out in sexually mixed public settings without fear of damaging their reputations or eliciting the anger of husbands or kinsmen.

Although many still veil heavily, others veil lightly, intermittently, or not at all (Makhlouf 1979:33-38). Sanᶜani women commonly chew *gāt* and smoke the water pipe. Furthermore, married couples occasionally go out together to picnic, view a parade, or shop. This is never done in ᶜAmran. Lastly, female educational and employment opportunities in the major cities far exceed those in ᶜAmran.

Most ᶜAmrani women are pleased that they do not have to work nearly as hard or as long as village women do. They would not trade the ease, comfort, and cleanliness of their town life for the lesser restrictions of village women. Many, however, are attracted by the expanded opportunities and comforts of women in the capital, and consider some, but not all, Sanᶜani ways better than their own. They disapprove, however, of laxness in veiling and think that jobs requiring a woman to go unveiled are not worth the cost in honor. Yet, most women are relatively uncritical of the women originally from ᶜAden or the southern region of North Yemen who forgo veils and work among men, recognizing the greater permissiveness of their traditions.

Very few ᶜAmrani women develop a clear idea of life in the capital. Most who return to ᶜAmran after having lived in Sanᶜa express relief to be home again. They describe Sanᶜani women as snobbish and say they suffered from isolation and loneliness while away, thus conveying to those who never left ᶜAmran that life is essentially better at home despite the greater ease, glamour, and sophistication of the big city. In fact, as Myntti (1979:71) has pointed out, city women, particularly in the newer housing areas where most migrants from the countryside live, have very limited social opportunities and, thus, compared to rural women "have a less pleasant life, and indeed, a less informed one."

Even less do ᶜAmrani women know of life in socialist South Yemen, where, in contrast to North Yemen, "there have been substantial changes in the position of women as a result of the revolution" (Molyneux 1979:6). They are unaware of the People's Democratic Republic of Yemen's activities through a Women's Union to educate, train, and employ women or of its reformist Family Code that places a near ban on polygyny, abolishes divorce by repudiation, and gives divorced women custody of their children. Rather, the propaganda to which they and ᶜAmrani men are exposed about South Yemen centers on the irreconcilability of socialism and Islam and the government usurpation of private property and intrusion into household affairs. Like men, they are hostile to and afraid of the government of the People's Democratic Republic of Yemen and the possibility of its growing influence on their own national government. In any case, the push to employ women in South Yemen is as related to a labor shortage (caused by male labor migration) as it is to a commitment to the emancipation of women (Halliday 1979:9; Ahmed 1982a:166). Because no serious efforts have been made to restructure relations between the sexes at home, South Yemeni working women have become like women in more advanced postcapitalist societies who "face the full burden of domestic labor on top of their new extra-domestic jobs: the double shift" (Halliday 1979:9). Given North Yemeni women's high evaluation of leisure and socializing, they would be unlikely to envy the situation of working women to the south. In Myntti's discussion (1984:15) of the effects of labor migration on women in a village in the southern Huggariya district of the YAR, it is clear that increased remittances in the 1970s have resulted in lighter work loads for the majority of women and a heightened evaluation of "leisure and home-bound activities." ꜥAmrani women almost without exception celebrate the reduction in their work load made possible by technological advances and purchase of imported goods, valuing particularly the greatly expanded opportunities for participating in female visiting networks. If, however, as Myntti suggests, North Yemen's economic boom is over, the trend toward increased female leisure may by necessity be reversed. Thanks to the discovery of oil in 1984, an intensification of the trend appears more likely. Women's lives in the 1990s may become similar to those of women in neighboring oil states.

The few ꜥAmrani women who recognize a need for greater educational and economic opportunities for women see themselves, and conduct themselves, as above and apart from ꜥAmrani female society. Consequently, their effectiveness as agents of change is limited. ꜥAmrani women resent being told what to do or being the objects of condescension. Given their proud, independent spirit, the high value placed on leisure and socializing and the limited exposure to alternative styles of existence for women, ꜥAmrani women can be expected to lag far behind the vanguard of any movement for the improvement of female rights that might develop in Yemen. Only if future advocates of change learn to present themselves in a more egalitarian, less overbearing manner and if the advantages of female education and employment are well conveyed to school children of both sexes, might a climate conducive to these changes develop in ᶜAmran.

The study of women of the Arab world has advanced over the last decade, but "we are still at the stage of exploring the tip of the iceberg" (Rassam 1984b:123). Recent research reveals considerable variation and complexity. We know a lot more than we did, but fundamental confusions endure. Clearly, sexual assymetry is pronounced in Arab countries, and it is not at all certain whether women's situation has always improved with socioeconomic development. Fernea (1985:2) tells us that "no longer is the example of the West seen as the answer to the problems of the Middle East." The recent trend among Egyptian university women to abandon Western dress for modest Muslim garb is just one illustration of Fernea's point. A large part of our difficulty understanding Arab women comes from perceiving them and their societies through ethnocentric Western constructs. We assume that the greater the extent of female exclusion from the public arena, the worse off women are. Yet, Ahmed (1982b) argues convincingly that when sexual segregation includes a separate female social world (as opposed to the case where women are kept apart from other women and totally under male control), women develop exceptional psychological strengths precisely because of their togetherness with other women. It is in the societies of the Arabian Peninsula that the separate female domain has been most fully developed. Speaking here of Saudi Arabia, Ahmed (1982b:528) claims:

> Although in its explicit formulations, Saudi society gives individual men control over individual women, nevertheless, the *shape* of that society allows men considerably less control over how women think, how they see and discuss themselves, and how they see and discuss men. Saudi society would seem to offer men less control than Western society [does], where women live dispersed and isolated among men.

Ahmed emphatically acknowledges that women of the Arabian Peninsula are subject to male authority and deplores the fact that they "generally have no control, except in the most circumscribed ways, over their own lives" (1982b:531). In no way an apologist for Islam, Ahmed is alerting us to the multiple dimensions and ambiguity of Arab women's lives.

This book presents a balanced account of the lives of women in one of the most traditional, underdeveloped countries of the Middle East. We have seen that ʿAmrani women derive psychological strength and emotional well-being both from their competent performance of clearly defined roles and from their extensive and intensive interaction with other women, despite the profound power differential between them and ʿAmrani men. They do not see themselves as men's moral or intellectual inferiors, and they are both freely critical of male failings and supportive of female moral deviance when male neglect or abuse necessitates it. Far from conforming to Western notions of the passive, vacuous victim behind the veil, they are, with few exceptions, strong, vital, self-confident women, abundantly capable of pursuing their own ends within the limits set for them and deriving great satisfaction from their lives.

Notes

Chapter 2. HISTORICAL BACKGROUND AND SOCIAL SETTING

1. Scholars disagree on whether Yemeni strata are best treated as classes or castes and on the order in which they should be ranked. According to Gerholm (1977:107):

> Some strata are defined by their occupation, others by their descent. . . . There is *no single* principle which could account for the levels of hierarchy in Yemen. To reduce them to an effect of either the division of labor or the division of ancestry misrepresents what I take to be the fundamental structure of Yemen society: the interlocking of tribes with two non-tribal institutions, the *suq* [market] and the *hijra* [sacred enclaves administered by a religious aristocracy that enjoyed the respect and protection of the tribes].

Gerholm (1977:108) criticizes those scholars who have described a rigid ranking of strata. There is, he claims, a real ambiguity in the relations between tribesmen and nontribal townspeople, which often leaves room for individual manipulation or "a subtle struggle over which definition is to prevail."

2. Most *sāda* were and still are very far from affluent. Some, but not all of those who were wealthy, have lost much or all of their fortune. However, even though *sāda* lost ascriptive access to high position, because of their established educational advantages they are still highly represented in government and other influential positions (Gerholm 1977:124).

Chapter 3. FIELDWORK: COLLECTING AND CONNECTING

1. The schedule covered areas such as ages at first marriage (pre- or postmenarche); bride-price received; separations (number, causes, resolutions); divorces (own and husband's); number of pregnancies, live births, surviving children; household composition; relations with parents, siblings, children, other kin, in-laws; and economic assets and sources of independent income.

Chapter 5. DAUGHTERS AND SONS

1. According to the Quran (Sura IV:23): "Forbidden to you are . . . your mothers who have given suck to you, your suckling sisters" (Arberry 1955, 1:103). A few

ʿAmrani women may have deliberately nursed the babies of their husbands' brothers to prevent a marriage between *ʿayāl ʿamm* (patrilateral parallel cousins). Although this form of marriage is usually seen as desirable, some women who dislike their in-laws try to avoid it.

2. Ethnocentrically concerned that infants might receive psychological damage from having their screams ignored, I asked in perhaps less than neutral tones about this practice. The answers were consistent: "I washed and fed and swaddled and dressed him, and waited until he fell asleep. I locked the door so his brothers and sisters can't get in and wake him or harm him. If he was sick or had refused to sleep, of course I would have stayed home with him."

When babies did awaken, their mothers usually saw it as unfortunate, but only mildly so. One woman's contrition was mixed with amusement as she told me that she arrived home to find the baby drenched with tears and perspiration. "Poor little thing woke up and cried and cried and sweated and no one was here."

3. This can be avoided, one woman told her pregnant daughter, by placing the new baby, the instant after it is born, on the naked back of his older brother. A powerful emotional bond will be created that prevents jealousy. The daughter seriously considered the suggestion, but feared that her young son would be dangerously *aftajʿa* (startled, frightened) by the blood and placenta. (*Aftajʿa* is a common cause of illness.) She did not implement the plan.

4. In Sanʿa where female education is taken more seriously among the upper classes, there are marked social differences between students and their older female kin. At afternoon gatherings the latter prefer visiting in a room apart from the others, and appear uncomfortable when joined by a married woman. Some students try to get out of paying formal visits altogether (Makhlouf 1979:73–75).

Chapter 6. Marriage: Arrangements, Celebrations and Consummation

1. Aswad (1967), Friedl (1967), and others discuss the importance of such informal female roles. Chinas (1973:108) describes the overt and covert nonformalized roles of Isthmus Zapotec (Mexico) women as valuable to both sexes. They "function to maintain the integrity of the household, to avoid conflict and violence, and more generally, to add oil to the social machinery."

2. The decision-making power of males and females is similarly unequal in Morocco (Maher 1974:164; Dwyer 1978:23–29). As in ʿAmran, in Taroudannt, southern Morocco, formerly married women have more of a voice than virgins. Makhlouf (1979:40) makes the same point for Sanʿa and quotes the Yemeni proverb: "Your first marriage is made by your parents, the second by yourself."

3. This fear was treated in a 1974 Sanʿa radio play, which propagandized in support of a government attempt to limit the maximum amount for marriage payments. It dealt with a woman who was afraid her husband was going to take advantage of the decree to take a second wife. "The moral of the story was that so long as a woman satisfies her husband and has a good relationship with him, he would not want another wife" (Makhlouf 1979:64). This perspective has not yet taken hold among ʿAmran women.

4. I asked a woman, whose fourteen-year-old daughter was soon to marry, what a bride does if she needs to relieve herself. She replied that this was no problem. "The bride simply descends from her platform, holds the *ṭarḥa* out enough so she can see downward and climbs and crawls over the guests and out of the reception

room. She pees and then comes right back. This is not at all shameful, not at all."
A little later, she turned to address her daughter in a half-serious, half-joking tone: "At your *mashjab*, don't you dare get down from the platform to go pee!" Later, she added in a clearly joking manner that the daughter need not worry, as she would have an empty can on her platform in case of emergency.

5. The announcements of the groom's gifts are also recorded when they are presented to him on the actual wedding day. Both recordings are replayed frequently by the bride and groom and by their relatives, partly for the pleasure of reliving the great events but also to learn and memorize the amount of each and every gift received.

6. See Chelhod (1973b) for a description of the procession and other aspects of male wedding celebrations in ᶜAmran and other parts of the Yemen Arab Republic.

7. In an exchange marriage between an ᶜAmran and a distant village family, each bride, accompanied only by a *muzayyina*, set off in the other's direction at a prearranged time. When the two cars met up, roughly halfway between the town and the village, the brides switched places. Each one, then, was required to enter her groom's house accompanied only by a *muzayyina* whom she had just met.

8. In a nearby town the bride will not enter her husband's house unless the neck of a freshly slaughtered animal is placed at the doorway for her to walk over. She steps over a dagger or automatic rifle as well.

9. This pattern is altered when one of the married couple is a virgin and the other not, since the former must be protected from supernatural contamination by the latter. The polluted one cannot stand above the virgin (just as an adult who is contaminated by various circumstances cannot stand above an infant until the infant is lifted over her/his head three times). If the bride is the virgin, she stands on her platform when the groom enters, or he meets her outside the front door of the house, so they may enter it at the same level. In one case of a virgin groom and a previously married bride, dirt was dropped on the bride's head from the rooftop as she first entered her husband's house. This act was also described as a decontamination measure.

10. The verb used to indicate the bride's loss of virginity is the same as or similar to that used in this morning greeting. Informants frequently point out the oddness of the morning salutation at this time. I never asked if a pun was intended, but think that may be the case.

11. Informants from a northern village say that in their area there is a public display of the bloody cloth at which kinsmen of the bride celebrate by firing automatic rifles. Informants from Taᶜiz (a large, relatively modern southern city) say that no one but the bride's mother sees the evidence there.

12. Informants say that about twenty-five years ago an unmarried village woman who lived in ᶜAmran became pregnant, and was brought before the *shaykh*, who banished her to her village for ten years, after which she returned to town. Now, they say, traditional and modern birth control techniques prevent many unwanted pregnancies. While one newborn infant corpse was found in a well, infanticide is considered extremely rare. Unmarried mothers carefully swaddle the newborn infant, and place it where it is sure to be discovered promptly. They sometimes attach money and/or a note to the covers. It is considered a blessing to raise a foundling (*lugṭa*).

13. On several occasions I was the not-so-innocuous family representative. I was eager to interview brides as soon as possible after their wedding night, and their mothers were even more eager for news of their daughters' adjustment. We were perfectly matched. Mothers assured me, "It's not ᶜ*ayb* for you to go since you're a

foreigner. Go ahead. Don't worry what people might say." The women of the grooms' household may have been unhappy to find me at their door, but politeness required that I be allowed to see the bride.

14. The spell is broken most quickly when the bride is inept at the prescribed dance style. Tradition requires that the bride open her *sābʿa* with the local dance, but most girls prefer the Sanʿa style of dancing and never master the ʿAmran style. Later in the afternoon the bride does dance the Sanʿa dance, unless she is also inept at that. If she can't dance at all, women are heard murmuring hopes that her talents for baking bread exceed her talents for dancing.

Chapter 7. MARRIAGE: RELATIONS AND CONFLICT

1. The data in this chapter are based primarily on the life histories of a few close informants and on the same informants' generalizations about conjugal relations in ʿAmran. The informants themselves point out that they do not really *know* about other women's sex lives, mainly because it is considered vulgar for a woman to discuss her sex life with others. Most women confide only in one or two intimate friends. Consequently, generalizations are not easy to make. Women joke about sex in informal (i.e., neighborhood) and even in more formal (i.e., wedding party) settings, but the jokes rarely reveal the teller's own sexual experience. Some women disapprove of such joking. They say that at Sanʿa women's gatherings, sex is never discussed. According to one informant, the disapproval of sexual topics was increased by my presence. There was a legitimate concern that "Susan will write all this down later!" On one occasion, a neighbor and I had each come separately to a large women's party in a remote part of town, and were not sitting near each other. My neighbor addressed a woman who had just returned with her husband from a trip to Cairo. "*Yā* Fatima, did your husband do it to you all day long? Wasn't he excited by seeing all those gorgeous unveiled women?" While many of those present laughed at the joke, a few told her to shut up and gestured meaningfully in my direction. They still wore kid gloves in their relations with me, and were shocked at my neighbor's apparent unconcern at my presence.

2. Keddie (1979:239) has suggested looking at sexual relationships as a microcosm of the general male-female relationship and has urged anthropologists studying Middle Eastern women to pursue this area of inquiry. Given the small number of ʿAmran informants on the subject of sex, any inference from my data must be extremely cautious. Their accounts clearly suggest, however, a more egalitarian pattern than might be expected for the culture area. Discussions of sexuality are very scarce in the literature on the Middle East, one exception being Vieille's article on Iran (1978:451–72). Iranian men, according to Vieille, are completely dominant in sexual relations and do not caress their partners before or during intercourse. Whether the differences between ʿAmran and Iran are real or simply reflect the fact that my informants were female and his most likely male is unfortunately impossible to determine.

3. None are serious about killing their husbands. Murder is perpetrated almost exclusively by men in ʿAmran. Most informants know of no female murderers, but a few spoke of a village *muzayyina* who long ago stabbed her husband to death. They think she was publicly executed but are uncertain of the veracity of the entire story.

4. The upper- and middle-class Sanʿani women studied by Makhlouf (1979:41)

appear to have considerably greater power than ʿAmrani women to terminate unwanted marriages. Through a father or brother a Sanʿani woman can become divorced by the court if the husband is unable to support her, if he is unjust to cowives, or is mentally ill or physically impaired. One ʿAmrani woman mentioned the possibility of the court granting a woman a divorce, but said this had not actually occurred in ʿAmran.

Chapter 8. Pregnancy, Birth, and Motherhood

1. Dwyer (1978:120–21) writes that in Taroudannt, Morocco, food cravings originate in the fetus: "What the foetus desires, the mother also desires." She recounts a folktale in which a butcher virtuously gives a pregnant woman the meat she craves. The woman's husband, however, becomes suspicious and enraged. When he slits open her stomach, "he finds his child with a piece of the butcher's liver still in its teeth." The righteousness of his wife was further proven:

> When the washers of the dead came for the dead woman's body, they found that it was gone. In the woman's place, they found a pair of silver scissors, the ones that the angels had used to cut her garments for the afterlife. They had left them behind as a sign that she had been taken directly to heaven, for she had done no earthly wrong.

2. Because of the secrecy about labor, I observed only one birth. The woman informed me at about six in the evening that her *lahīb* was intensifying. She suggested I go home and give my husband dinner, then return to her house at nine or half past nine. She told me to plan on spending the night, as she wasn't sure the birth would take place early enough for me to return home alone. As it turned out, I was home, and her baby born, by midnight.

3. Wives of merchants sometimes peddle their husbands' wares and some widows make a meager living off sales at women's gatherings. As discussed earlier, women are expected to avoid the *sūq* to a large degree. It is only through female sellers that most women can learn what is for sale and make purchases. They are often willing to pay the slightly higher price for the service and because, they say, most of the saleswomen have no source of income besides these transactions.

4. Also, on the thirtieth day after the birth, the women of the *walada*'s father's or brothers' household prepare lunch for the entire *walada*'s household. They deliver the lunch but do not always stay and eat with them. Sometimes there is a small *ḥalāfa* for female guests. From this day until the end of the postpartum confinement the *walada*'s father or brother is duty bound to provide all of her special food.

5. Aswad (1974, 1978) describes female visiting practices in Hatay, Turkey, which also operate on the principle of balanced reciprocity. There are differences, however. In Hatay, each member of the visiting system has a monthly reception day, whereas ʿAmrani women receive guests formally only in relation to the life crises of birth, marriage, and death. Furthermore, in Hatay only upper- and middle-class women (primarily the former) engage in these visiting practices; in ʿAmran all women do so. In ʿAmran, visiting crosscuts both traditional "status" and socioeconomic divisions and, according to all informants, has always done so. (In Khamir, a small town to the north of ʿAmran, the visiting patterns differ; lower-rank women call on higher-rank women, but the latter never return the visits.)

6. Dwyer (1978:114) believes that mothers in Taroudannt, Morocco, are fearful of losing the love and loyalty of their children. She suggests that the practice of threatening children with outside forces (like the ʿAmrani mother's boogeyman) is used to protect their image and relationship to their children.

Chapter 9. NEIGHBORS AND FRIENDSHIPS

1. It will be recalled that not only do ʿAmrani women interact closely with neighbors of all strata, their reciprocal visiting relationships cross-cut "status" lines as well. There is an equalizing tendency in this contrasting with the situation in Khamir, a northerly town which is the seat of the Hashid tribal confederation. In Khamir, *gabili* and *sayyid* women receive formal visits from women of the lower strata but never return them. Still, the equalization in ʿAmran should not be overstated. It does not appear to approach situations described elsewhere. Among poor, urban neighborhood friends in Lebanon (Joseph 1978:548–49), there is a norm of "total sharing"; friendships "become fragile" when one friend's economic situation improves over the other's. In an Arab village in Israel (Rosenfeld 1974), women have no hierarchies outside the household. Female reciprocity reflects equality between women in contrast to male reciprocity, reflecting men's hierarchical relations.

2. As "white lies" are endemic, the line between acceptable and unacceptable untruthfulness is not sharply drawn. It is perhaps because women are so dependent upon their reciprocal relations that they dissemble rather than refuse invitations or requests outright. They do so to avoid giving offense. In some social situations (when terminating a formal visit early, for example) politeness requires dishonesty. When I began to use the stock excuses available to me, friends and neighbors expressed amused approval that I was learning how to behave like them. They never called attention to my "white lies" in public settings, however, for doing so is rudeness toward dissembler and hostesses alike.

There is no doubt, however, that some women are thought to carry mendacity too far. They always have a reason why they cannot reciprocate and don't bother to offer a plausible excuse. Some lie about those who are thought to be close friends. Their stories are heard with interest, but they, as women, are judged.

Glossary

ᶜāgal   Rationality, responsibility, the ability to behave appropriately.

ᶜaūgari   A bizarre animal that is believed to enter the womb during pregnancy.

ᶜayāl ᶜamm   Literally, "father's brothers' children," the term may be extended beyond actual cousins to include any relatives on the father's side.

ᶜayn   Evil eye.

bint   Girl, unmarried woman, daughter of _____.

bint ᶜamm   Father's brother's daughter.

dawshān   A "poetic messenger," the bottom subgroup in the low-status *muzayyin* stratum.

gabīlī (m), *gabīliya* (f), *gabā'il* (pl)   Tribesman, tribeswoman, tribespeople; may sometimes have both complimentary and derogatory meanings simultaneously.

gahwa ghuda   Women's early afternoon visiting period.

gargūsh, *garāgush* (pl)   Bonnet worn by babies and by never-married girls and women.

gāt   *Catha edulis*, a shrub cultivated for its succulent leaves, which are chewed, producing a sense of euphoria.

ghāwi   Not having developed the ability to use reason or act responsibly; immature.

gishr   Coffee husks or the beverage brewed from them.

guriyya   Literally, a village; in ᶜAmran used to refer to the former Jewish quarter.

ḥākam   A judge schooled in Islamic law.

ḥalāfa   A special meal served to invited male guests, usually as part of a rite of passage.

ḥanag (vb), *ḥanagat* (adj)   The return of a wife to her father's house or otherwise leaving her husband's house; generally in response to maltreatment.

ḥarīwa   A bride.

ibn ᶜamm   Father's brother's son.

imam   Prior to the revolution, the political and religious head of state selected from among the *sāda*.

mahr   Portion of the bride-pride designated for, although not always given to, the bride.

majnūn (m), *majnūna* (f)   A crazy or insane person.

mashjab   Daylong prewedding party, one held at the bridegroom's home, another at the bride's home.

mawlid   A gathering where Quranic passages are recited.

muzayyin (m), *muzayyina* (f)   A member of the "barber-circumciser" social stratum; also female singer and wedding specialist from this group; a derogatory term applied to all low-status people associated with the marketplace or service trade.

rifd   Wedding gifts.

riyal   Unit of currency; one *riyal* equals US $.22.

sayyid, *sāda* (pl)   Descendents of ᶜAli, Muhammad's nephew from whom the imams of Yemen were elected; the social stratum associated with religious ancestry and expertise.

sharīfa   Honorable and respectable; also conventionally used when applied to a female *sayyid*.

sharshaf   Sanᶜa-style two-piece outer garment, worn by ᶜAmrani women for dressy occasions and trips to the capital.

shart   Bride-price.

shaykh   Tribal leader.

shikma   New bride's approximately weeklong visit with her relatives following first month of marriage.

sūq   Marketplace.

tūdara   Women's primary visiting period between the midafternoon and evening prayers.

ᶜūd   A lute.

walada   A new mother.

wasakh (m), *wasakha* (f)   Literally, dirty, filthy, improper, unrefined.

zamān   The past.

Bibliography

ʿAbd al-ʿAti, Hammudah
    1977   *The family structure of Islam*. American Trust Publications.
al-Abdin, al-Tayib Zein
    1975   The role of Islam in the state: Yemen Arab Republic 1940–1972. Ph.D. diss., Cambridge University.
Abdul-Rauf, Muhammed
    1977   *The Islamic view of women and the family*. New York: Robert Speller and Sons.
al-Abrāshī, Muhammad ʿAtiyyah
    1970   *Makanat al-mar'ah fi al-Islām*. Cairo.
Ahmed, Leila
    1982a   Feminism and feminist movements in the Middle East, a preliminary exploration: Turkey, Egypt, Algeria, People's Democratic Republic of Yemen. In *Women and Islam*, ed. Azizah al-Hibri, 153–68. Oxford: Pergamon Press.
    1982b   Western ethnocentrism and perceptions of the harem. *Feminist Studies* 8(3):521–34.
Ali, Parveen Shaukat
    1975   *Status of women in the Muslim world: A study in the feminist movements in Turkey, Egypt, Iran and Pakistan*. Lahore: Aziz Publishers.
Ammar, Hamed
    1954   *Growing up in an Egyptian village*. New York: Octagon Books.
Antoun, Richard T.
    1968   On the modesty of women in Arab villages. *American Anthropologist* 70:671–97.
    1972   *Arab village: A social structural study of a Transjordanian village*. Bloomington: Indiana University Press.
Arberry, A. J., trans.
    1955   *The Koran interpreted*. 2 vols. New York: The Macmillan Company.
Ardener, Edwin
    1972   Belief and the problem of women. In *Interpretation of ritual*, ed. J. S. LaFontaine. London: Tavistock Publications. Reprinted 1975 in *Perceiving women*, ed. S. Ardener, 1–17. London: Malaby Press.

Bibliography

Ardener, Shirley (cont.)
- 1975   The "problem" revisited. In *Perceiving women*, ed. S. Ardener, 19–27. London: Malaby Press.

Ardener, Shirley
- 1975   Introduction. In *Perceiving women*, ed. S. Ardener, vii–xxiii. London: Malaby Press.
- 1978   Introduction: The nature of women in society. In *Defining females*, ed. S. Ardener, 9–48. New York: Wiley and Sons.

Aswad, Barbara C.
- 1967   Key and peripheral roles of noble women in a Middle Eastern plains village. *Anthropological Quarterly* 40:139–52.
- 1974   Visiting patterns among women of the elite in a small Turkish city. *Anthropological Quarterly* 47:9–27.
- 1978   Women, class, and power: Examples from the Hatay, Turkey. In *Women in the Muslim world*, ed. L. Beck and N. Keddie, 473–81. Cambridge: Harvard University Press.

Barakat, Halim
- 1985   The Arab family and the challenge of social transformation. In *Women and the family in the Middle East*, ed. E. W. Fernea, 24–48. Austin: University of Texas Press.

al-Baydāwī, ʿAbd Allāh ibn ʿUman
- 1846   *Anwār al-tanzīl*. 2 vols. Ed. H. O. Fleischer. Leipzig.

Beck, Lois, and Nikki Keddie, eds.
- 1978   *Women in the Muslim world*. Cambridge: Harvard University Press.

Benedict, Peter
- 1974   The Kabul gunu: Structured visiting in an Anatolian provincial town. *Anthropological Quarterly* 47:28–47.

Bidwell, Robin
- 1983   *The two Yemens*. Boulder: Westview Press.

Boals, Kathryn
- 1971   *Modernization and intervention: Yemen as a theoretical case study*. Ann Arbor: University Microfilms International.

Bornstein, Annika
- 1974   *Food and society in the Yemen Arab Republic*. Rome: Food and Agriculture Organization of the United Nations.

Brohi, A. K.
- 1975   *Islam in the modern world*. Anarkali-Lahore, Pakistan: Publishers United.

Bujra, Janet
- 1975   Women and fieldwork. In *Women cross-culturally: Change and challenge*, ed. R. Rohrlich-Leavitt, 551–57. The Hague: Mouton Publishers.

Bullough, Vern L.
- 1973   *The subordinate sex*. Urbana: University of Illinois Press.

Bybee, Dorothy Ann
- 1978   *Muslim peasant women of the Middle East: Their sources and uses of power*. Ann Arbor: University Microfilms International.

Carmody, Denise
- 1979   *Women and world religions*. Nashville: Abingdon.

Chelhod, Joseph
- 1973a   La parenté et le mariage au Yémen. *L'Ethnographie* 67:47–90.
- 1973b   Les ceremonies du mariage au Yémen. *Objets et Mondes* 13:3–34.

Chinas, Beverly L.
   1973   *The Isthmus Zapotecs: Women's roles in cultural context.* New York: Holt, Rinehart and Winston.
Chodorow, Nancy
   1974   Family structure and feminine personality. In *Woman, culture and society*, ed. M. Rosaldo and L. Lamphere, 43–66. Stanford: Stanford University Press.
Cohen, Abner
   1965   *Arab border-villages in Israel.* Manchester: Manchester University Press.
Coulson, Noel, and Doreen Hinchliffe
   1978   Women and law reform in contemporary Iran. In *Women in the Muslim world*, ed. L. Beck and N. Keddie, 37–51. Cambridge: Harvard University Press.
Davis, Susan Schaefer
   1978   Working women in a Moroccan village. In *Women in the Muslim world*, ed. L. Beck and N. Keddie, 416–33. Cambridge: Harvard University Press.
Deffarge, Claude, and Gordier Troeller
   1969   *Yemen '62-'69.* Paris: Robert Laffont.
Divale, W. T., and M. Harris
   1976   Population, warfare, and the male supremacist complex. *American Anthropologist* 78:521–38.
Dwyer, Daisy Hilse
   1978   *Images and self-images: Male and female in Morocco.* New York: Columbia University Press.
Fayein, Claudie
   1957   *French doctor in the Yemen.* London: Robert Hale, Ltd.
Fernea, Elizabeth W.
   1969   *Guests of the sheik: An ethnography of an Iraqi village.* Garden City: Anchor Books.
   1976   *A street in Marrakech: A personal encounter with the lives of Moroccan women.* Garden City: Doubleday and Co.
   1985   Pt. I, Introduction. In *Women and the family in the Middle East: New voices of change*, ed. Elizabeth Fernea, 1–7. Austin: University of Texas Press.
Fernea, Elizabeth W., and Basima Q. Bezirgan
   1977   Introduction. In *Middle Eastern Muslim women speak*, ed. E. W. Fernea and B. Q. Bezirgan, xvii–xxxvi. Austin: University of Texas Press.
Fischer, Michael M. J.
   1978   On changing the concept and position of Persian women. In *Women in the Muslim world*, ed. L. Beck and N. Keddie, 189–215. Cambridge: Harvard University Press.
Friedl, Ernestine
   1967   Position of women: Appearance and reality. *Anthropological Quarterly* 40:97–128.
Fuller, Anne H.
   1961   *Buarij: Portrait of a Lebanese Muslim village.* Cambridge: Harvard University Press.

Geertz, Clifford
   1968   Thinking as a moral act: Ethical dimensions of anthropological fieldwork in the new states. *Antioch Review* 28:139-53.
   1976   "From the native point of view": On the nature of anthropological understanding. In *Meaning in anthropology*, ed. K. H. Basso and H. A. Selby, 221-37. Albuquerque: University of New Mexico Press.

Gerholm, Thomas
   1977   *Market, mosque, and mafraj: Social inequality in a Yemeni town*. Stockholm Studies in Social Anthropology, no. 5. Stockholm: Stockholm University.

Gerner, Debbie J.
   1984   Roles of transition: The evolving position of women in Arab-Islamic countries. In *Muslim women*, ed. F. Hussain, 71-99. London: Croom Helm, Ltd.

Gibb, H. A. R.
   1971   *Mohammedanism: An historical survey*. London: Oxford University Press.

Goldberg, H. I., J. E. Anderson, D. Miller, and O. Dawam
   1983   Contraception, marital fertility, and breast-feeding in the Yemen Arab Republic. *Journal of BioSocial Science* 15:67-82.

Goodale, Jane C.
   1971   *Tiwi wives*. Seattle: University of Washington Press.

Granqvist, Hilma
   1931   *Marriage conditions in a Palestinian village, I*. Helsinki: Societas Scientiarum Fennica.

Gulick, John, and Margaret E. Gulick
   1978   The domestic social environment of women and girls in Isfahan, Iran. In *Women in the Muslim world*, ed. L. Beck and N. Keddie, 501-21. Cambridge: Harvard University Press.

Haddad, Yvonne Yazbeck
   1980   Traditional affirmations concerning the role of women as found in contemporary Arab Islamic literature. In *Women in contemporary Muslim societies*, ed. J. I. Smith, 61-86. Lewisburg: Bucknell University Press.

Halliday, Fred
   1974   *Arabia without sultans: A political survey of instability in the Arab world*. New York: Vintage Books.
   1979   Yemen's unfinished revolution: Socialism in the south. MERIP (Middle East Research and Information Project) Reports no. 81, vol. 9(8):3-20.
   1985   North Yemen today. MERIP (Middle East Research and Information Project) Reports no. 130, vol. 15(2):3-9.

Harding, Susan
   1975   Women and words in a Spanish village. In *Toward an anthropology of women*, ed. R. Reiter, 283-308. New York: Monthly Review Press.

Henry, Jules
   1973   *Pathways to madness*. New York: Vintage Books.

al-Hibri, Azizah, ed.
   1982   *Women and Islam*. Oxford: Pergamon Press.

Hilal, Jamil M.
 1970 Father's brother's daughter marriage in Arab communities: A problem for sociological explanation. *Middle East Forum* 46:73-84.
Hussain, Freda, ed.
 1984 *Muslim women*. London: Croom Helm, Ltd.
Hussein, Aziza
 1953 The role of women in social reform in Egypt. *Middle East Journal* 7:440-58.
Jahan, Rounaq
 1975 Women in Bangladesh. In *Women cross-culturally: Change and challenge*, ed. R. Rohrlich-Leavitt, 5-30. The Hague: Mouton Publishers.
Jay, Robert
 1974 Personal and extrapersonal vision in anthropology. In *Reinventing anthropology*, ed. D. Hymes, 367-81. New York: Vintage Books.
Joseph, Suad
 1978 Women and the neighborhood street in Borj Hammoud, Lebanon. In *Women in the Muslim world*, ed. L. Beck and N. Keddie, 541-57. Cambridge: Harvard University Press.
Kaberry, Phyllis
 1952 *Women of the grassfields: A study of the economic position of women in Bamenda, British Cameroons*. London: H. M. Stationery Office.
Kader, Soha Abdel
 1984 A survey of trends in social sciences research on women in the Arab region, 1960-1980. In *Social science research and women in the Arab world*, 139-75. Paris: UNESCO.
Keddie, Nikki R.
 1979 Problems in the study of Middle Eastern women. *International Journal of Middle Eastern Studies* 10:225-40.
Khuri, Fuad T.
 1970 Parallel cousin marriage reconsidered: A Middle Eastern practice that nullifies the effects of marriage on the intensity of family relationships. *Man* (n.s.) 5:597-618.
Larguia, Isabel
 1975 The economic basis of the status of women. In *Women cross-culturally: Change and challenge*, ed. R. Rohrlich-Leavitt, 281-95. The Hague: Mouton Publishers.
Larson, Barbara K.
 1984 The status of women in a Tunisian village: Limits to autonomy, influence, and power. *Signs: Journal of Women in Culture and Society* 9(3):417-33.
Levy, Reuben
 1957 *The social structure of Islam*. Cambridge: Cambridge University Press.
Llewelyn-Davies, Melissa
 1978 Two contexts of solidarity among pastoral Maasai women. In *Women united, women divided*, ed. J. Bujra, 206-37. London: Tavistock Publications.
Lutfiyya, Abdulla M.
 1966 *Baytin: A Jordanian village*. The Hague: Mouton Publishers.

McClintock, David
- 1972 Yemen Arab Republic. In *The Middle East: Its governments and politics*, ed. A. A. al-Marayati, 317-32. Belmont, Calif.: Duxbury Press.

Maher, Vanessa
- 1974 *Women and property in Morocco: Their changing relation to the process of social stratification in the Middle Atlas*. London: Cambridge University Press.
- 1978 Women and social change in Morocco. In *Women in the Muslim world*, ed. L. Beck and Keddie, 100-124. Cambridge: Harvard University Press.

Makhlouf, Carla
- 1979 *Changing veils: Women and modernization in North Yemen*. London: Croom Helm, Ltd.

Mernissi, Fatima
- 1975 *Beyond the veil: Male-female dynamics in a modern Muslim society*. New York: John Wiley and Sons.

Messick, Brinkley
- 1978 *Transactions in Ibb: Economy and society in a Yemen highland town*. Ann Arbor: University Microfilms International.

Mikhail, Mona N.
- 1979 *Images of Arab women: Fact and fiction*. Washington, D.C.: Three Continents Press.

Milton, Kay
- 1979 Male bias in anthropology. *Man* (n.s.) 14:40-54.

Minces, Juliette
- 1980 *The house of obedience: Women in Arab society*. London: Zed Press.

Mohsen, Safia K.
- 1985 New images, old reflections: Working middle-class women in Egypt. In *Women and the family in the Middle East*, ed. E. W. Fernea, 56-71. Austin: University of Texas Press.

Molyneux, Maxine
- 1979 Women and revolution in the People's Democratic Republic of Yemen. *Feminist Review* no. 1. London.

Mundy, Martha
- 1975 *Yemen Arab Republic feeder road study: Report on phase II (Wadi Mawr)*. Vol. 2. Zurich: International Bank for Reconstruction and Development.

Musa, Nabawiyya
- 1923 *Al mar'a wa al-ʿAmal*. Cairo.

Myntti, Cynthia
- 1978 *Women in rural Yemen*. Sanʿa: United States Agency for International Development.
- 1979 *Women and development in the Yemen Arab Republic*. Eschborn, Federal Republic of Germany: German Agency for Technical Cooperation.
- 1984 Yemeni workers abroad: The impact on women. MERIP (Middle East Research and Information Project) Reports no. 124, vol. 14(5):11-16.

Nelson, Cynthia
- 1974 Public and private politics: Women in the Middle Eastern world. *American Ethnologist* 1:551-63.

Nordenstram, Ture
> 1968   *Sudanese ethics*. Uppsala: The Scandinavian Institute of African Studies.

Omvedt, Gail
> 1979   On the participant study of women's movements: Methodological, definitional, and action considerations. In *The politics of anthropology: From colonialism and sexism toward a view from below*, ed. G. Huizer and B. Mannheim, 373-93. The Hague: Mouton Publishers.

Ortner, Sherry
> 1974   Is female to male as nature is to culture? In *Woman, culture, and society*, ed. M. Rosaldo and L. Lamphere, 67-87. Stanford: Stanford University Press.

Padan-Eisenstark, Dorit
> 1975   Image and reality: Women's status in Israel. In *Women cross-culturally: Change and challenge*, ed. R. Rohrlich-Leavitt, 491-505. The Hague: Mouton Publishers.

Paulme, Denise
> 1963   Introduction. In *Women of tropical Africa*, trans. H. M. Wright, ed. D. Paulme, 1-16. Berkeley: University of California Press.

Pearl, David
> 1979   *A textbook on Muslim Law*. London: Croom Helm, Ltd.

Peterson, J. E.
> 1982   *Yemen: The search for a modern state*. Baltimore: The Johns Hopkins University Press.

Quinn, Naomi
> 1977   Anthropological studies on women's status. *Annual Review of Anthropology* 6:181-225.

Rapp, Rayna
> 1979   Anthropology. *Signs: Journal of Women in Culture and Society* 4:497-513.

Rassam, Amal
> 1984a   Introduction. Arab women: The status of research in the social sciences and the status of women. In *Social science research and women in the Arab world*, 1-13. Paris: UNESCO.
> 1984b   Toward a theoretical framework for the study of women in the Arab world. In *Social science research and women in the Arab world*, 122-38. Paris: UNESCO.

Reina, Ruben
> 1954   Two patterns of friendship in a Guatemalan community. *American Anthropologist* 61:44-50.

Reiter, Rayna Rapp
> 1975   Introduction. In *Toward an anthropology of women*, ed. R. R. Reiter, 11-19. New York: Monthly Review Press.

Rogers, Susan Carol
> 1978   Woman's place: A critical review of anthropological theory. *Comparative studies in society and history* 20:123-73.

Rohrlich-Leavitt, Ruby
> 1975   Conclusions. In *Women cross-culturally: Change and challenge*, ed. R. Rohrlich-Leavitt, 619-41. The Hague: Mouton Publishers.

Rosaldo, Michelle
: 1974 Woman, culture, and society: A theoretical overview. In *Woman, culture, and society*, ed. M. Rosaldo and L. Lamphere, 17–42. Stanford: Stanford University Press.

Rosenfeld, Henry
: 1974 Non-hierarchical, hierarchical and masked reciprocity in an Arab village. *Anthropological Quarterly* 47:139–66.

Rugh, Andrea B.
: 1985 Women and work: Strategies and choices in a lower-class quarter of Cairo. In *Women and the family in the Middle East*, ed. E. W. Fernea, 273–88. Austin: University of Texas Press.

al-Saadawy, Nawal
: 1972 *Al mar'aa wa al-jins*. Beirut: Al Mu'assassa al-ʿArabiyya lildirasaat wa al-Nashr.

Safa-Isfahani, Kaveh
: 1980 Female centered world views in Iranian culture: Symbolic representations of sexuality in dramatic games. *Signs: Journal of Women in Culture and Society* 6:33–53.

Saleh, Saneya
: 1972 Women in Islam: Their role in religious and traditional culture. *International Journal of Sociology of the Family* 2:193–201.

Salim, Mustafa S.
: 1962 *Marsh dwellers of the Euphrates delta*. London: The Athlone Press.

Schildkrout, Enid
: 1978 Age and gender in Hausa society: Socio-economic role of children in urban Kano. In *Sex and age as principles of social differentiation*, ed. J. S. LaFontaine, 109–39. London: Academic Press.

Schlegel, Alice
: 1977 Toward a theory of sexual stratification. In *Sexual stratification: A cross-cultural view*, ed. A. Schlegel, 1–40. New York: Columbia University Press.

Serjeant, R. B.
: 1973 The two Yemens: Historical perspectives and present attitudes. *Asian Affairs* 60:3–16.

Smith, Jane I., ed.
: 1980 *Women in contemporary Muslim societies*. Lewisburg: Bucknell University Press.

Stanford Research Institute
: 1971 *Area handbook for the peripheral states of the Arabian Peninsula*. Washington, D.C.: U.S. Government Printing Office.

Stevenson, Thomas B.
: 1985 *Social change in a Yemeni highlands town*. Salt Lake City: University of Utah Press.

Stookey, Robert W.
: 1978 *Yemen: The politics of the Yemen Arab Republic*. Boulder: Westview Press.
: 1984 Yemen: Revolution versus tradition. In *The Arabian Peninsula: Zone of ferment*, ed. R. W. Stookey, 79–108. Stanford, Calif.: Hoover Institution Press.

Swanson, Jon C.
    1979   *Emigration and economic development: The case of the Yemen Arab Republic*. Boulder: Westview Press.

Sweet, Louise E.
    1974   In reality: Some Middle Eastern women. In *Many sisters*, ed. J. Matthiasson, 379–97. London: The Free Press.

UNESCO (United Nations Educational, Scientific and Cultural Organization)
    1984   *Social science research and women in the Arab world*. London: Frances Pinter.

Vieille, Paul
    1978   Iranian women in family alliance and sexual politics. In *Women in the Muslim world*, ed. L. Beck and N. Keddie, 451–72. Cambridge: Harvard University Press.

Webber, Sabra
    1985   Women's folk narratives and social change. In *Women and the family in the Middle East*, ed. E. W. Fernea, 310–16. Austin: University of Texas Press.

Wenner, Manfred
    1967   *Modern Yemen: 1918–1966*. Baltimore: The Johns Hopkins University Press.

White, Elizabeth H.
    1978   Legal reforms as an indicator of women's status in Muslim nations. In *Women in the Muslim world*, ed. L. Beck and N. Keddie, 52–68. Cambridge: Harvard University Press.

Wikan, Unni
    1982   *Behind the veil in Arabia: Women in Oman*. Baltimore: The Johns Hopkins University Press.

Williams, Judith R.
    1968   *The youth of Haouch el Harimi: A Lebanese village*. Harvard Middle Eastern Monographs no. 20. Cambridge: Harvard University Press.

Yālgin, Miqdād
    1972   *Al-bayt al-Islāmī*. Cairo.

Yemen Arab Republic
    1978   *Final report on the airphoto interpretation project of the Swiss Technical Co-operation Service, Berne*. Zurich: Central Planning Organization of the Yemen Arab Republic.

Index

Abrid, 157
Al-ʿāda, 135
Aden, 28
ʿAdi, 137
ʿAdi ghāwiyya, 141
Adultery, 137, 181
ʿĀfiyya, 159
Aftajʿa, 208
ʿAgal: in daughters, 91; female views on, 84
Aggression training: of boys, 87; of girls, 87–88
Ahmad, Imam, treachery of, 28–29
Al-Ahmar, role of, in government, 29, 30
ʿAli, 25
Altizām, 144
ʿAmran: in civil war, 32, 34; cultural change in, 39; Jews in, 5; location of, 23; social history of, 32–40; Turks in, 5; and rest of Yemen, 202–5
Ashtughil, 136
ʿAūgari: antidotes to, 154; belief in, 41, 154–55
Authority. *See* Men, authority of
ʿAyal ʿamm, 104
ʿAyn, 82
ʿAzaba, 111

Badl, 104
Bakil tribal confederation, 25, 32, 34
Baraka, 123

Barber: as circumciser, 78–79; at wedding festivities, 119
Baths, public, 111
Beliefs, popular: childbirth, 50, 153, 154, 155, 157–58, 160–61, 208, 211; circumcision, 78, 79; evil eye, 82, 83; healers and, 45; influence of, 39, 41–42; mental illness, 190; swaddling, 80; wedding, 110–11, 113–14, 121, 209
Bin, 56
Bint, 111
Bint ʿamm, 104
Birth. *See* Childbirth
Birth control, 210
Bottle-feeding, 80–81
Boys. *See* Sons
Bread, preparation of, 6, 56, 65–66, 94
Breast-feeding, 83; beliefs about, 80–81; directly after childbirth, 157; duration of, 80
Bridal procession, participants in, 121–22
Bride-price: bride's share of, 107; divorce and, 152; exchange marriage and, 104, 106; father's/brothers' share of, 107; female support for, 107; limitation of, 208; negotiations for, 101, 103, 106, 108; size of, 106–7; value of, 19, 77
Brides, 111, 116–17, 121–24, 129–31, 135, 139, 208; at *mashjab*, 113–15; preparation of, 120–21; selecting, 99–100

Catha edulis. See *Gāt*
Childbirth: attendants at, 155; beliefs about, 155, 157–61, 208; customs surrounding, 50, 75–80, 158–64; folktale about, 157; husband's role during, 156; preparations for, 50; and postpartum recovery, 158–59; swaddling at, 79–80
Children: aggression training of, 87–89; behavior of, 58, 89; care of, 81–83, 172, 208; disciplining of, 84–85, 88–89, 165, 193, 212; dressing of, 87, 94; economic activities of, 91; games of, 89, 95; illness of, 39, 85, 87; indulgence of, 89; social access of, 53; socializing of, 12–13
Circumcision, 77–79; female, 79, 137
Civil war, 28–29; in ʿAmran, 34; female views of, 32, 35
Class difference: defining, 207; female views on, 6, 32–39, 175–77, 181. See also Social stratification
Clinic, female opinions of, 39, 80, 82–83, 153, 155, 156
Code: conduct, female views on, 202–3; dress, 3; Family, 203; tribal, 19
Commerce: in ʿAmran, 31, 34–35, 60, 68; petty, of children, 91; petty, of women, 43, 60, 64, 212; by Shafiʿis, 27
Confinement. See *Walada* period
Consumerism, in ʿAmran, 35, 37, 38–39
Consummation, marriage, 123–26; as proof of virginity, 127–28, 210
Co-wife: conflict with, 148, 150; status of, 146–47, 149
Cultural conflict, 39–40
Cultural devaluation, 18, effects of, 19
Cultural gap, in research, 198
Cultural ideology, female views on, 185–86

Daughters: aggression training of, 87, 89; benefits from, 76; confinement of, 95, 97; criticism of, 77, 166; dressing of, 87, 97; education of, 21–22, 91–94; family honor and, 95; goals of, 93; responsibilities of, 72, 77, 83, 85, 91, 94–95, 166; sacrifices of, 85, 91; socialization of, 12–13
Daughters-in-law, expectations of, 168
Dawshān, 119
Diet: ʿAmrani, 56, 58, 64, 71, 72; children's, 87, 94–95, 97; infants', 80–81, 83–84; new mothers', 158–59
Divorce, 211; children and, 105, 150; cost of, 143–44; ease of, 144, 151; family support during, 145, 151; fears of, 43; patrilateral parallel cousin, 105; proceedings of, 144–45, 151; reasons for, 147, 150; remarriage and, 145, 151–52; by repudiation, 144–45, 150, 203; stigma of, 152
Diwān, 68
Dominance, myth of male, 18
Dress: ʿAmrani children's, 87, 97; ʿAmrani women's, 3, 64, 70, 111–13, 174–75, 181; Sanʿa women's, 203

Eating habits, 66, 68, 72. See also Diet
Education: as an asset in marriage, 92; for boys, 91, 94; for girls, 91–94; for women, 21, 203, 205, 208
Ego boundaries, development of, 12–13
Egypt, in Yemeni civil war, 29
Employment of women, 22, 92, 200, 203, 205, 211; in South Yemen, 204
Engagements, breaking of, 103
Entertainment: during *walada* period, 160–63; wedding, 111–19, 120, 122, 128–31
Ethnography, research methods in, 41–51, 197–99, 207
Evil eye, 42; fear of, 87; infants and, 160; as a cause of mental illness, 189; protection from, 82–83, 113, 177; vulnerability to, 82–83; *walada* and, 160–61. See also Beliefs, popular
Extended households, preference for, 141
Extramarital relations, 137, 181

Family Code, 203
Family honor, 95
Farming, near ʿAmran, 34, 60
Fātḥa, 122
Father-child relationships, 14, 66, 86–87, 88, 133
Fatima, 25
Feminism, 199, 202; in ʿAmran, 205; effects of, on research, 10–11; in Arabian Peninsula, 21
Financial assistance, from sons, 166
Fitna, 16
Folktales: analysis of, 192–93; examples of, 185–91; fears expressed in, 190; female characters in, 186–89; love in, 187, 194; men's, 149–50; morality in, 186, 192–93; mother-son relationships in, 193–94; therapy in telling, 188–89; women's, 140, 148–49, 185–91
Free Yemenis' Movement, foundation of, 28
Friendships: evaluation of, 177–79; importance of, 43, 183; reasons for, 195; strength of, 176–78, 182, 212. See also Relationships, reciprocal
Fūṭa, definition of, 64
Fuwāṭ, definition of, 87

Gabāʾil, 34; social level of, 6; connotations of, 30–32
Gafu, 56
Gahwa ghuda, 70
Garāgush, 87
Gāt: aftereffects of, 68, 71, 136, 138; beliefs about, 68; chewing of, at *ḥalāfa*, 116–17, 118; chewing of, by boys, 94; chewing of, by women, 69, 182, 202, 203; costs of, 68; ritual surrounding, 58
Gāt sessions, 68–69
Ghāwī, 91
Girls. See Daughters
Gishr, 44, 85
Graining grinding, process of, 34–35
Grooms, 117–19, 122–24, 126; religious duties of, 118; vulnerability of, 110–11
Gurum, 56

Ḥākam, mediation by, 127, 144
Ḥalāfa, 78; cost of, 116, 119; *gāt* chewing at, 116; preparation of, 109, 116–17; women's role at, 119
Halba, 72
Al-Hamdi, 30; government control by, 29
Ḥanagat, 141; family support for, 142–43
Ḥariwa, 121
Hashid tribal confederation, 25, 28, 32, 183, 212
Healers, 42, 82–83; activities of, 45, 47; visiting, 53
Ḥirz, 113
Hodeida, 39
Hospitals: childbirth at, 156; female opinion of, 155. See also Clinic, female opinion of
Housework, 60, 64, 72, 204
Humor: importance and use of, 36, 44, 45, 47, 75, 76, 88, 142, 146–47, 162; at men's expense, 21, 104, 116, 138, 151; sexual, 44, 137, 138, 164, 181, 182, 210

Ibn ʿamm, 104
Illness: causes and prevention of, 39, 68, 78–85, 154–55, 158–61, 208; of children, 85, 87, 165; treatment of, 39, 42, 47, 168
Insanity, 84, 138, 146–47, 158, 189–90
Infanticide, rarity of, 210
Infants: care of, 81–84, 208; and evil eye, 82–83. See also Children
Interpersonal relationships. See Friendships; Relationships, reciprocal
Islam: divorce law in, 144–45; female evaluations in, 15–16, 193–94; sects of, in Yemen, 25–27; sexual code in, 10, 194, 202. See also Religious duties; Ritual impurities; Ritual prayer, importance of

Jahīn, 56
Jewish quarter (ʿAmran), 4–5
Jinn, 78

Khubz, 56
Kūfiya, 94

Laban, 64
Laḥūḥ, 118
Law: Islamic, 19, 110, 144, 150–51; in People's Democratic Republic of Yemen, 203; tribal, 19, 143; in Yemen government, 145
Legal reforms, for women, 9, 200, 204–5
London Women's Anthropology Group, 199
Lugta, 210

Madaʿa, 69
Madina, 4
Mafraj, 68
Mahr, 107
Majnūna dance, 162. See also Insanity
Male bias, double, in research, 10–11
Male dominance, myth of, 18
Maluj, 56
Manakha, 39
Marital conflict: divorce and, 150; mothers-in-law and, 139–40, 150; pregnancy and, 153; resolving, 133–34, 139–41, 143–44, 150; separation and, 141
Marriage, consummation of. See Consummation, marriage
Marriage, exchange, 104–6, 128, 143, 207
Marriage, repudiation of. See Divorce
Marriage arrangement, 99–101, 102–3, 106–7; contract and sealing of, 110; economic and political ties in, 100, 103; of nonvirgins, 100, 151–52, 208, 209; son's/daughter's approval of, 100–101; status differences in, 45. See also Mother-daughter relationships; Weddings
Martaba, 113
Mashjab: at bride's house, 113–15; entertainment at, 112–15; expenses of, 112–13; gift giving at, 113–15; at groom's house, 111–13; *muzayyina*'s function at, 112–15

Mashjab (flower), 112
Masturbation, practice of, 137
Mawlid, 176; during *walada* period, 162
Medicine, female opinion of, 39
Men: authority of, 14–15, 19, 99–101, 110, 139, 142–43, 152, 194; leisure activities of, 58, 60, 68–69, 71, 171; privileges of, 72, 144, 150–51; restrictions on, 21, 53, 158; work of, 31, 42, 60
Menstruation, 135
Mental illness, 189–90. See also Insanity
Midwives, 155
Mother-daughter relationships, 77, 91, 166–67
Mother-in-law–daughter-in-law relationships, 168–70
Mother-son relationships: daughters-in-law and, 169; in folktales, 193–94; importance of, 166, 168, 193–94
Muhammad, 25, 40
Mulk, 110
Muzayyin: social level of, 6; stereotypes about, 175; at wedding feasts, 117–19
Muzayyina, 32; hiring of, 109, 123; at *mashjab*, 111–15; status of, 38, 175; at *walada* parties, 162; at weddings, 37–38, 111, 120–22, 130, 209
Muzayyināt, 129

Naṣāra, 4
Naẓifa, 123
Neighbors. See Relationships, reciprocal
North-south conflict, origins of, 26–27
North Yemen. See Yemen Arab Republic

Oil, discovery of, 23, 204

Patrilateral parallel cousin marriage, 208–9; children of, 105; description of, 104; economic reasons for, 106; objections to, 105
People's Democratic Republic of Yemen: ʿAmranis' knowledge about, 203–4; feminism in, 21; influence of, 23

Polygyny, 203; children and, 147–48; costs of, 146–47, 150; deterrents to, 107, 145–48; divorce and, 147–48; economic reasons for, 146; female opinion of, 146; folktale about, 148–49

Pregnancy, 48, 49, 51; *ᶜaūgari* belief and, 154–55; cravings during, 153, 211; folktale about, 211; help during, 50; household duties during, 153; marital conflict and, 153; medical care and, 153; unwanted, 210. *See also* Childbirth

Public baths, 111, 117, 129

Rādhiya, 136
Ramadhan, 49, 158; fasting during, 153
Rape, 136
Rapport, during research, 197–98
Relationships, reciprocal, 5–7, 171–77, 195, 212. *See also* Friendships
Religious duties, 56, 68; female, 70; male, 66, 71
Rifd, 113; giving of, 119, 209
Ritual impurities, 70, 158
Ritual prayer, importance of, 56

Sābᶜa: celebration of, 129–31, 210
Ṣabaḥat, 126
Sāda/sayyid: in civil war, 29; influence of, 35; origins of, 25, 26; status of, 25, 45, 181, 207
Ṣadīqa, 137
Saleswomen, role of, 211
Samāta, 94
Samn, 64
Saudi Arabia: influence of, 23, 30; working in, 107; in Yemeni civil war, 29
Sayyid. *See Sāda; Sharīfa*
Separation: agreements on, 139, 144; polygyny and, 147; reasons for, 139–43
Sex differences: decision-making power, 14, 21, 99, 101, 208; eating patterns, 66; *gāt* use, 69, 71; mental maturation, 84, 91; moral worth, 21; pre- and extramarital sex, 135, 137; sleeping arrangements, 72
Sex roles, values derived from, 194
Sexual assault, 136
Sexual relations: beginning of, 123, 134–36; confiding about, 210–11; demands of, 139; extramarital, 137; female opinion of, 135; female role in, 136; frustration with, 138; Islamic theories on, 16; jokes about, 137, 210; magical papers and, 136; premarital, 135; resumption of, 164; studying, 210
Sexual stratification, 20, 200; evaluations of, 17–18; justification for, 194, 205–6; restrictions of, 199; theories of, 11–18
Shafiᶜi: in civil war, 29; discrimination against, 27; political resistance by, 27
Shafiᶜi school, 25; southern adherence to, 27
Shāl, 94
Sharīfa: restrictions upon, 36; status of, 32, 36–37, 181, 183
Sharshaf, 108
Sharṭ, 107
Shayāṭīn, 78
Shiᶜa Islam, Zaydi sect of, 25
Shikma, 131
Shopping, 58, 60
Sickness. *See* Illness
Sunni Islam, Shafiᶜi school of, 25
Social life: abstaining from, 182–83; in ᶜAmran, 42; female, 64–65, 69, 71–72, 171; importance of, 42, 43, 204; male, 53, 58, 60, 66, 68, 69, 71, 171; mother-daughter, 167; patterns of, 42, 44–46, 48, 71; during *walada* period, 163–64. *See also* Visiting
Social order: in ᶜAmran, 35; dissatisfaction with, 20; importance of, 6; theories of, 11–18
Social responsibility: changes in, 28; obligations of, 171; through reciprocal ties, 174–75
Social stratification, 25–32, 207; reciprocal ties and, 175–76, 212–13
Socialism, Islam and, 204
Socialization, patterns of, 12–15, 80–97

Sons: aggression training of, 87; dressing of, 87; education of, 91, 94; financial assistance from, 166; *gāt* chewing and, 94; preference for, 75–77; responsibilities of, 72; socialization of, 12–13, 94; treatment of, 166, 168
South Yemen. *See* People's Democratic Republic of Yemen
Sūq, 31; avoidance of, 53, 72, 212; shopping at, 49; social life at, 60, 68, 71, 171
Swaddling, 79–80, 83

Tanur, 65
Ṭarḥa, 113
Ṭariq, 182
Tribal confederations, northern, 25
Tribal images, 30–31
Tribal law, 19, 143
Trousseau, contents of, 108–9; delivery of, 129
Tūdara, 70–71
Turks: in ʿAmran, 5; in Yemen, 25

Unmarried women, restrictions upon, 71, 97, 178
Unwed mothers, 210

Virginity: confirmation of, 209; importance of, 125–29, 209; legal documenting of, 127; rumors about, 128
Visiting, 7, 20, 22, 64–65, 69, 183; conversation during, 46; informal, 42, 44–45, 64, 65, 71–72, 116, 172, 182; invitations for, 48; patterns of, 6, 42, 44–48, 70–71, 209, 212; during *walada* period, 50, 51, 159–64; wedding, 111–18, 120, 122–23, 126, 129–31, 139

Walada period: diet during, 158–59; ending of, 164; parties during, 159–64, 211; reciprocal relationships and, 173; restrictions and privileges of, 158–59, 165
Wasakha behavior: examples of, 179, 181–82, 190; mental illness and, 190; at women's gatherings, 181
Weaning, process of, 83–84
Wedding day, activities of, 120–22
Wedding feast. *See Ḥalāfa*
Wedding night, accounts of, 124–25
Wedding procession, participants in, 118
Weddings: beliefs about, 110–11, 113–14, 121, 209; costs of, 107–9; mother-daughter relationships and, 167; *muzayyina* function at, 37
Wet nurse, use of, 81
Women: devaluation and subordination of, 11–18, 202; and female education and employment, 21–22, 91–92, 94, 204–5; ideologies of, 16–17, 21, 171, 185–95, 202–3; and postrevolution change, 35, 39–40, 203, 204; psychological strengths of, 19, 205, 206; Sanʿa, and ʿAmrani, 69, 107, 109, 134, 200, 202–3, 208, 210, 211; sexuality of, 136–39, 210
Women's rights, ʿAmrani women and, 203, 205
Women's Union, 203

Yahya, Imam, 27; death of, 37
YAR. *See* Yemen Arab Republic
Yawm al sabʿa, celebration of, 129–31
Yemen: civil war in, 28–29; Egyptian influence in, 29; Saudi Arabian influence in, 30; Turkish influence in, 25
Yemen Arab Republic, 23, 25; feminism in, 21; leftism in, 30; modernization of, 30; oil production in, 23, 204; tribal conflict in, 30
Yemeni civil war. *See* Civil war
Yemeni Women's Association, 200, 202

Zannin, 87
Zaydis: in civil war, 29; influence of, 27
Zaydi Imamate, influence of, 25–27
Zaydi Islam, 25–26, 27; flexibility of, 70